T0131795

Reflection
of Selection

Jocelyne LeBlanc

BALBOA.
PRESS

A DIVISION OF HAY HOUSE

Balboa Press books may be ordered through booksellers or by contacting:

Balboa Press
A Division of Hay House
1663 Liberty Drive
Bloomington, IN 47403
www.balboapress.com
1 (877) 407-4847

Because of the dynamic nature of the Internet, any web addresses or links contained in this book may have changed since publication and may no longer be valid. The views expressed in this work are solely those of the author and do not necessarily reflect the views of the publisher, and the publisher hereby disclaims any responsibility for them.

The author of this book does not dispense medical advice or prescribe the use of any technique as a form of treatment for physical, emotional, or medical problems without the advice of a physician, either directly or indirectly. The intent of the author is only to offer information of a general nature to help you in your quest for emotional and spiritual well-being. In the event you use any of the information in this book for yourself, which is your constitutional right, the author and the publisher assume no responsibility for your actions.

Any people depicted in stock imagery provided by Thinkstock are models, and such images are being used for illustrative purposes only.
Certain stock imagery © Thinkstock.

Print information available on the last page.

ISBN: 978-1-5043-8258-8 (sc)
ISBN: 978-1-5043-8260-1 (hc)
ISBN: 978-1-5043-8259-5 (e)

Library of Congress Control Number: 2017909601

Balboa Press rev. date: 07/05/2017

To people who, despite adversity, manage to effectuate positive change.

Miraculous Body

We've been together from the start
Only at death will we part
When young, I felt invincible
Now older it seems impossible
To ignore all you do for me
Whether from the stars or the sea
It is still the greatest wonder
To just be

Disclaimer

The author assumes no responsibility for the information provided. Facts and sources have been provided as accurately as possible at the time of writing. The information is not intended to replace professional medical advice, and the author is not engaged in dispensing it.

Contents

Preface

Calling it a roller coaster ride trying to deal with all the emotions this disease can bring on is an understatement. It took years to accept it, and almost a lifetime of living with it brings me to this book. Multiple sclerosis didn't take over my mind, but it did take over my life for too long. It darkened my world in more ways than one. This left me not only shaken to my core—for a long time—it robbed me of any expectations that life was good. It felt like my last shreds of playfulness and anticipation were replaced with an emptiness and seriousness that have no purpose being part of a person's life on a daily basis.

It wasn't conventional medicine that led to my discovering the causes for so many of the distresses I endured. I had to dig deep to find the hidden dangers that were affecting my health. Eventually I was able to find some relief, and gradually I started to feel more like my old self again. I can honestly say I feel healthy for the most part. While people around me were hurriedly busy with their lives, I was learning to appreciate the now of every moment, all the while searching for meaning behind the condition. With a newfound appreciation, I have now come to believe that healing is possible.

There are no easy answers to be found trying to find reason when someone is suddenly faced with a chronic disease in the prime of his or her lives. Such a diagnosis brings with it a surreal feeling that takes over your psyche. You almost feel like you are drifting in a bad dream. Wishfully, you think you may come out of it unscathed. With the realization that life as it was will never be the same, your health—held in the background—suddenly jumps to top priority and becomes first in occupying your thoughts and existence. It's better late than never to realize there are always choices to be made to enhance wellness. In a better reality—and it is becoming so— as awareness grows, people give their physical and mental health the attention they deserve.

After years of reading, researching, and various life experiences, I have developed a certain understanding I would not have had I not been thrown into this MS journey. Over a decade later, with some in the medical profession questioning my proven MS diagnosis, I decided maybe I did have something to share with others. I don't have any professional credentials or star status. I am an ordinary person, like many of you, suffering with a disease with no cure in sight. Some say I have managed to cope well. I was inspired to write down some things that helped me and what I discovered along the way. As I delved deeper to support what I'm presenting and to reaffirm my position, I learned so much more. For that, I am extremely thankful.

Those in the limelight who are affected by disease or other health issues can be an inspiration to many. Sometimes the information or advice they convey on how they manage their diseases or overcame their health problems is difficult to get through. Granted, some information is useful; some of it is just not within reach of the majority of the population. Most people don't have the means to access the resources or support the well-to-dos can.

A growing sense of distrust is permeating the psyches of the general populations who witness blatant double standards from those we pay and elect to safeguard our well-being. This confuses rather than supports. Those in charge pass blame on anybody but themselves. Much like a two-year old found with hands in the cookie jar denying culpability, the powers-that-be are in denial of accountability; and that creates ongoing abuse.

It's in following the money trail that the hidden agendas and sinister views are often revealed. However, it's not all doom and gloom. Much is in our own hands. This gives us power to rise above the madness we've been entrenched in for too long. At the risk of being ostracized, I decided to go out on a limb—reveal some details I could leave out. However, to be as truthful and helpful as possible, I chose not to ignore uncomfortable parts that make up the whole of who I am.

Even as I write these words, I'm consciously telling myself I'm not reaffirming this condition I live with. I decided long ago I would not let this disease consume my every emotion. It's hard enough to physically feel its presence every day; I refuse to let it hijack my mind as well. Instead, I shift my focus to become aware of how food, emotions, and beliefs play important roles in our overall health.

With a chance of sounding redundant—I've gathered much information already out there. You've probably heard some of it more than once. It is my hope I'll be able to bring it home in such a way you'll never need to hear it again. I tried to compile it to deliver a clear message. I simplified much of the information to present it in an easy-to-understand manner. You, too, will feel informed and confident in your ability to reclaim your natural state and feel better.

Ultimately, the purpose of *Reflection of Selection* is to awaken your awareness by providing you with a foundation to build on. There's always more to learn as new advances are made on many fronts. During the years it took to write this book, I stumbled onto more interesting and relevant information. We can expect amazing discoveries on the horizon. Meanwhile, if I touch on something here that helps anyone, my time spent writing this will have been more than worth it. If you find I've left something out, I apologize.

Do not underestimate the power you can exert and experience by making changes. Whether big or small, taking one step, and then another, one day at a time, can lead to taking control of how your body feels. Days will turn into weeks, and before you know it, you'll feel better. Know and believe that how you feel is mostly what you choose it to be—not only because of the choices you make but also because of what you believe. Life throws enough at us that we have no control over. We don't need to add more hurt and uncertainty by ignoring our most precious resource—our health.

Never in imagining my life did I think I'd be faced with a chronic disease. I had just turned thirty-seven. How I choose to react and deal with it is my own personal choice. How you deal with your life situations is your choice. I am merely saying there is a choice to be made. Choose to greet the days with enthusiasm and anticipation instead of apprehension and fear. There will be days when this seems like a struggle. It's on those days it's important to turn things around. Fool your mind into a grateful state of consciousness—gradually you'll start to feel what you're feeding your mind. Eventually, these feelings become part of your nature—transform your existence. You'll live in appreciation and awareness of the choices you make in how you eat; feel; react; and, thus, live.

I'm not offering advice. I'm not professionally qualified to do so. Some of you will disagree with some of my views—isn't life a wonder of perceptions and interpretations? Everyone has a right to his or her opinions, as I have a right to mine. There's knowledge to be shared by everyone in one way or another. There's not one magic bullet guaranteed to fix whatever it is needing fixing. There are no easy quick fixes, no magical cures.

There are, however, step-by-step approaches that can bring about significant changes. For many of us, it took years to get to a state of bad health; it'll take some time to recover. I can only tell you what worked for me.

It's more than within reach to take charge of your well-being. It's really not as complicated as we have been led to believe. If you've been blessed with good health, it's far easier to maintain it than try to catch up later after disease has set in. Don't let yourself become one of the statistics. If you suffer from an illness or a chronic disease, like a great number of us do, it's even more urgent for you to control, as best you can, what you can.

CHAPTER 1

Diagnosis

Relapsing-Remitting Multiple Sclerosis (RRMS)

We have all heard the saying "one night can change your life forever." For me, it all happened in the space of one day in May, over twenty years ago. It was early one morning when I first noticed something was not right with my eyesight. I was getting ready to attend my young daughter's school concert, and while applying my makeup, I realized that my right eye was a bit blurry. I carefully ran one of my fingers over the lens of my eye, thinking it was a hair or something else obstructing my vision. As I did this, the vision in that eye didn't clear up.

I didn't have time to dwell on it then. I had to rush to make it on time for the school concert. During the concert, it became apparent that the vision in my eye was fading rapidly. It was becoming dimmer and darkened. I tried to enjoy the concert as best as I could. In the back of my mind, I was becoming increasingly worried and frantic about what was happening with my vision.

I was able to book an emergency eye appointment right away with an ophthalmologist, and there and then, my world as I knew it shattered. I was told point-blank that it was either multiple sclerosis (MS) or a brain tumor. As I sat there in shock, I thought, *How did my life come to this?* The ophthalmologist urgently referred me to the hospital to see a neurological eye specialist.

It was late afternoon by the time I arrived at the hospital appointment, and the vision in my right eye had completely disappeared. If I covered my other eye and tried to look only through the affected eye, my world was black. After an examination by the eye specialist at the hospital, I was told that it was optic neuritis. The inflammation of the optic nerve, located at the back of the eye extending to the brain, was, in all likelihood, caused by MS. The MS diagnosis was confirmed early the following year with an MRI.

As I sat in the eye specialist's office in disbelief, I felt relieved that it wasn't a brain tumor and wasn't fatal, at least not at that moment. The previous week, I had watched a television documentary on brain surgery, and it wasn't something I wanted to experience. Perhaps that initial reaction set the course for my dealing with this disease and how it affects my psychological mind and hence, my body.

The news left me numb. I knew a neurological disease was serious. I had seen the odd television commercials from the MS Society about multiple sclerosis. Other than that, I didn't know much about it. I didn't know anyone else affected with this disease.

Multiple sclerosis (MS) is an unpredictable and incurable disease. The body attacks the myelin, which is the insulating coat surrounding nerves. The lesions or scars left behind after these attacks cause the nerve impulses to malfunction, thereby creating disability in various nervous-system processes. There are four different classifications assigned to describe the severity and course of the disease—relapsing-remitting, primary-progressive, secondary-progressive, and progressive-relapsing. These were once called benign or mild, episodic, progressive, and chronic progressive.

At the time when this first happened, I was in the process of a move across the country. I didn't have time to let the reality of it all completely sink in. I was too busy packing and making arrangements. I didn't really know anything about MS and was not given any information on the disease. The neurologist told me that I should postpone my move. He never gave me an explanation of why. He simply told me that it was not a good idea for me to move at that time.

Ignorantly, I didn't realize that I was right in the middle of an MS attack. I had no clue that this was how MS was experienced—with attacks, or exacerbations as they can be called—and that things usually subsided in between assaults. I was not informed that the stress of moving was jeopardizing my recovery from this attack. I never fully recovered from it—not to say that one ever fully recovers from any of these attacks. Let's just say that, by being stressed and continuing with the process of moving, I was not helping my body heal.

As far as I was concerned, plans for the relocation were already set in motion, and things had to proceed as planned. For those of you who are not familiar with MS, optic neuritis often presents itself as one of the first symptoms of this disease. In the majority of cases, this first symptom usually resolves itself fairly quickly without any serious impairment to the person's visual acuity. However, for me, the attack was severe and painful. To this day, I have never regained clear vision in that eye. Tragically, the damage to the optic nerve was irreversible and became permanent.

A few weeks later, as the attack subsided, I felt the numbness on the right side of my face reach the tip of my nose and finally leave. Up until that point, I hadn't realized that the upper right side of my face was numb. It felt much like the sensation we experience after the numbing from a visit to the dentist gradually dissipates. The pain I had endured in both of my hands, which I had attributed to overuse because of packing, eventually improved. I had not given it any thought. It was minor compared to losing my eyesight.

After a bit of time passed, I began to suspect that I had had MS before this painful episode. A couple of years earlier, I had gone to see my doctor because I had abruptly started experiencing headaches and pain in the back of one of my eyes (troublingly, it was not the same eye that was affected when I lost my vision). Until those pains began, never in my life had I stocked pain medication for headaches. I'd never had reason to.

It was completely new for me, so my doctor ordered a nuclear scan. It failed to reveal anything. Since nothing showed up to indicate that there was any serious problem, the doctor prescribed pain and muscle-relaxant medication and told me that my headaches were stress-related. The medication helped with the pain behind my eye, so I thought that whatever it was was now cleared up. However, headaches became part of my life from then on.

It wasn't until I was a bit settled in my new location that the gravity of the diagnosis hit me. After the initial shock of it all wore off, my emotions ranged from anger to grief, back and forth like a pendulum, for a couple of years. I was able to keep busy and did my best to remain strong and positive, mostly for my young daughter. Any good mother will surely attest that it's always easier to do things for others rather than for herself.

This instinct comes naturally for most women, and for me, it was a good distraction. I don't want to get into a debate here about whether caring more for others is a strength or a curse of being a woman. For myself, it kept me focused on mothering rather than self-pity. I was starting a new life in a new location, and although things were not going as planned, I felt much excitement.

Like everyone who has ever faced a life-altering diagnosis, the question "Why me?" left me perplexed and dazed. It pierced through to the greatest depths of my being. Just when I thought my life was about to change for the better, I was faced with a new challenge. This new burden came with such finality. Life wasn't going to be that easy after all.

On some level, I believed it was my own fault. I hadn't been too kind to my body in my late teens and early twenties when'd I experimented with drugs or when I'd fallen short on providing myself with proper nutrition, not knowing how important it was. I just as easily could have been stricken with AIDS. I remember thinking that this was actually better than getting AIDS and the label that came with that disease at the time.

As the never-ending question of how I got MS consumed my mind, I kept going back over the distant and recent past to see if there was some type of precipitous event that had set off this disease. I acknowledged having stacked the odds in favor of a weakened immune system, but there were probably other factors at play. The last infectious virus I'd contracted had had me sick for weeks. Had it opened the door to MS?

I had been given two tetanus vaccines within three or four years of each other. It was shortly after the last one that my headaches had started. Did it go way back to the wood tick bites I'd gotten as a child? After all, I was the only one in the family who the bugs had feasted on. Had they infected and affected my body? Maybe it was from the skull injury I'd sustained when young, splitting my head open on the steel bar of a bedpost. Perhaps it was the cumulative effects of some or all of these experiences, or maybe it had nothing at all to do with any of these incidents. There were no answers then, and there aren't any now.

Not until Dr. Jean-Marie Charcot had dissected a brain and found lesions was the name "multiple sclerosis" assigned to this disease. MS causes lesions in the central nervous system (CNS)—namely, the brain and spinal cord. In early identification of MS, it was thought that a virus or toxin was responsible. Other than apparent neurological symptoms, the only other clue offered for diagnosing MS was from the results of a cerebrospinal tap test. These detect the presence of the antibody immunoglobin G in the fluid of the spinal column. The count for this antibody is high in people with MS. Today, neurologists use magnetic resonance imaging (MRI) to scan patients' central nervous systems to pinpoints location(s) of lesion(s). Those markers, along with other neurological tests, confirm the disease.

To this day, scientists haven't been able to identically reproduce MS in animal models. The closest they've come to doing so is with the autoimmune mediated condition, experimental allergic encephalomyelitis

(EAE), or with a virus-induced condition called the Theiler's Murine Encephalomyelitis Virus (TMEV). Neither represents this disease in its complexity. There is no true MS animal model for scientists to study.

Recently, researchers identified in animal models precisely how a protein that seeps from the blood into the brain sets off a response and, with time, causes the nerve cell damage that is the key indicator of MS. In vivo, meaning in live organisms rather than test tubes, imaging analysis observed in real time revealed what molecules cross the blood-brain barrier. They identified the protein *fibrinogen* as the main culprit in MS, entering the brain through leaky blood vessels and impacting the health of individual nerve cells.

The brain's immune cells and defense initiate a rapid response to the arrival of fibrinogen (a blood protein involved in coagulation). Fibrinogen is not found in healthy brain microglia. The response by the immune cells to this invading protein is to release large amounts of chemically reactive molecules, *reactive oxygen species*. This then creates a toxic environment within brain and nerve cells, leading to the debilitating symptoms of MS. One possible approach for treatment is to target fibrinogen microglia interactions halting nerve damage.

Acceptance

I didn't really know anything about this disease so I began reading and researching everything I could about it. The statistics were not good, but I decided back then I didn't have to be part of any statistics. The four different categories of MS eventually all lead to the same outcome. I wish I could remember which book I read this in so I could give credit where it is due because the following really stuck with me.

In a book written by a woman suffering from MS, she tells her readers with MS that it's them alone who can define who they are with the disease. Everyone is different—the afflicted are the only ones who feel how the disease is affecting them. I found this to be so true—each day brings with it its own set of circumstances and challenges.

There is no set course on how the disease affects each person. The plaques located in the brain or the spinal cord caused by the immune system attacking the nerves will only pinpoint where the impairment presents itself. How the disease progresses or what course it will take is unknown. Predicting outcomes can only be based on statistics or location of plaques—if these are apparent in the diagnostic imaging tests administered. The computed tomography (CT) scan of my head taken following my initial attack hadn't revealed any plaques. It was only the MRI taken the year later that showed the presence of plaques.

The fact remained—everything was very different now. It did take a couple of years for me to accept and come to terms with it. Many tell you to go on with the status quo and keep on with your normal life. For myself, at that time, that didn't make sense. My life had drastically changed. I was struggling to get past the denial to move on to acceptance.

I needed to accept that uncertainty had become the new norm. There was no going back. Pretending life was exactly the same as it had been before the disease struck seemed absurd and foolish to me. There is a period of grief one must go through when losing something as precious as health.

Reluctantly, after deep soul searching and weighing the pros and cons, I eventually gave up working outside the home. This was definitely not part of the original plan when I'd decided to move. I had so looked forward to starting fresh in a new job. I'd expected to be able to put in another twenty or thirty years at work until my retirement age. Not doing so left me feeling a loss of part of my identity.

The work I did entailed extensive use of my eyes using a computer. I didn't want to risk straining the vision I had left in only one eye. Deep down, I felt I didn't have the energy for performing at work either. I wouldn't be able to last day in and day out. It took a lot out of me to give up my independence. This had always been one of my most cherished qualities.

I remembered too well that, shortly prior to being stricken with MS, I had had a terrible flu bug hit me at work. It was the longest flu bout I'd ever experienced. Throughout my career of working in office buildings, I, like many others, had lived through and suffered from the virulent bugs making their rounds on a yearly basis. This last flu bug had taken a hold of my body for weeks. Now afflicted with MS, I was actually scared of exposing myself to viruses. I didn't want to chance picking up a virus in the fear it could precipitate another MS attack. I remembered how long I had endured the last one. I knew I was more vulnerable now because my immune system was compromised.

To this day, when going out in public, I'm very careful—always alert as to what is going on in my surroundings. I purposely change direction if I'm out and about and hear someone sneeze. I try to plan my shopping trips first thing in the morning when there aren't as many people out. I especially avoid any activities with large crowds in the winter months, when viruses are active.

Some people do or will think I am a bit paranoid. I decided long ago not to give much attention to what other people think. They are not the ones living with this disease. If they fail to respect the choices I make, it's not my responsibility to make them understand why I am a bit obsessed about maintaining my space the best I can.

Reassuring anyone that I am fine despite the restrictions I place on myself is not my concern. There was one time when I did have to convince the neurologist I was okay, despite the obvious confinement in regards to my social life or lack thereof. I make the choices I have to make because I'm more than aware of what this disease leads to. It is my sole responsibility to control adverse conditions that are threatening to my physical wellness. Some things we should and must control. This is one area where at least I had and have a choice; I choose to minimize my exposure if I can.

Two years after my initial MS attack, I did suffer another optic neuritis attack in my good eye. My eyesight almost totally disappeared. To say that I was terrified is an understatement. Fortunately, I knew by then, most optic neuritis attacks are never as ravaging as mine had been. I hung on to that thought as I went to the emergency department at the hospital. Luckily, this episode was indeed short-lived. I didn't lose any more vision than I'd already lost. The fright was enough; my decision to give up work was final.

Oddly enough, the roles of the home felt demanding. This was, without a doubt, my new reality. After being independent and working two jobs to make a living—it wasn't easy for me to give up working for my livelihood. Fortunately, I was able to choose this option with the support of my family. Still, I struggled with it for years. Even to this day, I miss work and the interaction and satisfaction that go with it. For the most part, I had always enjoyed my work. I was good at my job and had built a reputation to go with it. I understand fully that not everyone wants or is able to leave his or her work behind.

Looking back now, I can honestly say giving up work was the best and wisest decision for me at the time. I needed to just be and come to terms with what was lost and learn to appreciate and love every moment. Things looked very different. I couldn't ignore that stark reality. I had to learn to make the best of it and not stress by minimizing overreactions, keeping a grateful outlook, denying frustrations, and letting many things go.

I made lifestyle adjustments to compensate for the shortfall in income my not working created. There was no need for the expense of a second family automobile. I mostly was happy being housebound.

One difficult aspect of dealing with not working was the inadequacy I felt when responding to people who asked what I did for a living. As much as we don't realize it, we do judge people by what they do for a living. I'm guilty of this discrimination myself. As my daughter grew older, the awkwardness I felt when asked what I did for a living was amplified.

Unless a woman is at home with young children, today's society values her out in the workforce. I have never answered that question by saying I was disabled. I'd answer saying I was forced into early retirement for medical reasons. Most people didn't pry. If they did, my response was, "It's a long story." As the years went by and I aged, I got away with simply answering that I was retired.

I instead found purpose in the little things in life that I had been too busy to appreciate when I was working. It's regretful it took a chronic illness for me to slow down—learn to live in the moment. I was grateful to be able to walk my daughter to school, wait with her for the bus, and be there when she came home from school at the end of the day and for lunch.

These times I would never have experienced had I been working. I took correspondence courses, found new interests, and discovered new hobbies. I dove into gardening—from herbs to flowers to vegetables. I immersed myself in learning as much as I could about various topics. I particularly enjoyed and appreciated having the time to learn about nutrition and healing.

Many years later, after a near emotional breakdown, I realized I should've returned to some type of work sooner rather than later. By then, my skills were really outdated. I needed retraining if I wanted to reenter the workforce. My recommendation to anyone facing this type of dilemma: Do take time to let whatever you're facing sink in and to adjust—but not too much time.

There is still a need for balance. If work is something you rather enjoy, as I did, it's better not to totally give up that part of yourself. Do not wait too long to get back in the routine. Otherwise, you run the risk of feeling too isolated. That is not something you want to experience.

Awakening

Many do learn what works and what doesn't to manage their disease. The doctors and specialists give you information they think might be helpful depending on your particular situation. Medications are administered to alleviate symptoms as best as they can. There are support and therapies offered to cope according to the severity of the symptoms.

Like many other diseases, MS's management can become cumbersome and seem futile. Coping mechanisms are not uniform; adaptations differ according to life circumstances and difficulties experienced. Uncertainties of the disease course challenge even the most levelheaded of personalities. Post-traumatic stress disorder (PTSD) is also possible for people facing serious medical conditions.

I remember attending a seminar on newer drug treatments available and hearing that, for people with MS, these were exciting times. Medical doctors were saying that, if you had to pick a time to become afflicted with this disease, this was the best time. Twenty or thirty years prior, there were no drugs available to help control relapses.

Neurologists from the MS Clinic claimed the drugs they were promoting reduced not only the rate of relapses but their severity as well. Hearing that at the time made me somewhat hopeful. It wouldn't surprise me if they are saying exactly the same thing today. There is never a good time to become afflicted with this disease or any disease for that matter. Anyone implying otherwise is putting up a front or selling something.

Eventually, I decided to take one of the newly available medications, a beta-interferon, for RRMS. This drug is prescribed to reduce the number of MS attacks. I took it for years. Apart from the side effects of flu-like symptoms, injection-site rashes, and internal fibrous scar tissue, I was rather well while on it. I won't dispute any of the claims made about it.

After approximately seven years, I felt it was time to give my body a break from the medication. I gradually stopped taking this drug treatment. I feared the long-term side effects. These hadn't, and still haven't, been determined. This medication was fairly new—the data was not available. It's a bit perturbing when the drug makers and the doctors can't tell you exactly how the drugs work. All they can say is they do work.

Recent medical news headlines reported certain popular medications used for decades were contributing to development of other conditions. One example, the contraception pill, used for decades by women, was now declared more harmful than previously thought. Honestly, no one can really say with certainty how these new drugs will affect our bodies. It's unnerving enough to realize that, when you are taking MS medications, you've suppressed your immune system, leaving yourself vulnerable to other illnesses.

Some of us have come to realize we need to become proactive, rather than reactive with regards to our health. As information is made readily available through media, specifically the World Wide Web, people can make informed choices. There is still, however, a reactive type of mentality among many in the government-regulated, profit-driven medical communities. As much as advancements are made on numerous fronts, major diseases have yet to be cured.

Insofar as health is concerned, it appears the most popular proactive approach available from governments comes in the form of vaccines. Everything else is left for individuals to deal with. Coverage for the basics of care—dental, visual, physiotherapy, and others are not provided unless people can pay out of their own pockets. Many of these services are classified as extended benefits under certain health care plans.

Thankfully, the pace at which new discoveries are made is rapid, as geneticists unlock the mysteries of the human genome. Expectantly, as our understanding deepens, advanced awareness will give rise to ensuring basic needs are met—bringing a healthy collective consciousness and enhancing health as a mindset rather than a burden. Sadly, a society that does not assist in effectively meeting the basic needs of its citizens creates a fragmented diseased outlook to health.

Health, which should be at the forefront of our vision, is not so evident in an uncooperative, oppressive, distorted, and confining reality. Would society not fare better overall in an incorporated, disciplined, and proactive environment? It's in offering abundant varieties of prevention assistance and advanced monitoring and, thereby, helping to maintain health that we'll celebrate optimum collective health. This is realistic and attainable in this day and age. The present reactive, restrictive, and selective attitude to health is outdated.

In the United States, the right to bear arms is one area where the public is fiercely involved in fighting the government. I understand it is about freedom to choose. Why is the right to health care for all being ignored? Instead of demanding these human rights for our well-being, we let ourselves be ruled by corporations that care only about their bottom lines.

How can the big pharma companies raking in millions in profits each year justify misleading and using the poor of India for drug trials? These are the companies we here on the other side of the world trust with our health. The shareholders of these multimillion-dollar businesses are either unaware or don't care. They, too, are contributing to the goings-on behind the scenes. They should demand better ethics from the companies they invest in.

We the public are many, and we must not consciously support these types of abuses. At present, the poor are left with few other options. The dispensary of drugs is a much easier process than providing alternatives. Those of us with the means to make better choices need to start tightening the screws on these companies by not purchasing their products.

Conventional medicine does screen urine samples for the presence of blood, elevated levels of glucose, proteins, or hormones. From these a number of health issues like kidney stones, urinary tract infections, pregnancy, and on and on are diagnosed. However, unless something questionable prompts attention, requests for specific medical tests are not performed. The tests in annual medical exams do not depict the whole picture of someone's health.

Rather than a complete picture, fractions of information often lead to misguided results. Simple analyses, such as total vitamin and mineral levels and stress tests, are usually not requested in regular screening. Vitamin B$_{12}$ deficiency includes vague symptoms of fatigue, heart palpitations, and shortness of breath. Signs are subtle, as they are with most vitamin deficiencies. It takes several years to progress into something serious like anemia. Vitamin B$_{12}$ is essential for proper reproduction of our red blood cells. Apparently rare, this deficiency could lead a person to requiring supplements for the rest of their life. Early detection makes it possible to eliminate such outcomes.

It makes sense to screen for vitamin and mineral levels—possibly preventing lifetime dependencies on treatments. Avoiding irreparable damage with early detection and promptly addressing the shortfall is proactive. Rather than prescribing drugs, it's possible to treat certain afflictions with a change in diet or supplementation of vitamins. A good example of how this might work is adding extra magnesium to alleviate muscle spasms.

Vitamins and minerals play key roles in our bodies. Most of us are, in all probability, not getting enough of these from the foods we eat. This is not just because we're not eating enough of the right foods. The soil our plant-sourced foods are grown in might not be providing sufficient nutrients or could be laden with pesticides or other chemicals. The reasons we have shortfalls are many.

Only specific and evident symptoms bring about the will to dig deeper into one's state of health. Without obtaining and gathering important details for a clearer, more accurate picture of health, individuals are left with no preventative treatment until manifestations are visible. These old standards and practices let illnesses take hold rather than halt their development. Many are put through unnecessary suffering for years. Proper diagnoses and the early identification of problems, via more expensive screening tests, are not made available. Better screening might not only avoid complications and alleviate suffering, it would reduce costs in the long run.

Individuals are mostly left to their own demise insofar as applying preventative measures for good health. While many do welcome this responsibility, I suspect most just don't have the time, the inclination, or the resources to become too involved. If we are well, we believe how we feel physically will continue at least until we become old. For some people, it remains so.

For many of us, this does change sooner than we think. The busy demands of life, for many, especially those without adequate support, leaves health to chance. As stress levels become harder to cope with, the physical and emotional distresses experienced increase the susceptibility of our bodies to triggers like viruses and bacteria, making them prime environments for developing illness. This is magnified if our diets are lacking in nutrition.

Maintaining a healthy lifestyle does require work and awareness. One is going against the wave of simplicity and convenience when adopting a healthier way of living. Incentives must be found within—they are not forthcoming elsewhere. Privileges afforded to only a few do nothing to instill esteem for a direction of appreciation and respect of health in the general population. Those who have are able to pay for services to direct their choices and assist them in leading healthy lifestyles. Others who have not are left restricted to choose poorly. Consequently, the rate of disease increases, as does the cost of health care. The cycle of treating symptoms persists.

As links are made between poor health and limited choices, the best we hear from the mainstream, another study is being commissioned. Monies, especially public monies, spent on these types of studies is better used to effect real and immediate changes, exactly at the determinant cause for the study.

One example that comes to mind left me bewildered when I first heard it. Get this, "Study Supports Link between Obesity, Cavities in Homeless Kids." This study was to provide further evidence on reports from the US Centers for Disease Control and Prevention. They had linked obesity and poor oral health to increased risks of health problems and self-esteem issues in the homeless population. Really? It took another study to affirm these conclusions!

I do not profess to know the reasons behind this study or any other studies. Was it simply to provide more evidence to support the reports, or was it to bring attention to the problems of homelessness? Last I heard, more studies were planned. Honestly, do you think this helped in any way?

Wouldn't the simplest of actions—provide a new toothbrush and floss—serve the public good better than these types of studies? In cases like this, the results could speak for themselves. It would be a start. I doubt when Doctors without Borders decide to allocate themselves and their resources in war-torn or disease-ravaged nations, they ordered a study to discern precisely what their roles there were going to be. They see a need; they try to fill it as best as they can. They make a real difference!

Studies dissect information to provide statistics on how exactly the proposed change will affect the outcome. Problems are dragged out and become more complex when the solution, or at least part of it, is in plain view. What is needed are actions to stop the suffering of our fellow human beings. The majority of medical studies are beneficial and crucial for research and the advancement of medical science. There seem to be many that are simply unnecessary. Launching a study might be a prudent route to take in some instances where further evidence is warranted. In many cases, the end result has already been determined.

Stakeholders will order studies in order to reaffirm and assert their positions on a particular claim or product. If studies produce different outcomes than previous ones, they are rebutted and called into question. It's often the studies done by third parties—yielding results not anticipated or supportive of the status quo—that are disputed.

In September 2012, the government of France requested a health watchdog conduct an investigation after results of a study done by researchers linked genetically modified corn to cancer in rats. Earlier, a study led by Gilles-Eric Séralini, "Long term toxicity of a Roundup herbicide and a Roundup-tolerant genetically modified maize" is a perfect example. It was immediately disputed because it produced unexpected results. A greater number of studies assert this grain is safe. I leave you to speculate by whom they were commissioned.

There is much activity on the nanotechnology front. Micro-electromechanical systems (MEMS) and silicon chips implantable in the human body is a field that has seen fast growth, especially in the last decade. The chips in development will be implanted in and used to monitor the human body. This is way beyond the fitness tracker wearables we have now. They'll be able to detect diseases or conditions at the microscopic level. It looks promising as a proactive tool. However, it does raise questions of how the information will be used. Is it going to be used to help us? Or will it further divide the *haves* from the *have-nots*?

The people who can afford it will have timely surgeries and prompt treatments. For those who are without means, the chips will observe while diseases take their tolls and study drugs used in treatments. Some of these chips are specifically developed to administer drugs. This new technology has the potential to only serve the purpose of promoting and, quite possibly, imposing the use of medications.

One need not be a believer in conspiracy theories, and I am not, to realize there's an exorbitant amount of money to be made keeping with the status quo. Let's face it; when choices made are to treat symptoms not cure illnesses before they develop, there is only one loser—the consumer/patient.

Smart technology brings us phones we can use to check our blood pressure or, if diabetic, keep an eye on our blood glucose levels. Dr. Eric Topol, author of *The Creative Destruction of Medicine*, appeared on NBC,

January 25, 2013. He predicts that, someday, smartphones will let users run routine medical tests themselves and share data with their physicians. Hopefully this facilitates and frees up doctors to practice preventative medicine dedicated to accurately diagnosing illnesses.

We try to eat better and, meanwhile, discover our food is contaminated, recalled, or genetically modified. The mass production of plant foods has eroded and altered the soil, leaving it deficient in minerals. Once isolated instances, recalls on food items have become all too common. Some foods thought to be harmless or even beneficial are eventually proven harmful. Our healthiest foods make us sick and have killed. Even water, our most basic need, has claimed lives due to contamination. In May 2000, seven people died from the Escherichia coli (E. coli) bacteria-contaminated water supply of the town of Walkerton, Ontario, Canada.

Some of these tragedies are the result of human error or negligence. They are rightfully condemned. What about the intentional integration of harmful chemicals into our foods and almost everything we consume? We are informed that some of the vitamins we have been taking may be creating more harm than good. The artificial dyes used in the majority of these pills are wreaking havoc in our bodies. Many people now consciously avoid foods with dyes in them, only to then pop vitamins made colorful with these synthetic dyes.

The enteric coating on some medications to ensure they transit through the stomach to the intestinal track intact in order to avoid stomach upsets includes artificial dyes. The chemicals used to make these dyes can create a range of problems, not limited to gastrointestinal troubles. Rashes often develop when the dyes are released through the skin. Many of these products are consumed on a daily basis.

As difficult as it is to overlook the shortcomings imposed by sectarian, outdated methods, we really need to answer for ourselves. It's up to us individually to make better choices. Eventually the powers that be will have no choice but to change with the rest of us.

There are already small changes taking place. Product labels are used by more and more producers. Healthier menu items are offered in some restaurants and fast food chains. Caloric and nutritional values are frequently displayed. As each of us make small health conscious choices, we, altogether, will create a big ripple effect in the overall scheme of things. Gradually, we'll tip the scales in a new direction of health.

Something as simple as choosing water over sweetened drinks more often than not will ultimately affect companies' profit margins. This is probably the only way they'll respond. It's the choices we make that will bring change. If the demand is still there—things will remain as they are.

A major food manufacturer launched an organic baby food line at the same or better price than its regular variety. Baby steps are gradually bringing us change. We still have a long way to go. Steadily, we can increase the stride by demanding better and not settling for less.

It's bad enough that a lot of the foods we consume are genetically modified. We must not let our bodies become prisoners to fast, convenient, manufactured foods. We really don't want to end up trapped, having to take meds for ongoing conditions that become endless. Certain medications lead to other conditions. It's disturbing when the lists of side effects of some drugs go on and on.

In Canada, prescribed medications take the second largest share of the health care budget after hospitals. We need to realize what this actually says about our lifestyles and the society we live in. Among seniors, the top three pharmaceuticals used are for treatment of high cholesterol, hypertension, and acid reflux.

The word *polypharmacy* is given to describe the use of multiple medications. In 2010–11 this term applied to 69 percent of Canadian seniors' medicating practices. At the ages of eighty-five and beyond, the number of prescription drugs taken reaches a staggering number of fifteen plus. We can assume this number has grown yearly. It's expected to continue increasing exponentially in the coming decades—the majority of the population here will be in the senior range.

We have to take charge of our health to avoid afflictions before there's no other recourse but to be at the mercy of drugs in order to exist (and then, when we're older, to be lodged in facilities using exactly the same methods in care that got us there in the first place). At this time in our evolution, it's pitiful to grasp that a dog groomer is better paid than a personal support worker. I'm not saying either does not deserve to be well paid—both involve care. However, it's obviously a bit more complicated and intensive to care for elderly people than it is to groom pets.

There is effort required in taking back control. It's not without reward though! It's the greatest gift you can give yourself. We've all heard the term reborn Christian. What if we could be reborn healthy? Our bodies are extraordinary in their capacity to heal and regenerate. As we take better care of our bodies, our minds will respond accordingly. It starts with understanding how the foods we eat, the physical activity we exert, and the thoughts we focus on all have a compounding role in our health.

CHAPTER 2

Understanding Some Basics

Renewal

A quick overview of white blood cells (WBCs), or leukocytes, gives us a glimpse into just how complex and intricate our bodies' immune system is. It has to be—it protects us from invading organisms, fights infections, and heals. These warrior cells that seek, identify, and kill foreign microbes are mostly made in our bone marrow. A higher than normal count of WBCs in our blood indicates infection. The measurement of their levels is normally included in routine blood tests. A prolonged extremely high number of WBCs, in the range of fifty thousand per drop of blood, indicates leukemia.

Without getting too bogged down in the biology of cells, it's still worth taking a look at the major types of cells constantly active in our body's defense. Neutrophils outnumber the others, taking up between 50 to 70 percent of the total WBCs. They are our body's first defense against bacteria and fungi. They're able to kill bad bacteria by completely surrounding and then digesting them with digestive enzymes.

The eosinophils kill parasites and have a role in allergic reactions. Basophils are involved in inflammatory reactions. They also have a role in parasitic infections and allergies. Lymphocytes produce antibodies providing resistance to prior infections. They can be found in the lymph nodes, tonsils, gastrointestinal tract, and the spleen. Monocytes, the largest of the WBCs, produce macrophages that are scavengers. They eat up bacteria and dead neutrophils—they clean up after an infection is killed.

As amazing as all that, there's another important role our warrior cells participate in that was only recently discovered. They're very much implicated in the regeneration of our red blood cells. The red cells' basic function is to carry blood oxygen throughout the body and bring carbon dioxide to our lungs to be released as we breathe. The WBCs were reported to play a key role in controlling red blood cell levels. The researchers were able to demonstrate that macrophages nurture production of new red blood cells, all the while they're remove aging red cells from circulation.

To this day, there are still many questions yet to be answered. With an estimated count of 85 billion neurons, gone are the days when we thought we only used 10 percent of our brains. Today's technology enables us to view the brain as it responds to different stimuli. It's mapped out a better understanding of how our brains work.

We are far from knowing, and may never know, how each element is interrelated and affected by the foods we feed our bodies with and our thoughts and actions/lifestyles. There are always new discoveries made and a great anticipation of the possibility our brain might be able to heal and repair itself.

The human body has ten times more bacteria cells than human cells. Human cells are estimated at about ten trillion—bacteria cells at about one hundred trillion. These bacteria cells inhabit our bodies mostly in the intestines and other parts of our digestive system. There are about five hundred to a thousand species of bacteria and yeasts in our gut and an equal amount for the skin, eyes, and saliva. Even with most of these organisms proven useful and crucial, the effects of many are still unknown.

How our immune systems react with these bacteria plays a role in diseases such as Crohn's. To assist our digestive system, we can supplement with probiotics or eat fermented foods like yogurt. There are other bacteria we know we need to avoid at all costs. We are aware we have to handle our raw meats carefully to avoid cross-contamination. We know to cook our meats to a high temperature in order to kill salmonella and E. coli bacteria.

Our human cells reside with a majority of bacteria, and now we have introduced an enormous array of man-made chemicals to the mix. It could take a generation or longer to discover the effects all these chemicals will have on our bodies. It is a well-known fact that our red blood cells regenerate every four months.

It is known that a deficiency in vitamin B_{12} affects our body's ability to produce red blood cells. Now there are chemicals added to our bloodstream affecting this process—probably not in a good way. We don't know how all the chemicals we drink in our water, eat in our foods, and slather all over our bodies react with our cells, disturb the bacteria equilibrium, and impair our body's regeneration capabilities. There is no way to know all this.

Every minute, within our bodies, new cells are made and others are dying. Similar to our nails and hair regrowth, there is other regeneration occurring inside our bodies. Exceptionally, insofar as what we know up to now—the liver's regeneration capabilities are nothing short of miraculous. Only a quarter of it needs to be available for the regeneration to take place. The rate at which it regenerates, too, is fast depending on the extent of damage. Sources say the total regeneration of a liver takes between one to five months.

A lot of research is being done to understand the apoptosis (programmed self-destruction of cells) and the rebirth of cells throughout the human body. Research by KL Spalding et al. observed one-third of the subpopulation of hippocampal neurons are subject to exchange. Seven hundred new neurons are added to each hippocampus per day, with a slight decline seen in aging.

Moreover, it has been determined for some time now that learning something new like a new language or even just doing crossword puzzles benefits our brain health by creating new pathways. This is an important fact to keep in mind as our populations age, perhaps helping prolong independence. Technology fits in well with this, bringing new subjects, games, and an endless array of other stimuli to get our brain active.

Previous animal research showed injecting younger blood into older animals improved stem cells functionality at various locations in the bodies of mice. In trying to figure out if similar effects could be demonstrated on an aging human brain, scientists identified the youth protein, GDF11, that is present in plenty when we're young and disappears as we age.

Where all this leads should prove very interesting indeed. Another exciting development follows investigations into the science of molecular biology. These investigations supported the concept that our genes are as changeable as our brain cells if given the right signals. Should this hold true, it's impossible to imagine the vast implications of this discovery.

Then and Now

One hundred years ago, the life expectancy for the majority of people was forty years. The leading cause of human deaths was infectious diseases. Tuberculosis, as it is called today, has plagued humans for thousands of years. It took the majority of human lives when it was known as consumption. It has now morphed into a strain resistant to the antibiotics used to treat it. It is still very much a threat.

The catastrophic flu pandemic of 1918 took an estimated fifty million lives. Whether the cause was the flu or the vaccines developed to prevent it, number of deaths was horrific (it's not unreal to think both took their toll on the populations). Given the urgency to mass-produce vaccines, compromised integrity in one form or another was probable.

As much as we try to prevent infection from pathogenic bacteria, we ourselves may be carriers without even knowing it. There are bacteria that reside in a person's body that do not create any physical symptoms. These are then transmittable in one way or another and cause illnesses in others.

One case in point on the subject of unsuspecting carriers of bacteria was famous in the early 1900s. A woman carrying the deadly typhoid fever bacteria was responsible for the death of many. Typhoid Mary, as she became known, held a job as a cook and thus, unknowingly, transmitted the bacteria to others. It's an interesting story in that she couldn't be held responsible for her guilt in the initial outbreaks. Defiantly, she returned to cooking years later, ignoring her deadly reach, and caused further outbreaks, claiming more victims.

It's from the animal kingdom that many bacteria are transmitted to humans. From mosquitoes, fleas, houseflies, rodents, and our beloved pets, infectious bacteria find entry into human hosts, where they cause diseases and deaths. The fourteenth-century bubonic plague in Europe was transmitted to humans by fleas carrying bacteria from rats. The great pestilence, or the Black Death as it was called, killed a third of seventy-five million people in four years. It returned every eight years for over three-quarters of a century, wiping out over half of the population. The *yersinia pestis* bacterium still lives today, affecting rodents. It's transmitted by fleas and cats that have been in contact with infected rodents.

It's believed the Black Death started in Asia's infected rats that hitched a ride on ships during the silk trade between China and Europe. Native to central Asia, the large marmot rodent is believed to have played a key role in spreading the bacteria. Infected trapped furs sold along the river to ports of thriving communities, including rat populations, helped distribute the organism. It went to Sicily, to France, to Britain, and on to Denmark, Germany, and Poland.

We live in a day and age when we have access to a multitude of drugs, vaccines, and antibiotics. Regrettably, some treatments inadvertently create other ailments—even cause death—so many are not without risks.

Modernization, with its dismissive attitude and failure to investigate ancient natural methods, has substantially delayed antibiotic development.

A secret government report revealed eighteen child deaths occurred within four years following vaccinations. Rare and serious reactions to vaccinations are a fact of living these days. For those who are affected, these can be devastating or fatal. There've been times when batches of vaccines supposed to prevent illnesses were recalled due to contamination.

In late summer and fall 2012, a drug administered to treat back pain in US patients was contaminated with a fungus. It caused a national meningitis outbreak killing thirty-nine people and leaving many others compromised. It's estimated around fourteen thousand people nationwide received injections with this black mold steroid. It's unknown what the future will bring for many of the recipients because the fungus is known to create problems only later on.

Not only errors but also some side effects can be life threatening. A cancer drug used to treat a type of brain cancer, used in chemotherapy for metastasized cancers, is linked to the bacterial infection necrotizing fasciitis, commonly known as flesh-eating disease. More common drugs, antibiotics called fluoroquinolones, used to treat urinary tract and other bacterial infections are having damaging consequences on the eyes—in some patients leading to retinal detachment.

It's very much like playing Russian roulette when we're subjected to some of these treatments. Although the treatments are, no doubt, helpful and lifesaving for many, there is no way to accurately predict the outcome for everyone. There are many heart-wrenching stories of people whose lives were adversely or tragically affected when they became part of the statistical few who did react to the drugs prescribed. A person needs to look no further than to Terence Young's book, *A Death by Prescription*, about his daughter's sudden death after taking prescribed medication for a stomach ailment.

New vaccines are not without controversy. There were reports of one particular vaccine being fast-tracked in order to beat the competition. Further research revealed disturbing information on this controversial vaccine. I really can't say on which side of the fence I stand on this subject. It's clear many deadly diseases have been kept at bay because of vaccinations. I would probably opt to take a vaccine if ever there was a case of a deadly outbreak. As it stands now—I haven't had a vaccine in decades.

What is unclear is whether there's a need for so many. It's for that reason I choose not to roll up my sleeve every time a new vaccine is offered. This is purely a personal choice, as it should be for everyone. You have to decide for yourself if this is something you believe benefits you.

There are people who question whether vaccinations are implicated in children with autism. The number of vaccines administered today is far greater than it was when I was a child. Perhaps there's a link with some babes being more sensitive to the numerous types of vaccines administered so early after birth—all within a short period of time of each other. It is unfortunate the mother's antibodies passed on to her babies decrease after the age of two months.

As I said earlier, I'd been given two tetanus vaccines within approximately three years of each other. Since my body had already produced the antibodies necessary from the first administration of the vaccine, maybe the second vaccine sent my immune system in overkill. Whether the double dose of the tetanus vaccine had anything to do with precipitating MS is a question that's likely to remain unanswered.

Parents with autistic children may never get their answers either regarding possible vaccine implications in autism. Is it possible that, once an immune system has developed antibodies to a specific disease, administering more of the same vaccines within a specific period of time creates an overload that compromises the immune defenses? Is it only in certain people the immune system overreacts and causes damage?

In the last few decades, yearly flu vaccines are offered and recommended to the general population. This now includes babies over six months of age. It is highly recommended that people with chronic diseases and compromised immune systems get the yearly flu vaccines. In many circumstances this practice is being forced on workers.

In some lines of work, taking the vaccine is mandatory. Refusing to do so imparts upon employees unpleasant consequences. Those who work with the elderly, in hospitals, medical clinics, and others are often left with no choice. They must adhere to the guidelines on working with the public and accept the yearly flu vaccinations. If they don't, they run the risk of losing sick pay benefits should they become ill during the flu season.

I find it hard to wrap my head around the advice given to those with MS on staying away from anything stimulating to the immune system, such as the herb Echinacea, while on the other hand we're told to get the yearly flu shot. It's claimed that having the yearly flu shots helps people develop the immunity to fight off the viruses. Even if true, as someone who needs to keep my immune system in check, I choose not to participate. Again, this is my personal choice. I'm not advocating it for anyone else. This needs to be a decision everyone makes on his or her own, rather than enforced—taking away our freedom to choose.

The overuse of antibiotics to treat infections the human body has the ability to successfully clear itself of has narrowed the effectiveness of their lifesaving potentials. Fever, a normal reaction of the body's immune system dealing with infections, was, for a period of time, treated as a condition to immediately and entirely suppress with drugs. During those times, parents with young, feverish children flocked to emergency rooms of hospitals and were widely prescribed antibiotics. Moderate fevers that eventually and naturally run their courses were unnecessarily treated.

It's been established for some time now that illnesses of viral origins are not treatable with antibiotics. Wisely, doctors are now much more cautious in prescribing them. That change in trend is a bit late for some, as it's come to light that taking only one course of some broad-spectrum antibiotics can wipe out the entire array of good bacteria from our guts permanently. Some doctors do recommend their patients replenish their gut flora with good bacteria after taking an antibiotic. Patients will not always follow through if they lack the information on how to proceed or don't have the means to. Probiotics are not prescribed medications—their cost is not covered.

As it was in the last century, the deaths of so many were, in the majority, related to infections. The diseases killing many today are mostly related too. They are the direct result of inflammation. We must not kid ourselves; infection outbreaks can hit us out of left field without time to react or means to eradicate them before they take lives. In a world where billions travel across the globe on a daily basis, it's not inconceivable a fast spreading infection makes its way here.

What one population has developed immunity to may not be so easily tolerated by others who have not had the same exposure. These potential threats make it all the more important we strive to maintain optimum health as best we can. We have to keep our bodies free from the stresses of constant inflammation.

Inflammation

Inflammation is an essential natural part of the body's healing process. We see this acute inflammatory immune system response at its best when the body reacts to an injury such as a bruise or a cut. The healing begins instantly. The bump we see and feel after an insect bite is our body's reaction to the intrusion. It's the amazing immune system doing its job. It protects against outside agents so we don't fall extremely ill when subjected to hazardous compounds and provides healing when harm is inflicted.

It's chronic inflammation or systemic inflammation that's harmful to the human body. What causes this chronic inflammation in the body? So far we do know stress, poor diet, lack of sleep and exercise, undetected infections or allergens, excessive use of alcohol, and toxins all lead to inflammation. Basically it boils down to diet and lifestyle. This is not news. We've heard this over and over again. Some of you will roll your eyes in defiance and yawn. It doesn't take away from the fact intricate complex processes are taking place 24-7 in our immune systems, keeping us alive.

The constant inflammation often undetected until serious damage has occurred is active in many diseases and speeds up the aging process. The link between gum disease and heart disease was made some time ago. MS is an inflammatory autoimmune disease in which the body turns on itself. Inflammation in the joints is common in many types of arthritis. Allergies are inflammatory responses by the body to pathogens. Asthma is inflammation in the respiratory system. The list goes on and on. What is disconcerting is many of the diseases associated with inflammation are or will become life threatening.

As people age, this type of inflammation becomes apparent with more involved screening offered, when diseases begin to take hold, and when functions decline. This is, by no means, only a condition of the old. Unfortunately, uncovering hidden inflammation before symptoms are obvious is not standard.

Proteins are markers for disease. There's a blood test to detect inflammation in the body. However, it is not part of the usual yearly routine gamut when blood is collected for analyzing. The test measures the amount of the protein C-reactive (CRP) in the blood, indicating the degree of inflammation present. Usually this test has to be specifically requested by doctors.

How are we to know if we don't have access to this hidden knowledge? Since inflammation is easily identifiable in the blood, consistently screening for it to determine susceptibility to disease is common sense. Discovering this marker early would provide people with direction; and real support on how to adjust and change their lifestyles and diets might go a long way in disease prevention.

What's All the Gut About?

Although this area of health is largely uncharted, unstudied territory, we are aware many diseases begin in the gut. The research to support this claim is well underway. The US National Institutes of Health initiative, started in 2008, identifies and characterizes microorganisms found in healthy and diseased humans. The Human Microbiome Project's goal is to test how changes in the human microbiome are associated with human health or disease. You can visit HMP's website at www.hmpdacc.org for further information.

Questions on the role of gastrointestinal (GI) health and its part in different diseases including neurological diseases are being raised. Hopefully, as research advances, answers will follow promptly. The vagus (Latin for wandering) nerve is actually two cranial nerves originating in the brain stem that travel and branch out throughout the human body. From the brain to the tongue, the ears, the heart, the lungs, and then to the digestive organs—this wandering nerve sends a variety of signals to and from the brain.

In the abdomen branches, it enters the stomach, pancreas, small intestine, large intestine, and the colon. The vagus nerve regulates the chemical levels in the digestive system to assist in the processing of food and nutrient absorption. It's further involved in regulating a variety of body functions, including the heartbeat, breathing, and muscle movement.

Research shows Parkinson's disease (PD) early stages center on the nucleus of the vagus nerve sending vagrant connections to the gastrointestinal tract. There were two studies in which the protein a-synuclein (aSYN) was identified as a biomarker in the development of PD. The protein was found in patients' tissues of specimens from colonoscopy biopsies, collected years before they even presented with early PD symptoms.

Further research is needed to back this up. Testing for PD during routine colonoscopy screening is a definite possibility. In another study, increased levels of aSYN oligomers, macromolecular complex, were observed in the blood plasma of PD patients. This looks promising for easier diagnosing of PD, now only identifiable through brain imaging.

Important for people with demyelination diseases, researchers identified through observations a sequence of events triggering organ-specific autoimmune diseases. In one model of encephalomyelitis, a microbial infection triggered auto-aggressive responses from the immune system's T and B cells. The autoantibody-producing T cells depend on availability of target autoantigen and commensal gut bacteria. In ecological terms, commensal is a class of relationship between two organisms—where one benefits without affecting the other. Microbiota means microscopic living organisms of a region.

Disorders of the vagus nerve, overactive or underactive, resulting from damage were seen in diabetes, post-surgery, and trauma, patients, as well as in those presenting with viral infections, chronic illnesses, and alcoholism. Symptoms of vagus nerve disorders vary greatly, since it reaches many organs and parts in the body. These range from difficulty swallowing, voice changes, ringing in the ears, pain, or a drop in heart rate and blood pressure to urinary incontinence and constipation. A person's increased susceptibly to develop peptic ulcers because the stomach is producing too much acid is another indication of vagus nerve damage.

Some specific larger-than-normal populations of gut bacteria are possible causes of diseases like rheumatoid arthritis (RA). Long suspected to play a role in RA, gut microbiome could now be used as a biomarker for predisposition. Apart from genetic susceptibility, hormonal changes and aging precipitate inflammatory conditions.

The latest news on Crohn's disease is it's more than likely fungus related. Individuals with Crohn's have a higher than normal interaction between two types of bacteria and the fungus *candida tropicalis*. This creates a biofilm leading to inflammation. One involved bacteria, *serratia marcescens*—responsible for turning our toilet bowls pink—thrives in moist environments. It's already been detected in numerous ailments, from urinary tract and respiratory infections and arthritis to more serious infections like meningitis, sepsis, and so on.

Irritable bowel syndrome (IBS)

The term *irritable bowel system* (IBS) is used to describe a number of digestive issues resulting from inflamed bowels. I was diagnosed with this disorder in my midthirties, shortly before I got MS. I was suffering from discomfort in my upper left bowel area, which the doctor promptly labeled as IBS. There were no specific tests ordered; nor was any further investigation undertaken. I took my doctor's word for it. I didn't bother informing myself as to the specifics of this disorder. It wasn't until a decade and a half later that I was enlightened as to exactly what IBS meant.

This could be where I turn a lot of readers off, but I ask you to bear with me, as this is significant. If you've been watching any medical doctor programs on the television as of late, you may not be as offended. This subject has been approached on a few occasions. It's a good idea to observe our bowel movements to possibly uncover potential hidden health problems. Constitutionally speaking, a healthy bowel produces a toothpaste-like, smooth brown tube that torpedoes to the bottom of the toilet bowl. Do not panic if you see something out of the ordinary. What we eat has an effect on the outcome.

Beets imprint a red tinge, too much iron or Pepto-Bismol blacken, and asparagus leaves a peculiar smell. There are many other foods that alter the texture and coloration of our excretions. If something is out of the normal for an extended period of time, and you can't relate it to anything you've consumed, it's time to set up an appointment with your doctor. You wouldn't ignore your car if it spewed off strange fumes or pellets from its exhaust system. Ignoring any abnormalities here is not going to change the matter.

I suffered from loose bowel movements for some time. I hadn't given it much thought. I figured it was the norm for me. I attributed it to the large volume of fiber in my diet. It wasn't until, by accident, I discovered something strange in the toilet bowl that I decided to pay attention. Having just come in from the garden outside, I thought perhaps something had fallen off of my clothes, my body, or my hair.

I made it a point to examine the toilet bowl on a regular basis. At about the same time, I was experiencing severe abdominal pain every night at bedtime. It got to the point where I had to take Advil every night to get any sleep. The pain was exactly the same as the menstrual pain women experience at that time of the month. However, the pain was nightly and unrelenting, no matter whether or not I was on my period. Every night I doubled over, waiting in agony for the pain reliever to take effect. Strangely, if I napped during the day, I didn't feel any pain.

After researching on the Internet to find answers, I came upon a possible diagnosis that appeared to fit. I know what some of you are thinking; this is no way to diagnose illness. Let me assure you I am far from being a hypochondriac. I'm not one to run to the doctor every time some little thing is wrong with me. I go for my checkups when I have to. That's the extent of my presence at the doctor's office. Even that is a stretch for me. I have skipped appointments here and there. I do not really want to go there unless I absolutely have to.

The possible cause gradually became clear. Including the nightly pain, I had almost all the other symptoms but none of any others pointing to something else. After what I'd observed and what I felt, I concluded I possibly had a parasite infection. I confirmed this with the samples I got. A couple of years earlier, I had a copy of my blood test in hand to bring to another doctor's appointment. It was then I noticed that a couple of areas in the results were flagged. At the time, I'd only concerned myself with the low sodium alert. I hadn't concerned myself with the high level in another area. It seemed to be related to allergies.

Now revisiting these results, it jumped out at me. The category that had been flagged as high was the EOS level. I had scribbled parasitic infections or allergies beside the box. When I'd originally looked this up, I'd had no idea a parasitic infection, rather than allergies, could be the culprit. The concept was way beyond my scope of thinking. Frankly, I'd always believed I had allergies, although it was never confirmed with medical tests. I took it the doctor chalked the results up to high level to allergies, and that is why the high EOS level was never addressed.

Armed with what I knew and after a few weeks of nightly pain, I decided to book an appointment to see my family physician. I'd already started taking natural remedies. I was hoping for some reinforcement to eradicate the problem as quickly as possible. She told me my last blood test was normal.

I really wanted to check the EOS level myself. I was sent home with a request for stool samples. The samples came back negative. I convinced the doctor to give me a dose of medication anyways. An appointment with a specialist was booked.

The internist specialist turned out to be an absolute godsend to me. She point-blank told me, "IBS is a term thrown around after someone's suffered an infestation." I showed her some specimens and, even though we both agreed they were definitely bugs of some kind, only a laboratory equipped to analyze these sorts of things can identify them. Unfortunately, there was no such lab in the vicinity. Their origins were never determined.

Nevertheless, because of the long duration of the pain I experienced, it was deemed prudent to undergo further testing with a colonoscopy. The test didn't show any conclusive evidence. That was a good thing in a way. Had cysts been located, it would've meant the infection was severe. The possibility of undergoing some type of surgery was avoided. I was given another small dose of medication. Due to my condition, my family physician was alerted to be watchful for these types of occurrences. With a compromised immune system and the immune-suppressing drugs I had been on for years, my likelihood for infection is greater than that of the average person.

I call this miraculous because, for me, it felt like it at the time. After suffering from sinus congestion for years and chalking it up to allergies, I took the antiparasite drugs, and my sinuses cleared up almost overnight. This was a huge relief. I'd thought I'd have to live with this condition for the rest of my life.

Even more astounding, following the initial first dose of the medication, the nightly abdominal pain disappeared too. For me, even if there was never any laboratory substantiated evidence as far as the doctors were concerned, it confirmed my suspicions. If I had any doubt, it vanished after experiencing relief of so many aggravating inflammatory symptoms.

It shouldn't have been so farfetched to think I might be infected with some type of pathogen, given some of the conditions I subjected myself to. In my pursuit to satisfy my taste buds for exotic cuisines, I occasionally frequented food establishments leaving a bit to be desired insofar as cleanliness. Being an avid gardener, I had never given much thought to wearing gloves while digging in the dirt, compost, or even manure.

Usually, I only put a pair of gloves on if they were readily available. I never made it a point to always protect myself by wearing gloves. I thought washing my hands after was good enough. I never ever would've guessed I might have been exposing myself to nasty microorganisms. I've owned cats from time to time and have always owned dogs. There was one occasion when I was bitten by a mosquito while vacationing in Mexico that I never reported to my doctor. Living in the developed world in highly civilized societies with almost impeccable hygiene practices doesn't guarantee these types of incidents are rare. Infections from parasites happen and do more often than we might think.

What used to be a normal precaution has faded with deniability and arrogance. I remember my mother, bless her soul, every year like clockwork, readied all her children for back to school with a week's daily dose of cod liver oil. This was a preventative for parasitic infections. It was the responsible thing to do, akin to farmers treating their livestock and pet owners treating their animals. The populations of industrialized nations now believe that, being privy to more sanitized practices, we aren't exposed to pathogens.

Back in 2012, an article in the newspapers brought this threat home. Foxes, coyotes and rodents roaming the cities could be transmitting tapeworms to dogs and they, in turn, infecting humans. The *echinococcus multilocularis* (e. multi) parasite used to be confined to China. It was reported in nine countries of Europe during the past decade.

Startling to animal researchers is the fact this strain is now in North America with an expanding range. In 2012, it was reported in Alberta, Canada, about half of the 250 coyotes studied carried the parasite. Dogs were always believed to only carry the adult tapeworm. They're now found to have larvae cysts in their bodies. This potentially dangerous parasite, which can take years to develop into cysts, mimics liver cancer.

The cysts are located in the lungs or even the brains of humans. Available treatment is lengthy and expensive. I suspect arriving at a diagnosis isn't easy, since the majority of people have their heads in the sand regarding these types of issues. It becomes even more challenging to detect if infected individuals are not pet owners.

Another disturbing case follows the largest scale study of its kind in Canada. Tests done on prewashed leafy greens reported contamination with parasites. Out of 544 samples purchased between April 2009 and March 2010, one-tenth of the samples had *cyclospora, cryptosporidium*, or *giardia*. This wasn't an isolated incident, and it was not confined to one location.

The highest rate of contamination was in US samples, where the majority of the samples came from. Out of twenty-three samples grown in Canada, three tested positive for parasites. The seven samples from Mexico did not test positive for any. Consumers think because these vegetables are washed they are clean. Some of the samples were said to have been triple-washed. Water doesn't remove these organisms, and refrigeration only stops the growth of more. A bit of vinegar in water is a natural option used by some people for cleaning produce. What presents itself mildly in most people as a short bout of diarrhea could have severe consequences in those who are sick, elderly, or in pregnant women.

Another widespread food contamination incident was reported in the US in 2013. The Center for Disease Control (CDC) received 353 cases of *cyclospora* infection, a stomach parasite seen with fresh produce. Infections were reported in the city of New York and fourteen states—Arkansas, Connecticut, Florida, Georgia, Illinois, Iowa, Kansas, Minnesota, Missouri, Nebraska, New Jersey, Ohio, Texas, and Wisconsin. These were not linked, and the source was never identified. The symptoms associated with this illness include diarrhea, which could last up to fifty-seven days. That wasn't a typo—fifty-seven days is right.

Uninvited Guests

Claims have been made for people with autoimmune diseases that inviting some species of helminthes (intestinal worms) into their bodies may prevent the immune system from overreacting. The intention is to switch the immune system's activity to fighting off invaders, stopping it from destroying its own tissues. Those of us suffering from these diseases or disorders hope it was so simple. There are some success stories with this therapy in alleviation of symptoms.

However, there were other factors involved in those successes (such as a change in diet) that I believe might have influenced the efficacy of the therapy. This raises the question of whether the relief was indeed a result of the therapy itself or of the changes in lifestyles. The data on the long-term impact for this therapy is not yet in. I'm not challenging the reports that some individuals felt better using this therapy. For myself, I know firsthand how the parasites in my body affected my health in many ways irrelevant to MS. My gut health is not something I am prepared to gamble with.

It's been suggested the eggs of the pig whipworms have anti-inflammatory properties. A study by the US National MS Society saw a reduction in the size of brain lesions in MS patients. Participants are to ingest a number of eggs that will grow to develop into larvae in their intestines. The larvae aren't supposed to survive longer than two weeks in human hosts. This wouldn't be enough time for them to mature fully into worms colonizing our insides and stealing our nutrients. During the study, four out of five patients saw a decrease in their brain lesion sizes—only to have them rebound or rise after the study ended.

The worm of choice used in this study was the pig whipworm, the *trichuris suis*, at the egg stage. Infections from this roundworm shaped like a whip, hence the name whipworm, are common in warmer climates. The microscopic eggs are often found in contaminated soil; water; or dry goods like grains, rice, and beans. In another study funded by the United Kingdom MS Society, at the University of Nottingham in Britain, human hookworms are to be used because their biology is better understood.

Conversely, too many worms are cause of tissue damage. The same *Wall Street Journal* article discloses, according to research firm Espicom, the MS drug market for 2010 was $12.6 billion.

Medications to slow the disease progression do not come cheap and are not without some serious risks. The helminthic treatment approach falls right in line with the way some medications are presented. We are often told that, although the exact processes on how these drugs work are not known, we're to believe they do work. MS symptoms could subside using helminthic therapy; but what about what else is going on inside the body?

I do not want to minimize what some, or any relief, from debilitating symptoms of MS means for someone afflicted with this disease. I only want to present facts about what we know so far about these pathogens. Whether this becomes a safe, cheap, controllable therapy in the future is unknown. At first glance, this treatment looks easy. However, the essential and crucial monitoring of patients that needs to be provided could well prove too elaborate a task to be done efficiently and cost-effectively.

Since everyone reacts differently to these types of invasions, the administration of helminthic therapies will create a type of hit-and-miss scenario until a suitable protocol is established. How will the immune systems of patients who've been on immune-suppressing drugs for years fair with this new assault? What works for many might not help some. For others, worse symptoms could appear, perhaps not right away, but down the line. If you open the door for one parasite, are you opening it for others to straggle in and become dangerous?

Helminthic therapy looks to be based on a "hygienic hypothesis." It's believed the rise in allergies and autoimmune disorders in developed countries is due to the elimination of parasites. In developing countries, where hygiene is still lacking and exposure to parasites infections are common, the incidence of allergies and autoimmune disorders is low. I don't buy into the "hygienic hypothesis" behind the therapy.

I realize I am far from understanding the microbiologic processes going on; I can only go by what I experienced myself. Proponents of helminthic therapy argue that, because we've evolved alongside these parasites, they protect us by keeping our immune system busy. They claim introduction of certain parasites into our system has the potential to reset our immune system so that it functions properly. Some parasites are believed to feed on the garbage accumulated in our bodies.

Is it a coincidence that, in the days when preventative treatments for parasites were administered on a regular basis, allergies were unheard of? Exposures to such organisms were an unpleasant fact of life. They were dealt with preemptively and defensively. Today, there are not many people who'll not have some type of allergy at one time or another.

If you agree with the helminthic theory proposed, you'd say that my immune system is overreacting because I'm no longer exposed to pathogens. This does make sense—but I believe the opposite is true. Apart from all the other possible scenarios, just by way of gardening and owning dogs most of my life, I am, I know, still very much exposed to pathogens. It's the preventative measures I was accustomed to that fell to the wayside. Now, globalization has brought more pathogens, as well as parasites, home.

I'm more inclined to believe it's rather a proliferation of too many parasites, along with other pathogens, that compromises health. So why did society move away from maintaining vigilance over organisms harmful to our bodies? Let's not forget the timing of this, which coincides with pet ownership evolving into a bond as cherished as the bonds between humans. Pets are no longer kept outdoors. They're in the homes and in our beds. Recalling the previously mentioned report on wild animals infecting dog parks, it might be time pet owners seriously consider treating themselves alongside their pets—as a preventative.

The advent of fast foods not only gives us convenience, it brings with it a broader exposure from the handling and preparation of foods. Reliance on health regulations and codes of conducts has falsely secured our beliefs that enforceable laws protect and release us from scrutiny over what we eat. There are other reasons why we have come to think we need not bother with prevention. It's time we reconsider our position and start keeping our guards up.

We have the ability to travel and reach remote parts of the world, and along with it, we must realize this global freedom didn't only bring the zebra mussels and the Asian carps to our waters. There are other dangers at the microscopic level being introduced. In 1997's *Nature Wars*, we were told that, in North America, there were around two thousand foreign insect and mite species, and the number increases annually by an average of 11 percent. Overspraying our food crops with chemical pesticides killed off any beneficial organisms available in natural pest control.

The frequency of air travel to foreign and exotic locations definitely increases our risks of contracting many types of infections. As much as we think the vaccinations imposed on us before we travel ensure our safety from certain organisms, there are many others left unchecked. They're ready to invade our bodies and hitch a ride back home with us. Then it'll be like searching for a needle in a haystack, trying to figure out causes of illnesses.

One of my dear lady friends came back from visiting her country of origin, Vietnam, and almost died upon her return back home to Canada. She spent a week in the intensive care unit of the hospital, while doctors frantically tried to figure out what her body was battling with. After five days, having exhausted nearly every possible test, the doctors finally figured out a virus had invaded her bladder. Luckily, she had landed back home before the virus took control of her body. There's a very real possibility she would've succumbed to its fatal tendency had she not been back in Alberta.

Her husband, who was by her side during the entire trip, ate and drank from the exact same places but never showed any signs of infection. I wasn't there at the time, and given the language barrier with hospital officials, all she and her husband were able to gather from the ordeal was that she'd contracted a bug. When I say it was a virus, I could be wrong. Whatever it was, it was virulent in its attack and almost killed her. In her case, the vaccinations she took prior to her trip abroad were of no help. Did they instead create an imbalance in her body so she experienced difficulty in fighting infections? This is an intriguing question with no answer.

In February 2016, India reported a massive national campaign was underway to deworm some 270 million schoolchildren to prevent mental and physical impairment. There was no mention of adults who work with these children participating in the program. If they didn't take part, we can only hope they were otherwise protected.

"Invasion of the Brain Snatchers," an episode of the CBC documentary series *The Nature of Things*, goes so far as to allege that, not only do these buggers invade, they actually affect whole societies negatively. It showed that we need only look at impoverished and malnourished nations. The unstable, unruly, and even warring behaviors exhibited across the board are directly related to the effects of pathogenic parasite overburdens on human bodies.

We think we're invincible because we're adults now. Funny, we don't feel that way when it's time for vaccinations. We keep going back for more. Next time you travel to these faraway places, especially if you are bringing young children along, do take some extra precautions in this regard.

Infections are the new reality, which needs to be faced not ignored or denied. The only way we'll ever get the upper hand is by dealing with them. For MS sufferers, helminthic therapy goes against the previous advice given to avoid immune system stimulants. Granted, the reaction of the immune system to various stimulants differs depending on what it's exposed to. Exposing oneself to helminthic therapy still creates an immune response. Whether your immune system is able to keep the bugs in check is another matter.

Some very effective drugs previously administered to treat parasites have since been banned because of their toxicity. Today, many infestations are treated with antibiotics. These new treatments do not come without risks either. It's disconcerting because we now know some antibiotics destroy our friendly gut bacteria. Our immune system is then depleted of some of the natural defenses usually present to protect us. There's probably an urgent need to repopulate good bacteria in many people, depending on how many courses of antibiotics they've taken and how they eat.

In this day and age of globalization, with antibacterial soaps and gels, stress, and antibiotic overuse, along with manufactured diets, soil depletion, overconsumption of sugar, and alcohol and substance abuse, it shouldn't surprise us to discover our bodies are hosting uninvited organisms. With foreigners taking space, our helpful natural bacteria are diminished. It is bacteria, in fact, that offer the best opportunities for further antibiotic development.

Bacteria are very evolved and complex organisms. The not-so-friendly types have come up with ingenious ways of defending themselves against death. Some can destroy the antibiotic before it reaches them, and others are capable of ejecting the antibiotic out of their cell. There are countless ways they've evolved to avoid destruction. Much of the seen and unseen worlds of microbes, including algae, bacteria, fungi, and protozoa, remains a mystery.

The ailments we suffer through and try to appease with this or that medication could be directly related to the load we're carrying. I'm not suggesting all illnesses are a result of invasion. I'm only stating this is the hidden cause of many especially in individuals who are already immune compromised. I want to say health, but I say better health for myself, was experienced after I targeted these problematic, obscure enemies.

The immune system's reaction to vaccinations is different than the immune system's reaction to pathogens. Vaccinations initiate a response by the body to produce antibodies. If confronted by same agents in the future, it'll have ready the tools to rid itself of the invaders. When the immune system is fighting a pathogen, it reacts by sending in the troops to kill and clean up. It seems logical to deduce that, if this battle is never ending, it creates a state of constant inflammation.

When confronted with images from aid organizations of starving children in third world countries, the distended stomachs we see are not only a mark of starvation. They're apparent as a result of parasite overloads. For us in the developed world, it's much harder to grasp from the images the children are severely infested with parasites. While we don't comprehend those images, for the people who are there and see those images up close and personal, it's clear as day.

It's evident in the myriad of digestive issues people suffer from that our modern diet—which consists of too much manufactured foods with empty calories lacking in nutritional value—is putting a strain on our bodies. Everyone's immune system probably reacts a bit differently when neutralizing and killing pathogens. While many have no clue they've been infected, others react violently, sending their immune systems in turmoil. Some end up fighting for their lives. It's no coincidence the recommended herbs for digestive issues are antiparasitic herbs. For example, fennel seeds help alleviate gas and bloating.

Hosting cancer

Much more than just the viruses and bacteria we are aware of play a role in triggering some cancers. Parasite infections can fester silently, leading to cellular changes resulting in malignancies. It rarely causes symptoms but a common sexually transmitted infection by the parasite *trichomonas vaginalis* increases men's risk of developing a lethal form of prostate cancer. In women *trichomonas vaginalis* is silent.

At cancer.org it is reported *opisthorchis viverrini* and *clonorchis sinensis* liver flukes can lead to bile duct cancer. The *schistosoma haematobuim* is linked to bladder cancer and possible links to other cancers are being studied. In the developing world, 22 percent of cancers are of parasitic origins, and the percentage in industrialized countries is reported at 6 percent. I would venture to say 6 percent is low and is not the actual amount.

The antiparasitic, antibiotic drug Ivermectin was observed to determine the susceptibility of certain cancers to the anticancer molecular mechanism of the drug. Years prior, Russia reported Ivermectin almost totally suppressed the growth of melanoma and a few other cancer xenografts in mice with no adverse effects. However, the anticancer mechanism at the molecular level was still unknown. Following is what researchers found out.

The kinase PAK-1—kinases are enzymes that convert a proenzyme to be active—is required for growth in 70 percent of human cancers. These include pancreatic, colon, breast, and prostate cancers, as well as neurofibromatosis tumors. This new study showed the drug blocked the kinase PAK-1 in human ovarian cancer. Some antivirals work by inactivating viral or tumor kinases.

This does add proof regarding the lead role of pathogens in development of some of the deadliest cancers. According to one molecular and cell biology professor, Peter Duesberg, cancers are newly evolved parasitic species. Whereas oncologists and pharmaceutical researchers are focusing on gene therapy to block mutations, Duesberg hopes treatments target chromosomal disruptions, rather than turning genes on or off. Pathogens that have a lead role in development of cancers are those of the flatworm type called flukes. They are the cause of some bladder and liver cancers.

Burdens in unruliness

This is where it becomes a bit more interesting rather than macabre. It's still very disturbing. The parasite that inspires the recommendations to pregnant women on avoiding cat litter boxes, *toxoplasma gondii,* is one that alters human behavior. It's been shown that the toxoplasmosis parasite affects the production levels of dopamine and triggers schizophrenia and bipolar disorders. It's more common than we think. It is estimated that the parasite cysts are carried in 22 percent of the US population and in 10 to 20 percent of the UK population. Who knows what the percentages are for the rest of the world?

This parasite, capable of making rats lose their fear of cats, causes reckless behavior in humans. It's believed to be a factor in traffic fatalities and suicides. There's a potential link in neurological conditions, including attention deficit disorder. Many people don't suffer with any more than flu-like symptoms and improve after a few weeks or months. The *toxoplasma gondii* is a major threat for people with weakened immune system and can even prove fatal.

It's also being investigated for its possible part in irritable bowel disease, rheumatoid arthritis, and autism. This might explain why the majority of children with autism suffer from some type of gastrointestinal distress.

Studies in mice showed that, when the organisms were introduced, the mice's immune systems began overreacting to beneficial bacteria.

In contrast, it looks promising for treating PD by raising dopamine levels, which fall with this disease.

Dientamoeba fragilis, classified as a nonpathogen based on its source of nutrition, the commensal bacteria of the gut, not the host tissue, is now recognized as a very real gastrointestinal pathogen. Coinfections with other pathogens are common. Because of its new pathogenic classification, its role in intestinal diseases is now clear. Its mode(s) of transmission haven't yet been identified.

It's essential for all IBS patients to be screened for parasites. The parasites cause symptoms that are chronic—IBS. Diagnosis can be made with smear tests but are not being performed. Patients with IBS are left on their own to try to deal with these issues. *Blastocystis hominis*, *Entamoeba histolytica, giardi intestinalis*, and others are causative agents in IBS. *Blastocystis* appears to dominate, perhaps due to its ability to avoid detection. Given the controversy surrounding pathogenic conditions, it's had free roam displacing others.

Scientists used CT scans and deoxyribonucleic acid (DNA) sequencing to reveal microbial infections while studying mummies. They're investigating an illness known as Chagas disease transmitted by the parasite *Trypanasoma cruzi*, which causes heart failure and swelling of digestive organs. The parasite infects almost ten million people, mainly in Latin America and is reported to be spreading. This parasite was found in bone remains from as far back as seven thousand years ago. It's hoped the mummies will provide a wealth of information leading to better treatments. Evidence of everything from tuberculosis to heart disease to malaria to prostate cancer was revealed.

Microscopic universe

Microbes confined to some parts of the world are slowly making their way around the globe. In May 2013, a Canadian news agency reported, an Alberta tourist returning home from Thailand had contracted the Zika virus. She was tested for numerous illnesses, such as dengue fever, malaria, and measles. This rare pathogen took longer to diagnose because it's not part of regular testing. Transmission is similar to dengue; the two viruses are easily confused. Zika virus, which was confined to Africa and Asia, was detected in a 2007 outbreak on a remote island in the southwestern Pacific Ocean.

Scientists sounded the alarm on this one as an emerging threat back in 2009. It must have fell on deaf ears because look at where we are today—scrambling to find a vaccine, which takes five to ten years to develop. We might have had one ready by now and, along with it, a clearer understanding of Zika's pathology.

Another case of a mosquito-borne virus showing up where it had never appeared before was reported in a travel advisory to the island of St. Martin by the CDC in December 2013. It was the first time the chikungunya virus was observed in the Western hemisphere. According to the World Health Organization (WHO), the virus, usually seen in Africa, Asia, and India, was imported to Europe in 2006 following the peak of an outbreak in the Indian Ocean islands.

It was then the CDC started working with the Pan American Health Organization (PAHO) to get ready for the arrival of the chikungunya to the Americas. There were 109 laboratory-confirmed, travel-related cases identified between 1995 and 2009. There's never been an actual outbreak in the United States. Will some of these eventually become common hazards in our daily lives? Some may already be infiltrating.

Medicine has come a long way since the days when administering treatments rarely cured patients. A popular remedy up to the mid-1900s, calomel (known as mercurous chloride)—used to treat numerous conditions, from malaria and syphilis to scurvy and yellow fever—was finally discontinued after it proved too toxic. The mercury preparation known as worm chocolate or worm candy would cause a violent purging of the bowels.

It was used to expel intestinal worms. Long-term toxic effects were seen in an ashen appearance, excessive salivation, gum inflammation, loosening of the teeth, and gastrointestinal disturbances, as well as neurological symptoms including tremors, loss of coordination, and behavioral changes.

Not meaning to veer off course, it's important for some to know that calomel was an ingredient in a few teething powders until 1954. It was also used as a fungicide in the agricultural industry until recently. Another powerful remedy used to remove intestinal worms, except for tapeworms, santonin, included the herbs senna and artemisia. It is no longer available.

For those of us living in North America, we've been warned that one of the effects of global warming will be thriving illnesses from the south making their way farther up. Sadly, here too, we remain in reactionary mode. Since this is one consequence we're anticipating, we hope to be prepared for its arrival. Awareness is not always enough to avoid infections. We learned this lesson all too well with the West Nile virus.

Monetary issues likely dictate whether action is directed into preparedness for pathological conditions. No way will monies be allocated to possible threats. We are stretched enough trying to deal with what we know is real—like the yearly flu vaccine that, as of late, misses the mark rather than match its target. While we learn about the prevalence of all these microorganisms, we can be sure that, as much as we've evolved, so have they.

As advancements are made with our understanding of the microscopic realities, the rate of old and young chronically ill people need not keep climbing. Even as our human capacity to fight disease diminishes with age, learning to keep harmful microbes out could very well offer unprecedented health. As scientific discoveries and medical advancements assist us in effectively maintaining our immune system and keeping our minds sharp, we'll be able to fend off invaders and take better control of our bodies.

Many doctors only look for common signs, such as anal irritation, to investigate possible infection. No disrespect intended; some infestations are dangerously more complex. Not all parasites fall in the category of worms that migrate to that part of our body or make their presences felt undoubtedly. In this global world, faraway unknowns can easily be brought to our part of the world. The denial attitudes many people carry can influence how deep doctors probe to find causes. Telltale signs are not always there, and diagnosis tools are not readily available. If tests are timed during the reproduction cycle of some parasites, they're hibernating— making detection nearly impossible.

In a brochure distributed by a big drug store chain, parents were informed that highly contagious pinworms and roundworms are spread in day cares and schools occasionally. The company was advertising its over-the-counter medication. If parents do happen to read these types of brochures, it's probably the extent to which they'll think of pathogens, other than the typical fleas and lice. Convincing family physicians to order tests out of the ordinary can be extremely trying and embarrassing for parents.

There are many natural remedies out there, and often times this is the only place we have left to turn to. You'll have to experiment to find the one(s) that help you best. Introducing a new unfamiliar herb was the knockout punch I needed.

The herb with the most effect for me was *Azadirachta indica*, also known as Neem. I did find taking methylsufolnylmethane (MSM) also helpful. A naturopathic doctor recommended I take olive leaf from the *Olea europaea* tree extract for some time as part of my treatment, along with probiotics. He informed me that, where there are parasites, there is usually fungus as well. Olive leaf is used in the treatment of fungal infections. A change in diet during treatment or longer is necessary. Eliminating sugar is crucial for treatments to be effective. I chose a total change in lifestyle after that nightmare. If my guts start to rumble, I take an herb for a period of time.

Some signs and symptoms to look for depending on the type of parasitic infection include:

- abdominal discomfort or pain and distension or bloating
- agitation
- anemia
- behavioral changes
- blindness
- constipation
- coughing or wheezing
- diarrhea
- disturbed sleep
- dysentery (bloody, watery stools)
- eggs or worms in stool
- enlargement of liver and spleen
- eye inflammation
- fever
- flatulence
- flu-like symptoms
- frequent urination
- headaches
- hives
- itchy anus
- loss of appetite
- muscle aches
- nausea
- nutrient deficiencies
- seizures

- shortness of breath
- subcutaneous nodules
- teeth grinding during sleep
- tinnitus (ringing in the ears)
- vomiting
- weakness
- weight gain or loss

Some of these symptoms are subtle, many are more serious in nature, and others are life threatening. If any are persistent, it does merit a discussion with your doctor.

Following are some preventive guidelines:

- Do not eat raw meat or fish.
- Cook meats at high temperature until well done.
- Inspect, wash, peel, or cook all fruits and vegetables before eating.
- Wash hands after bathroom use, before eating, and prior to and after handling food.
- Keep fingernails clean and short.
- Do not share towels, washcloths, or other personal care items.
- When traveling, drink bottled water and use it to brush your teeth.
- Beware of food or water that could've been contaminated with human waste.
- Wear gloves when in contact with soil.
- Dispose of diapers properly.
- Wash hands after handling pets.
- Ensure pets are dewormed and maintained on preventative medications.
- Do not defecate outdoors. If you absolutely have to, pick it up and dispose of it properly. Infected waste is hazardous to other humans and animals.

CHAPTER 3

The Goods on Goods

Say No to Sugar

A warning—sugar is toxic; it should be regulated like tobacco and alcohol. If you haven't heard it yet or perhaps you have but have dismissed it as some rhetoric, I assure you the evidence is mounting, proving sugar's starring role in developing sickness. The rate of per capita consumption of sugar has rapidly and steadily increased, as has the rate of diseases. Sugar is the taste of choice for most people; it has taken too much of a place in the daily diets of too many people. Sweets, at one time consumed only as a treat, are now the pacifiers for every age. From trying to comfort babies and children to indulging oneself for pleasures, sweets are the preferred choice.

Another discovery with important implication for MS and other demyelination diseases points to the involvement of a sugar molecule in CNS lesions. Researchers discovered blocking a particular enzyme in the brain can help repair the brain damage associated with MS and other demyelination diseases. The research team found the sugar molecule called hyaluronic acid accumulates in areas of damage in brains of humans and animals with demyelination brain and spinal cord lesions. It's not the hyaluronic acid that prevents differentiation of myelin forming cells.

Rather, breakdown products generated by a specific enzyme chewing up hyaluronic acid called *hyaluronidase* contributes to remyelination failure.

How the human body uses sugar in the body involves many processes, with major organs having important roles including the brain. Glucose is the name given to the chemical made when the body breaks down starches and sugars from carbohydrates. All foods deliver glucose to the body by one process or another. This is not the man-made glucose we see on lists of ingredients. This is the naturally occurring glucose in the human body. Glucose is an important energy source for every cell in the body and is essential for the human brain.

Too much sugar, though, creates a reaction that actually starves the brain of glucose. When an abundance of sugar is detected, the pancreas secretes the hormone insulin. The process of taking it away from the blood is started. It is then stored in the liver and muscles in the form of glycogen. Consequently, the brain is then deprived of one of its major sources of energy; the body is in storage mode. This would explain why people experience not just a physical but also a mental fatigue type of crash shortly after consuming large amounts of sugar. What's important to ponder is the insulin reaction by the body that controls blood glucose levels may eventually fail because of the rapid, continual delivery of too much sugar.

As a consequence of our sweet-filled diets, the body, which is designed to store excess glucose in case levels fall low, is in overdrive, storing the excess. Is this why many of us feel fatigued and groggy? It's hard to get away from eating sugar. It's in the majority of the foods we consume.

I know some of you will resist, but this sabotage to health, is the most urgent to give up. In return, it's perhaps the one with the greatest dramatic visible reward—not to mention the internal benefits experienced once the body isn't taxed to the limit trying to process enormous amounts of sugar. It's not like we can never eat it again. It's just taking back control by deciding it's of no benefit to our bodies. Doing this should be easy after feeling the difference of functioning without it.

The many years of taking an immune suppressing drug for RRMS left me susceptible to infections. It wasn't until I was treating myself for one that I decided to give up sugar. Lucky for me, I'd already switched over to drinking my coffee black. It happened quite by accident that, as I gave up sugar, I started to lose weight. I was able to shed the extra pounds I'd carried around my midsection since my pregnancy over twenty years earlier. Suddenly, losing weight wasn't as complicated as rocket science. It came as an unexpected pleasant side effect of making a healthy choice. Once you experience the benefits of giving up this drug-like substance, I'm positive you'll, at the very least, choose to keep it under control.

Whether we are knowingly consuming it or whether it is hidden in the foods we're choosing, we need to become aware of sugar's presence. It's in the majority of the foods we consume throughout the day. It's foolish to think our bodies have miraculously evolved, in less than a generation, to cope with the large quantities of sugar we now ingest. This excessive consumption puts a strain on the body's digestion—part of our immune system. I'd never made this connection until long after I became sick. I honestly hadn't given much thought to what exactly my immune system was. I don't recall learning about it in school. I never bothered learning about it later either. It had protected me without fail throughout my entire life until MS.

Sugar, chemically named sucrose, has an acidic effect on the body, which in turn, produces inflammation. It's important not to forget that, if inflammation becomes chronic, it leads to disease. Fructose is the sugar that occurs naturally in fruits and vegetables. This fructose is not to be mistaken with the highly processed fructose added in manufactured foods.

It can be confusing and difficult to remember all the different names given to sugar; its refining processes are many. Other than fructose, sugar from natural foods, any ingredient listed that ends with the letters *ose* is a sugar-like substance. There are many sugar concoctions used in a lot of the processed foods we consume. From ketchup to peanut butter to the sweetest treats, sugar is often present in one form or another.

Too much fructose interferes with various bodily functions. Consuming large amounts of fructose messes with our brain's ability to regulate appetite, our hormones, and our digestion. Remember our brains are deprived when there is too much sugar. Furthermore, because fructose doesn't stimulate the pancreas's production of necessary appetite-regulating hormones, our bodies are unable to know when we've eaten enough. With sugar collecting in the blood, the pancreas releases more insulin, and the liver accumulates fat. All this leads to type 2 diabetes.

The soft drink industry really took off in the 1920s, to grow into a $61 billion-a-year industry. This number is on a decline, with more people being conscious of the foods they consume. The choice beverage of convenience for many people, the soda pop, contains sugar or a replacement chemical. We quench our thirst with these beverages without thinking they lack in nutritional value—not to mention that they possibly pose a threat to our health. Even when it comes to drinks that have some nutritional value, the sugar infusion in most drinks, including many fruit juices, surely negates any health benefits.

If we moderated our consumption of sugar, maybe we'd avoid some of the negative effects sugar has on the body. It's not just diabetes that sugar is implicated in; other possible connections between disease and sugar intake include Alzheimer's, metabolic and cardiovascular dysregulation, and obesity. I'm sure there are many others. We can get the picture from those few. It's time we start paying attention to how much sugar is in our diets.

When I was a child growing up, sugar was indeed a treat. Other than its presence in the white bread we consumed, sugar was basically absent from our everyday diet. Obesity and diabetes were not at all the norm as they are today. Sugar's prevalence in today's food preparation is to please the taste buds to move more products. This leads to overconsumption and addiction. Rather than appreciating its pleasure-rendering properties on occasion, our blood is saturated with glucose and our bodies are overtaxed trying to process this excess. This leaves us vulnerable to a host of afflictions. We know we can't keep running an engine at full capacity endlessly. It's unrealistic to expect our bodies to keep functioning properly under steady duress due to excess sugar.

Over seven years later, my body lets me know when I have eaten too many sweets. I manage to stay away from sugar—I have good control over that weakness. On those occasions when I do indulge, I will usually feel it right away with an upset stomach and/or congested sinuses. For those reasons, I am able to simply watch others satisfy their cravings.

Adding it all up

Becoming more aware and recognizing how much sugar we put into our bodies in a day can be as simple as reading the ingredients list. It is not uncommon to find sugar holding second or third place in lists. This means it's a major constituent in the food. Ingredients are listed starting from the most to the least.

To find out how much sugar is in a particular food, it helps to look at grams of sugar in relation to a teaspoon. This gives a good picture of how much sugar is consumed. A teaspoon of sugar holds four grams of sugar. To check the sugar grams in a food, divide the amount by four. The result is the teaspoon(s) of sugar amount.

A 20-ounce bottle of soda pop can have up to 69 grams of sugar. To convert grams to teaspoons, divide 69 grams by four; again, this is how many grams are in a teaspoon. This comes to almost fifteen teaspoons of sugar. To better visualize what fifteen teaspoons of sugar looks like, consider this—it takes up over a quarter of an 8-ounce or 250-milliliter measuring cup.

Some other names for added sugars on food labels include brown sugar, cane sugar, corn sweetener, corn syrup, corn syrup fructose, dextrose, fructose, fruit juice concentrate, galactose, glucose, high-fructose corn syrup, honey, invert sugar, lactose, maltose, malt syrup, molasses, raw sugar, sucrose, sugar, syrup, and others.

Unless you're preparing the majority of the foods you consume and control the incorporation of this ingredient, chances are you're consuming too much sugar. This can happen even if the only sugar you get is from drinking sweetened beverages. It's shocking the sum total we come up with at the end of the day. Don't forget that all the food you eat converts to glucose in the body. Is it any wonder our bodies become riddled with disease before their time?

Let's look at what the average person consumes in a typical day, starting with breakfast. Even unsweetened, an average glass of orange juice has at least 20 grams of sugar. If you drink coffee or tea with a couple teaspoons of sugar, you've already started your day with 28 grams, or over seven teaspoons of sugar.

Some brands of milk contain 12 grams of sugar per cup. Add another three teaspoons if you have it with your cereal. If you eat sugared cereal or add sugar, add that amount also. Spreading jam on toast adds another 6 grams per tablespoon. Bread slices and bagels have about four grams apiece, so slightly over one teaspoon. Eating a muffin adds anywhere between 14 to 28 grams. That's another three to seven teaspoons. In this typical scenario, a person would've already ingested about seventeen teaspoons of sugar. That's over a quarter cup! Pancakes with maple syrup can pack almost 60 grams of sugar with only the maple syrup—another quarter cup.

Lunch might consist of drinking a 355-milliliter can of soda with your food, so add another eight plus teaspoons. If you used any sweetened condiments, such as ketchup, listing sugar or high fructose corn syrup as an ingredient, add 4 grams of sugar per tablespoon. Another popular condiment, salad dressing, has a minimum of 1 gram per tablespoon. This needs to be added up too. In another few hours, when eating dinner, consumption of more sugar in the form of a drink, condiments, and/or desserts is par for the course.

Inconspicuously, we quite possibly have consumed about thirty teaspoons of sugar throughout the day. Any foods with naturally occurring sugar such as fruits because they, in and of themselves, pack a lot of fructose need to be added too. An average apple or orange give us about 23 grams of sugar, a banana 17 grams, a peach 15 grams, and a ripe fig 10 grams. If snacking on sweet foods such as granola or fruit bars, we're taking in about 8 grams per serving. Fruit cups, jellies, or yogurt with added sugar add another 15 to 19 grams per serving. Candy bars, often eaten as snacks, can pack as much as 30 grams per bar—over seven teaspoons of sugar in one snack.

Experts report there's no connection between sugar and hyperactivity in children. This does make sense since we know eating too much sugar causes a crash when our brains are starved of glucose. Some experts say other added ingredients accompanying sugar, such as caffeine and food dyes, are causing hyperactivity behavior.

Psychiatrists instead look at the dynamics involved, such as parties or the like, as cause for children's hyperactivity. Many experts now challenge the belief that food is the underlying root cause of hyper behavior. Are they saying a diet of sipping on soda pop or eating processed foods doesn't affect a child's demeanor?

In Britain, recommendations were heard to half the recommended "five a day" fruit portions. This reduced from 10 percent to 5 percent the total caloric intake of sugar recommended. The recommendation was aimed directly at limiting consumption of the fruit juices and smoothies fueling the nation's obesity crisis. Portions for these were to be reevaluated depending on their total sugar content.

There is a dispute over the assumption that the brain and CNS need 130 grams of dietary carbohydrates to function well. It's been proposed that the liver and kidneys are capable of producing that amount of glucose from protein. Except for the red blood cells, the retina, and a remote part of the kidneys, everything in our bodies can run on fat.

If we need another reason to think twice before we put sweet stuff in our mouths, disturbing news was recently released about sugar and its link to deadly heart problems. Over thirty thousand American adults, with an average age of forty-four, were involved in one of the largest study of its kind. Previous studies already associated diets high in sugar with obesity and nonfatal heart problems. The results of this new study found diets with added sugar increased risk of premature death from heart conditions. The increased risk wasn't limited to the obese; it included normal-weight people who ate added sugar. There was three times a greater risk of dying for adults who consumed a quarter of their calories from added sugar than for those who consumed the least, 10 percent.

With today's modern diet, it's very easy to unassumingly consume way more sugar than our bodies can use. It's only the fructose from fruits our bodies are designed to process, not the mass-produced versions added in manufactured foods. Rather than feeding our bodies and our brains when eating sugar, we may be feeding pathogens or causing irreparable damage to ourselves. Regulating our sugar consumption has become an urgent concern we need to address sooner rather than later.

That it took so long for sugar to be viewed as toxic when obesity and diabetes rates are skyrocketing everywhere is a great injustice.

Now, in all fairness, I do have to say a small amount of sugar may not prove harmful. However, statistics say individuals consume on average ten teaspoons of sugar daily. That's a lot of sugar on a daily basis. If left unchecked, the excessive, ongoing consumption of too much sugar leads to disease. Period. It's only a matter of time.

Salt Is Not All Sodium

Salt has got to be the most taboo food ingredient out there. It is good up to a point. It can also be bad, depending entirely on the type and the total amount consumed. Salt has been getting a bad reputation for a lot longer than sugar because of its implication in hypertension. Without getting too technical here, the table salt we consume every day is a crystalline compound. It's comprised of a mixture of sodium at approximately 40 percent and chloride at approximately 60 percent. Both of these minerals are necessary and crucial for the proper functioning of the cells in our bodies.

The general consensus seems to be that adults need to consume and aim for the minimum of 1,500 milligrams daily. The maximum of 2,300 milligram of sodium is acceptable. However, experts are now taking a more conservative stance, recommending the minimum of 1,500 mg as the optimum maximum amount.

The following measurements take no account of the aforementioned ratios. Thus, the acceptable level of sodium, at 2,000 mg per teaspoon, is about a teaspoon. It's easier to imagine what 2,300 mg looks like in the context of a teaspoon. And that means, in a teaspoon, you're getting over 3,000 mg of chloride.

Since 1 milligram equals 0.001 of a gram, 2,300 milligrams equals 2.30 grams. As it stands in the culinary world, one teaspoon of salt holds 5 ml or 5 grams—unlike sugar, which weighs in at 4 grams per teaspoon. A half teaspoon holding 2.5 grams is a little over the maximum daily recommendation of 2.3 gm.

The chloride daily requirement for adults is the same as sodium at 2.3 gm. Adults who consume one teaspoon of salt daily are well within the required daily chloride allowance. If you aim for the daily minimum allowance of 1,500 mg of sodium, consuming three-quarters of a teaspoon of salt daily is acceptable.

The human body needs chloride for metabolism and to help balance the acid base. The kidneys regulate the amount of chloride in our blood. The findings of a study out of the University of Glasgow revealed low levels of chloride in the blood is an indicator of mortality risk for people with hypertension. Data from thirteen thousand high blood pressure patients was analyzed and followed up over a thirty-five-year period. There was a 20 percent higher mortality rate in those with the lowest levels of chloride.

It's important to note that all table salts are not created equal. You need to check the content labels of the salt you use. Surprisingly, one popular table salt product includes sugar in its ingredients' list. It is supposedly added as an anticaking agent. Who knew you had to check the labels of even the simplest of foods like salt.

Most of us know and accept that too much salt is bad for us. The exact causes of high blood pressure are not known, but too much salt intake is a known factor in its development. On the flip side, too little salt can also be just as bad for our bodies. In the human body, salt has a crucial role in maintaining the water balance of cells and in the function of nerve impulses and muscles.

Some people go to extremes, claiming the human body needs only a daily minimum of 200 mg of sodium to function. Elsewhere, this number is 500 mg. It's argued the recommended daily allowances are way too high. Again, we're left wondering what exactly is best. The contradictions abound—there are no definite answers. Three signs indicative of too much salt in the body are bloating, thirst, and puffy eyes.

A recent study out of Yale claims dietary salt is a prime suspect in the rise of incidences in autoimmune diseases like MS. Researchers said when salt was added to the diet of mice, they developed a more severe form of the animal model of MS. The deduction by experts, who are now leaning toward a more conservative daily sodium intake recommendation, is that the wrong amounts of salt were used in past experiments. Patient trials are planned.

Adding to the confusion on what are acceptable levels of sodium to consume, another study brought forward evidence that the recommended daily intake amount for salt is too low. The results of the meta-analysis are a follow-up to the 2013 Institute of Medicine report that had cast doubt on the CDC recommendations on salt. The latest study determined a range of 2,645 to 4,945 mg a day of salt is a healthier amount. Deviation on either side is harmful. To this day, it's not clear what the right numbers for salt are.

I was in my early thirties when I started restricting the amount of salt I consume. I was heeding the warnings we all heard at one time or another on limiting the amount of salt we consume. I had entirely stopped adding salt to the foods I prepared, thinking I was doing something good for my body. I didn't know back then that the body still needs a minimum amount of salt daily. I figured I was getting enough sodium from the processed staple foods I was eating. I wasn't eating too many on a daily basis or in large quantities. Looking back and knowing what I now know, I realize totally giving up salt was creating a great strain on my system, rather than benefiting it.

This realization came to me years later when my blood test result was flagged at low sodium. Foolishly, I had abstained from adding salt to my food without any clear direction to do so. I was not following doctor's advice. I didn't have high blood pressure. The few extra pounds I'd put on were definitely not all water because of too much sodium. I was just listening to the messages broadcast by the media, blindly placing my trust in information delivered to the general public.

Even my family physician was perplexed as to why I'd stopped using salt altogether. The look on her face gave me the impression I was not her only patient who had eliminated salt without justification. I believe it was the lack of this important mineral in my body that aggravated many of my health issues, such as sinus congestion and low blood pressure. There are exceptions when one needs to take control by eliminating some items from their diets, such as in the case of diabetics and sugar. For the most part, by way of allergies or intolerances, our bodies are good at letting us know when something is not right.

If we are consuming manufactured foods loaded with many different types of sodium, we're probably way over our daily allowable intake level. It's not the packaged bowl of soup, popcorn, or chips, we eat from manufacturers that deliver the minerals in salt the body needs. There is good reason why athletes supplement with sodium water to avoid muscle cramping. Sodium is lost during sweating and must be replaced to maintain optimum performance.

The table salt we use isn't made up entirely of sodium. This makes it impossible to verify the actual sodium content of the salt. When we eat healthy and prepare our own foods, we need to take into account the actual sodium content in the particular salt we're using. As stated earlier, sodium is usually at a ratio of 40%.

The sodium amount is usually readily available when checking food labels of prepared products. It, too, like sugar, comes in many forms. Some are less than desirable. Names for sodium include celery salt, onion salt, seasoning salt, sodium citrate, monosodium glutamate, and the like. The total amount also includes the amount of naturally occurring sodium in the food. Please refer to the section entitled "Macho Micronutrients" in chapter 4, "Conscious Choices" for a list of the foods with the most naturally occurring sodium.

On a promising note with regards to salt, scientists demonstrated how targeting cancer cells with a surge of salt made the cells die. The chloride and sodium work together to disrupt the ion balance of cells, causing them to self-destruct. Even though there's still work to be done, as this procedure kills other cells—it offers some hope in the fight against cancer.

To finish on another positive note, a possible milestone has been reached in the fight against superbug infections in hospitals with one man's ingenious experiments with salt. The fixture product line, Outbreaker, made out of salt was first developed in a garage. It's now patented in twelve countries. Methicillin-resistant staphylococcus aureus (MRSA) can only survive five minutes on salt, whereas it lives much longer on other surfaces.

Testing in two hospitals is set to begin shortly. This is a clear example of one man wanting to make a difference.

Iodine

Classified as a mineral, iodine was added to table salt in the early 1900s in order to prevent mental retardation and goiter (enlarged thyroid gland). Iodine is a very important trace mineral for our bodies. It's crucial for the production of the thyroid hormones. Important not only for pregnant women and people with MS, thyroid hormones are key in the myelination process of the central nervous system.

When people reduce their intake of salt, they need to realize they're reducing their intake of this important mineral as well. It does occur naturally in seafood like fish and sea vegetables. It's in plants grown in iodine-rich soil and in dairy products, if cattle feed was supplemented with iodine or salt licks. Salt of the sea delivers iodine just like iodine is generously supplied in sea vegetables such as kelp, nori, arame, kombu, and dulse.

Iodized salt is not in processed foods. As people eat out and/or consume processed foods, raising their sodium levels, their iodine levels have dropped enough to create negative effects on their health. Unless you reside in sea coastal areas where seafood and sea vegetables are consumed as part of your diet, chances are you are probably not regularly consuming these iodine-delivering foods. With industrialized agriculture practices having raped the soil of essential nutrient-delivering properties, diets low in seafood and dependent on fruits and vegetables for iodine may be lacking this essential mineral.

Regions surrounding the Great Lakes, as well as other geographical locations, are known to have no, or low levels of, iodine in the soil. There are maps online showing these locations if you are curious about your locale. Fruits, especially strawberries, and vegetables grown in iodine-rich soil, do capture some of this element. It's better found in vegetables, including spinach, summer squash, Swiss chard, and turnip greens. It is in garlic, lima beans, sesame seeds, and soybeans. Again, all this does depend on whether the soil used for cultivation contains iodine or is being enriched with iodine.

Having suffered from sporadic itchy, bumpy skin rashes for years, I found relief after a girlfriend introduced me to an iodine liquid soap used for scrubbing by those in the medical profession. She told me to use the solution on the affected area. Not only did it offer relief in more ways than one, I started using it on a weekly basis for my fibrocystic breasts. I remembered reading more than once that iodine supplementation is helpful in treating fibrocystic breasts. I decided to try this type of delivery, and it worked.

Given that fibrocystic breasts are often associated with the development of breast cancer, it might be worthwhile for women who suffer from this condition to try supplementing with iodine. Do investigate this further if you are on a restricted salt diet or feel your level of iodine is low. The symptoms of low iodine are listed in the section on iodine in chapter 4's "Macho Micronutrients."

The recommended daily intake (RDI) of iodine for adults is 150 micrograms (mcg) minimum up to 900 mcg maximum. Multivitamins usually include this mineral in their preparations. Whether our bodies are able to assimilate it in the forms it's delivered in is question. People who take their multivitamins in tablet forms may not be digesting them entirely. It is recommended when taking vitamin tablets to cut the pills in half and take separately.

Altered States

Most foods are processed to make it to market. I prefer the term *manufactured foods.* To me this describes best products coming off an assembly line. Again it's no coincidence that, as our rates of consumption of processed foods and sugar rise, so do the rates of disease. The process of refining sugar cane to crystals, to give us refined sugar, was first started in India. Evidently, as modernization of the continent grows, so do the ill effects that can come with it. India, which has recently been surpassed by China, long held the largest population of people with diabetes. However, according to *The Diabetes Atlas*, as of 2007, the highest per capita rate of diabetes was in the United States. It remains there as of this date.

As nations' economies flourish, food trends veer to convenience as people scramble to get their fair share of the prosperity that's become attainable. The marketplaces expand, fast food outlets and vending machines take up locations, and the eating experience is reinvented. Long-standing eating customs and rituals are replaced with new habits and changed behaviors reflecting the fast pace of the new economies.

People are sacrificing nutrition for convenience. Younger generations are none the wiser of the developing consequences of such upbringing. The firsthand effects of these types of diets are just now becoming apparent, and it's not pretty.

There is some good news. A growing number of individuals are educating themselves and making the necessary changes. They avoid the convenience of manufactured foods. Some go so far as steering clear of any packaged products. This is the point where I try to stay at right now.

In the modern world, we are bombarded with an assortment of harmful chemicals used in almost all manufactured goods—from the toothpastes we brush our teeth with to the vehicles we drive. We are constantly exposed to toxins in one form or another—in the air we breathe, in the foods we eat, in the items we handle, and so on. Unfortunately, these chemicals are likely to remain, until and unless each is individually proven dangerous. It's just the way the system works.

Some big food manufacturers advertise beneficial ingredients in some of their products by displaying pictures of fruits on the packages. When consumers take the time to read the food labels on these products, they'll notice the names of the supposedly included fruits have been formulated. I blindly consumed these for a period.

Blueberries are surprisingly renamed blueberry crunchlets or something of the sort. They're a mix of sugars (glucose or fructose, corn syrup, starch, and cellulose), along with artificial coloring with food dyes such as blue #1 or #2 or red #40, combined to imitate berries. I wasn't able to find the definition of crunchlet in a dictionary. Its definition in the urban dictionary relates to food after it's been digested by the body. I will not include it here. Do not believe the healthy hype certain food packages portray. A higher price doesn't mean it is any better either.

One of the most confusing food choices to be made has to be yogurt. Varieties for flavored yogurt appear endless. There are numerous brands to choose from with sugar or different types of sweeteners added. If the yogurt is flavored and the container states that it's all natural, it has sugar (considered a natural ingredient). Greek yogurt provides more protein and a creamier texture because it's been strained. If it's flavored, beware of the sugary goop that could be hiding in its body.

One pricier brand advertises blueberry and pomegranate fruits. Consumers, who think they're getting excellent antioxidant value, do willingly pay more for it. Quantities of real fruits are just an illusion. On the label, the second ingredient after skim milk is blueberry and pomegranate fruit preparation. This is prepared with sugar, water, blueberries, concentrated pomegranate juice, natural flavor, pectin, and concentrated lemon juice. This does not sound so bad, except sugar is the first ingredient listed.

Berries with their correct names should be well proportioned throughout the product. They should be listed as one of the first ingredients, instead of found at the end of the list. These companies cut costs by substituting sugar concoctions for real berries. Unless consumers read the labels, they are fooled by the deceptive packaging pictures. If glucose and/or fructose are listed in a product showing fruit content as one of the first ingredients, it's almost guaranteed the majority of the following ingredients will not be real.

There are many disguises for chemicals that have been added to foods. It's only by reading the food labels that consumers can learn about food additives and preservatives incorporated during processing. The words that stand out or the pictures popping out on the packaging are only there to appeal and entice consumers. They show the foods shoppers expect to dominate a product when making their selections, but companies using these promotions are deceptive. Don't be fooled by the packaging.

When choosing a food, it's the ingredients list we really need to pay attention to. These are the only available tools we have to make an informed choice at that moment. It's in our best interest to pause and read the labels before choosing. It is something we must do to avoid being grossly deceived and ripped off.

Many foods believed to be healthier (and actually healthier in some aspects) are pricier. Certain pricier foods, though, fail miserably on delivering entirely beneficial ingredients, with companies cutting value in favor of reduced operating costs.

Food manufacturers are legally obliged to provide labels. They cannot make us read or understand them though. Just getting started with the habit of checking ingredients lists while shopping will raise awareness. Eventually reading food labels becomes second nature; this teaches the children to do the same. I can't help but smile when I see people doing this. It shows progress in the direction of a health-conscious society.

If you struggle to read and pronounce some of the ingredients in a list, it's probably better to avoid the product altogether. Anything with a number indicates artificial colors have been added in the preparation of the food. The word *hydroxide* following an item on a product's ingredients' list—for example, calcium hydroxide or sodium hydroxide—reveals an added chemical compound is present. Hydroxide is a chemical compound belonging to the hydroxyl group. Hydroxyl, according to Mosby's Medical

Dictionary, 8th edition, is a monovalent radical consisting of an oxygen and hydrogen atom—an extremely reactive radical species capable of damaging DNA.

Sodium hydroxide is listed on more than food labels. It's listed in drain opener, paint stripper, oven cleaner, and so on. These two items couldn't be one and the same. It's not the only chemical present in processed food that's found in other products. You only need to compare manufactured food products with other product labels around the house. One you might find is disodium EDTA—found in many personal care products, as well as some salad dressings. The ingredient azodicarbonamide, used as a bleaching agent, is served in some foods at many popular fast food restaurants and is found in yoga mats too.

A little while ago, there was a lot of controversy because an ingredient classified as a carcinogen was in the products of two of the soda pop giants—namely Coke and Pepsi. Coke did remove this ingredient from its products. As of this writing, Pepsi had not followed suit. According to the US Center for Science in the Public Interest, the ingredient, 4-methylimidazole (or 4-MEI), used for the sodas' caramel color is dangerous. The toxic chemical is formed during the heating, roasting, or cooking processes of soy sauce, caramel, and molasses.

The FDA said consumers would have to drink more than a thousand cans of soda a day to match doses proven cancer-causing in rodents. Health Canada does not think the chemical traces of 4-MEI in foods are a risk to Canadians. Do they really know the cumulative effect of this chemical in the human body?

There has to be a better option than having this chemical in some foods. Without a doubt, consumers would gladly adapt and accept a change in color, if it meant the food was safer.

Patch jobs

It's a sad realization that the systems supposedly in place to protect citizens operate mostly in reactionary mode. Many of the food additives we consume require approval at the federal level. In the United States, the FDA has approved seventy thousand food additives, ranging from natural to genetically modified to GRAS, generally recognized as safe. There are no such approvals required for cosmetics and personal care products.

I will go a bit off track here. I do so only to expand your views. I only ask you the following question: Do you honestly think governments who choose to engineer the climate instead of implementing necessary changes for a sustainable earth willingly commit sufficient resources to fully protecting individuals' health?

If you have not heard of geoengineering, you might want to read up on it. It could have great impact, possibly not a positive one, on not just our weather but on our food crops and—ultimately—our health.

Rather than resolve difficult issues by providing corrective, remedial, realistic, and sustainable actions, much of the world plays around with only one aspect at a time. We need only to look at the answer to blindness in starving nations—produce a new rice species called "golden rice." This new rice, genetically designed to deliver vitamin A, will prevent blindness. Hopefully, it will alleviate suffering due to blindness and prevent the two million yearly deaths due to vitamin A deficiency. This solution will alleviate the feelings of hunger, but it is far from providing a balanced diet. Too much of one thing and too little of another can be damaging.

We can do better and should expect and demand it in this day and age. This seems like a step in the right direction. In true reality, we need to implement a wider range of applications to address the issue of starvation. This is not only a problem in faraway places. It's right under our noses here at home. This reflects on the world as a whole, the world you and I are a part of.

On this side of the world, we're offered the first ever genetically modified animal—the salmon. Grown in containment, it matures and grows at almost double the rate of its wild counterpart. As a precautionary measure against possible contamination, in the event of accidental escape from their inland farms, only sterile females are produced. The go-ahead for human consumption has been given. Just like the food crops, the new genetically modified animal will not be clearly identified as such when it makes it to the supermarkets or restaurants in North America. Have you taken a close look at your salmon lately?

We've moved past consuming genetically modified plants to genetically modified creatures. All this without really knowing the long-term effects on the overall scheme of the food chain—let alone human health.

Coming soon, trees designed to make it easier to produce pulp. I don't want to minimize this commendable work. Is it not the result of planting only male species of trees to avoid dealing with spent flowers and fruits the reason the air is overloaded with pollen? What does one have to do with the other? Maybe nothing. It's just an example of how unintended consequences can dramatically alter environmental balances.

Even with strict safeguard measures in place, this has the potential to become another Pandora's box. A perfectly unknown environmental impact—unintended spread of genetically modified corn seeds by the wind taking over unsuspecting farmers' crops. The farmers ended up being forced to pay for seeds they never wanted in the first place. Even in this digital age, we can't simulate the outcomes of all potential natural repercussions.

Let's not take it at face value that all that is available to eat is actually good for us. Yes, we in the Western world are privileged to have such a vast array of food choices. They come not all with guarantees for good health. Simple is the safest and best choice—meaning stay away from manufactured foods.

A television documentary revealed that, even in smaller venues of the industrialized world, food preparation is contracted out and dispensed by assembly lines and machinery. I was a bit surprised when I first heard this. I shouldn't have been because this is something I'd already experienced myself. As a result of the recent collapse of the economy, restaurants are now serving up manufactured frozen dishes.

Not only is this a cheaper alternative, it's a convenience imposed after staff reductions have taken away the capacities and time required for basic food preparation in kitchens. This is not something only encountered randomly here and there. Surprisingly, this practice has become relatively common, even in places where people wouldn't expect it. Many of the fancier, renowned European restaurants have incorporated prepared frozen foods in their menus. Their clientele is none the wiser when the food is presented in an elegant fashion.

Some argue that, since taste is not compromised and the customers are still happy, it is of no concern how and where the food was prepared. What clients expect to have been prepared with only the freshest of ingredients might actually contain preservatives. Even in classier restaurants, patrons are left in the dark as to what it is they're actually ingesting.

Here it is again—convenient and cheaper alternatives replace value. We'll never know unless we ask specifically, or can find out otherwise, how our food was prepared. Customer service employees are trained to dodge and distract from customer concerns. The company profits come first. Responses to avoid full disclosure on such matters are more than likely scripted or rehearsed.

Chemical generation

What's in a word? A lot it seems. *Obesogens* is a relatively new term given to a group of chemicals that mimic the hormone estrogen in the body. Obesogens disrupt lipid metabolism and can lead to obesity. Metabolism is the cells' chemical processes that break down substances for energy or synthesize the buildup of these for later use.

At least twenty obesogens have been identified so far. These obesogens are not used by the body. They remain therein, tucked away in fat cells and making those cells reproduce. Furthermore, they are not removed like other toxins from the body during urination, defecation, breathing, or sweating. The three letters, *gen*, added at the end of the word obesogen could stand for "obese generator."

By now, everyone is aware of the dangers of using plastic containers to microwave food. Bisphenol-A (BPA) used in food packages, plastic bottles, and can liners is proven to seriously disrupt hormones. It was removed from baby bottles a little while back. It's also important to avoid exposing any food prepared in plastic containers to heat. This does not just apply to the use of a microwave; submerging any plastic receptacle in boiling water releases toxins as well. Samples of water from bottles left in automobiles during the heat of the day were analyzed and found to have high amounts of BPA.

When grocery shopping, it's next to impossible to know if there are plastic liners in canned foods from looking at the cans. Many canned goods still have them. I'm not aware of anything in the coding of cans indicating whether or not liners were used. Unless we know which cans are lined, short of opening them or contacting the companies directly to ask, I don't know how we can tell. Plastic liners in cans were introduced after aluminum was determined harmful to the human body. The liners are now believed even more toxic to humans. I try to avoid cans as much as possible. On the occasions when I do use cans, I try to remember and avoid the ones that are lined.

Any replacement for BPA will be more of the same—another chemical to be used until it is proven harmful. Rather than finding natural alternatives, chemicals are the go-to choice when it comes to packaging and giving food longer shelf life. Not only are some foods overloading our bodies with excesses of sodium and sugar, some can deliver toxic chemicals our bodies just can't process.

Consumers are left with little choice, even though they're the ones who'll deal firsthand with the repercussions of ill health brought on by these goods. Governments will say, as they always do, that there are benefits to consuming these foods whether they come in a plastic container or not. As a result of all the years of exposure to these toxins, the problem is then passed on to the health care systems. Then, it is they who are left trying to deal with the bizarre conditions and diseases that show up. Consumers lose again as costs escalate and are passed onto them in the form of taxes.

Furthermore, there are many environmental obesogens. They are the ones we're all exposed to in one form or another. We're exposing ourselves to a variety of these chemicals by extensive use of plastics in our everyday lives. From the plastic toothbrushes to the electronics we cling to throughout our day, our bodies are almost constantly in contact with chemicals. Environmental obesogens were detected in drinking water, contaminated seafood, and agricultural products. These chemicals have inconspicuously made their way into our environment as a result of our careless behaviors.

Shockingly, there are pharmaceutical obesogens in some of the drugs we take. Particularly disturbing are the obesogens found in the drugs used to treat diabetes. These were shown to cause weight gain with prolonged use. This is especially alarming given the discovery of the link between diabetes and obesity. It makes it nearly impossible for a person to attain a healthy weight while taking the available medication needed to control his or her disease.

There's a common misconception, and I have fallen victim to this on more than one occasion. Simply because a company has a good reputation does not mean all its products are consistently of quality. I purchased a supposedly safe hand and body lotion from a popular brand, only to discover later it contained parabens. This company usually advertises its natural products.

The fact that we can't even rely on brand selection makes the process of choosing safe and healthy (nontoxic) products to apply to our skin—our largest organ—not only discouraging but also challenging and confusing. Our skin not only keeps us assembled; it's a big help in our health—keeping microbes out and eliminating toxins. Another common additive found in cosmetics and lotions, listed as PEG-100 stearate, has been shown to cause kidney toxicity if applied to damaged skin.

The Environmental Working Group (EWG) warns of organ, reproductive, and developmental toxicity, cancer, and irritation. Experimental results from a study published by the *International Journal of Toxicity* pointed to an increased risk of brain, breast, and uterine cancers and leukemia from the impurities found in some PEGs. You can easily check toxicity ranking of products you use on your skin at the EWG website. The lists of ingredients on some of these products are extensive and replete with chemicals. You might also want to look up the products used around the house.

Any concern brought forth regarding products seems to only dictate that further research is needed. As consumers, we can make up our own minds. Consumer demand drives the marketplace. There's no need to wait for more studies or research. The human body is not designed to process these substances. Even if our bodies eliminate many toxins, it's irresponsible to use products we know have little to no benefit. These chemicals could seriously impair the body's ability to use other beneficial compounds. Rather than keep feeding the hands of those who cause harm, choose natural and stay away from chemicals that have no business being in our products in the first place.

Wheat, Wheat, It Is Everywhere

Wheat is incorporated into many of the foods we eat. It is alleged by some professionals that this is a contributing factor in various health issues many people are experiencing. I happened on an article in the newspaper about a book written by US cardiologist Dr. William Davis at the same time I had given up all grains for a time. In his book, he advises avoiding wheat.

It was good timing. I haven't read the book myself, as I don't need to be convinced. I already knew the bloating I felt after eating was not due to overeating. It came on after I had eaten any wheat. I could hear and feel my insides churning as soon as I ate any wheat.

Wheat was hybridized to increase yields. It is claimed to be a healthier choice for breads, pastas, and the like. Wheat flour has replaced white flour in the lists of ingredients of most prepared foods. It is the preferred nutritional choice of many. According to Western food guides, it is purported that humans need to consume many servings of grains daily to ensure adequate fiber intake. Most of us have heard about the benefits of grains.

For a period of time, I did not eat wheat. I was trying to figure out the source of my digestive discomfort. I am now able to and do consume grains. They are, for the most part, whole or sprouted. I try to stay away from overly refined grains as much as possible. I do prefer to get the bulk of my fiber from vegetables and fruits.

Again, it looks like the food industry has gone overboard with this one too. Instead of consumers having a choice of whether or not they want to consume it, it's included as filler in many foods we wouldn't expect. Wheat, thought of as healthy, is left unchecked until digestive issues manifest. Individuals develop gluten sensitivities, and wheat and other grains are avoided at all costs. What is to be marginally consumed is, instead, unknowingly consumed throughout the day. Digestive distresses are experienced in some sensitive people.

Gluten, eaten for decades, becomes the new villain, and a whole new food industry is born providing gluten free products. The alternatives are well tolerated by the gluten-sensitive consumers. However, many of them are not the best food choices to make anyways. Avoiding some and replacing them with other overly processed grains in manufactured foods is not healthier.

There is now the question of whether governments' food guides' high daily intake recommendation on grains have been wrong all along.

Alcohol

Although we are being told moderate consumption of alcohol has some health benefits, it is recognized that excess alcohol intake can have the opposite effect. It can even be deadly. It's not rare to hear of someone suffocating in his or her vomit and succumbing to death because he or she was intoxicated to the point of losing all control.

Cultures who include wine in their daily diet are said to live healthier and longer lives. Is it the wine they drink or is it their healthy diet of good fats, fruits, and vegetables, along with good habits and good attitudes that are the keys to their good health? There are way too many variables to pinpoint with certainty one particular reason. Let's face it; it is never one thing.

The combination of many factors, including wholesome foods, physical activity, healthy social relations, and other things that comprise the complete lifestyle is the real reason for such health and longevity.

Claims have been made for some time now that having a daily glass of red wine is good for heart health. Even so, if I remember correctly, confusion arose not long after those guidelines came out. They warned women that consuming wine was putting them at an increased risk of breast cancer.

As with all the other recommendations that are good for us one day and bad the next, the guidelines about wine and alcohol aren't easy to understand; it's hard to figure out what is what. If you choose to drink alcohol to decompress after a hard day's work or use it to alleviate stress or are consuming it because of its health claims, moderation is definitely wiser. Whether this benefits you as an individual is best discussed with a health care practitioner, particularly if other health conditions are involved.

I never acquired a taste for alcohol enough to become a regular drinker. Of course, like many, I went through a period in my younger years when going out drinking was the in thing to do on weekends. I was not in a financial position to sustain it as part of my lifestyle. Now when I think back, I realize that was a good thing.

It was not until much later in life, after a couple of years of increased drinking habits, that I was hit with MS. It wasn't a daily habit, but alcohol, whether in the form of beer or hard liquor, had become a fairly regular weekend indulgence. It was for the overall enjoyment of leisurely activities.

I remember, clear as day, the night before I woke up half-blind from optic neuritis. I had had a few drinks early in the evening and begun to experience the hangover headache one expects the morning after a night of serious drinking. I distinctly remember feeling a sharp jolt in my brain. It was not painful but was definitely bizarre and unlike anything I had ever experienced before. The best way I can explain it is that it felt like there was a short circuit of some kind or something had snapped. That's exactly how I described it in my mind at the time. I was thinking I had pulled a nerve inside my head—if that was even possible. It became clear the next day—that was not the case at all.

Not long after the relocation, regular alcohol drinking was a thing of the past. Alcohol consumption became reserved for special occasions. It's rare I feel a desire to partake in alcohol drinking. I've lived long enough with MS to know the hangover headache I feel sometimes without drinking would only become more pronounced if I did drink. Consuming alcohol is no longer enjoyable. It affects my physical wellness negatively.

It's estimated that three-quarters of the adult American population use some form of alcohol. Out of that number, 10 percent have the potential to become dependent on this legal drug. Since so many are alcohol drinkers, I believe 10 percent is an underestimation of the likelihood of dependency.

Your body on alcohol

Alcohol, known as ethanol, is made from fermentation. Yeast breaks down sugar into ethanol and carbon dioxide. As alcohol is broken down in our bodies during the metabolic process, it produces acetaldehyde, which is more toxic than the alcohol itself. Alcohol, a depressant, starts off a stimulant arousing feel-good chemicals and slows down brain function. Inflammation follows as the body's antioxidants defense abilities are repressed by the alcohol.

It was once believed that alcohol killed brain cells. This has now been disproven. Even if brain cells on alcohol do not die, changes in neuronal structures can disrupt brain function. Dehydration due to the effects of the alcohol causes permanent damage. Findings have repeatedly confirmed the brain shrinks as a result of chronic alcohol consumption.

Researchers were able to see what (and how) parts of the brain behave under the influence of alcohol. They pinpointed the exact receptor involved. PET scans were done on a group of subjects so the active regions in the brain could be identified. The largest decrease in brain activity was observed in the following areas—the prefrontal cortex region responsible for decision making and rational thought and the temporal cortex, which houses the hippocampus, the brain region responsible for forming new memories. Decreased activity was also observed in the cerebellum, a structure responsible for coordinating motor function.

This helps us understand why we behave the way we do on alcohol. The areas of our brains responsible for various functions are either stimulated or depressed and malfunction, altering our behaviors. Most people reflect on how their body feels on alcohol. They likely don't think about what is occurring in their brains to bring about these experiences. Alcohol creates a less than ideal environment for the proper functioning of our brain.

High blood pressure or hypertension as it is called is another side effect of drinking over the recommended amounts of alcohol. The recommended daily limits are one drink for women of any age and men over sixty-five and two drinks for men under sixty-five. Chances are, if you're a woman who drinks more than seven drinks per week or if you're a man under sixty-five drinking more than fourteen drinks per week, you suffer from hypertension.

There's no banking up extra drinks for later use if you didn't drink on some days to overindulge at another time. Alcohol-induced hypertension is usually easily reversible with the abstinence of alcohol. Continual alcohol overuse, though, puts a person at risk—this risk climbs steadily as consumption increases. Excessive and extended alcohol consumption can permanently damage heart muscle cells and lead to cardiomyopathy.

There are high caloric contents to alcohol drinks. What we mix in adds more calories and sugar. Individuals who follow particular diets count the calories from the liquor they drink. Generally, we don't pay attention to the calories in booze and continue to put on weight as time goes on. There's no way to get around it; drinking alcohol does contribute to weight gain in some people. This creates another risk factor for hypertension.

Wine has now grown in popularity outside of Europe. It's preferred over beer for its antioxidant properties. These come from the flavonoids it contains. Even though having a daily glass of wine offers antioxidant benefits, it still raises your blood pressure. If you're already suffering from hypertension, regularly consuming alcohol could keep your blood pressure spiked to the point that it eventually requires medication to keep stable. We need to determine whether we are placing ourselves in jeopardy while we presumably reduce our risk for heart disease. Drinking over the maximum recommended daily limits cancels out any of the benefits of wine. We are kidding ourselves if we believe otherwise.

Is alcohol actually and accurately included when studies such as the Western diets are performed, presented, and discussed? Yes, we know alcohol use has been studied in Mediterranean and other diets. Is it properly addressed and assessed, as it ought to be, in all studies involving the diets of adults? Statistics show the majority of adults are regular alcohol drinkers, and many of them are exceeding the recommended daily limits. We can rightly assume this affects factual evidence for analyzing outcomes of research encompassing adult diets and lifestyles. This is a sensitive issue many evade. People are reluctant to disclose precisely the amount of alcohol they actually consume. This factor alone renders most studies involving diets useless.

Knowing the risk factors and how our bodies react to drinking alcohol should help us to err on the side of caution when it comes to this lifestyle choice. We know moderation is key to reap any of the benefits associated with alcohol drinking, and we know excess creates inflammation. This is one time when following guidelines proposed by health officials is sensible. Just because we're able to develop a tolerance to drinking with regular use doesn't mean it is okay to push our limits or make it a daily habit.

In case we need another reason to think twice before keeping alcohol in our diet staple—it's now classed as a Class 1 carcinogen with asbestos. There's a steady influx of new evidence linking alcohol consumption to many cancers. Let us not forget that drinking alcohol is dehydrating, which in itself causes a wide range of problems.

Be Real, Eat Real

I am thankful I did have a good foundation to build on with respect to my relationship with food. Although hard for some to imagine, there was life before the conveniences of modern-day foods. The majority of households found space to grow a vegetable garden and prepared a lot of their own foods. It was then and can still be for some more economical and convenient. Those who weren't able to grow their own produce would shop locally to support their communities. Visits to fast food outlets or restaurants were special outings rather than regular quick fixes.

The natural way of eating is slowly making a comeback as more people realize and experience its benefits. Not only do you know what you're putting in your mouth is real and good for you, you can tell the difference in how your body feels. Real food gives you energy because it provides the nourishment your body needs to function properly. Instead of leaving the body drained trying to digest unusable elements in manufactured foods, real foods are easily assimilated and used.

There's no list of ingredients to read if you chose natural foods like fruits, vegetables, nuts, and legumes. It is beneficial to know where the food comes from. It's always best to buy locally and in season. Seasonally available produce is probably grown nearby and will be priced fairly. Locally grown foods have less of an impact on the environment. They haven't been hauled from great distances. Hopefully, they are pesticide free. You might be able to ask the grower just that when shopping at local fruit and vegetable markets. Here, too, we need to be watchful. If you notice out of season produce, it might have been purchased from supermarkets for resale.

Some vegetables easily regrown in water include bok choy, cabbage, carrot greens, celery, fennel, garlic chives, green onions, leeks, lemon grass, and lettuce. Guidelines on how to grow these can be found online. All you need is a bit of water, a window nearby, either a shallow dish or a glass, and a piece of the vegetable you want to grow. Some of these grow from the center out; it's from there they can be harvested.

If you do or have to consume produce from a distance, choose the 100 percent organic variety if at all possible. Some people protest this notion, insisting organic isn't any better—the pests you can encounter with organic foods are not worth it. As far as I am aware, and I may be wrong, in past recalls due to contamination, the majority of cases did not involve organic produce.

A contaminated cantaloupe that hadn't been washed prior to cutting caused severe abdominal distress in a few people gathered at a catered company function. The outer skin of the fruit had E. coli bacteria. The bacteria contaminated the inside of the fruit when the knife used to cut it pierced through. Some people are now advocating soaking your produce in vinegar and water to remove any unwanted residues, such as pesticides, waxes, bacteria, and the like.

There are those who say the world's food demand cannot be sustained with simply organic produce. I'm not here to debate that. All I'm saying is, if you're in an area where you can buy fresh produce from your local farmers, then you really should. If you manage to adjust your taste buds with the seasons, you can consume nutritious, fresh produce year-round at a reasonable cost. Just skipping the junk food aisle easily offsets any extra costs incurred.

Simply, the word *nutrition* can confuse. What does it really mean? Just the word can conjure up an array of numbers and values requiring memorizing and retention to become useful. Regrettably, many of us won't give any thought to nutrition until we are faced with a health issue requiring a change in our diet. Other than learning some basics through various media, I suspect the majority of people's knowledge of nutrition does not extend farther than their country's food guide. There's just too much for the average person to learn and retain. Nutrition requires a great deal of study; it's a full-time career for some. By choosing real food, you're feeding your body the nutrition it needs.

Even with people's busy schedules, it is becoming more common to see people taking the time to read the ingredients' lists on the packages they place in their grocery carts. People are taking more control over their food choices. They look beyond the packaging. Still, there are so many contradictory messages out there that it's difficult to know which choice is correct. For years, we were told margarine was a healthier choice over butter. Now food experts tell us butter is better, provided you don't eat too much of it.

Vegetable oils, all the rave for years, now have become bad for us. They, along with other cooking oils, have been linked to lung diseases including asthma. We now know choosing extra virgin olive oil over plain olive oil is better. Extra virgin olive oil means it's as unprocessed as it can be. When I first heard those two words I had no clue what they meant. We're also to choose cold-pressed olive oil. This tells us the oil hasn't been expressed using heat, which destroys most of the oil's beneficial qualities.

All this time, we were not informed that other vegetable oils they kept promoting and recommending are processed to the max and extracted from heat. Unless we took the time to put two and two together, or were aware of the practices used for oil extraction, many of us were simply unaware. Again, it's a question of the integrity of the product. If it doesn't state "cold-pressed" or "extra virgin" on the bottle, the oil has, in all likelihood, been expressed using the easiest and fastest possible way, through heating.

One of the easiest and simplest ways to determine whether you are making a healthier food choice is by looking at the list of ingredients. That alone shows how pure the food is. Many ingredients on the list indicate the food has been overly processed. I use the term overly processed here because most foods are processed. At the very least, they have been processed to make it to market. Even the simplest of food like butter has to be processed. It's not a naturally occurring food. It is cream processed into butter. Its list of ingredients is minimal compared to margarine's list, which go on and on.

CHAPTER 4

Conscious Choices

Between the deceptions and the misrepresentations, it's become almost impossible to make healthy choices in food. So what is a person to do? One thing we can do is stop being enablers. The term *enabler* is commonly used in addiction lifestyle classes. It describes a person who enables another to keep behaving in ways that support their addictions, whether in a physical or emotional manner. We, as a society, have enabled companies and businesses to keep feeding us crap by our continuing consumption of their products and goods. We have become entrapped by food conveniences, in the meantime sacrificing our health to eventually become slaves to pharmaceuticals.

There's a constant bombardment of media advertising everywhere and anywhere trying to get our attention. From the billboards on the back of benches to the television, consumers are being targeted everywhere they turn. Unless you live in a remote or secluded location, you cannot escape the advertising bombardment invading everyone's daily life. Gradually people are becoming more conscientious—companies are scrambling to find innovative ways to market their products.

As side effects of manufactured foods come into public perception, emotional advertising is amped up. Causes dear to consumers' hearts are commonly attached to products. The ads aim for a reaction of support from consumers. This tactic targets emotions—the main motivator in purchasing. Many will throw caution to the wind thinking they're helping a cause and end up buying products they really had no use for.

There's a need to disconnect from the feelings brought on by advertisements. Take notice of how you come to the decisions you do regarding the food you choose to eat. Are you giving in to temptation? One way to deal with the feelings of hunger or desire provoked by advertising is to stop to ponder why you feel the need to eat. Just this one conscious pause might be enough to help you put an end to the automatic eating reaction brought on by ads.

If you're leaning toward eating prepared foods, read the labels to find out what is in the foods you choose. Again, just the act of stopping for a moment to consciously select what you put in your mouth may lead to denying reactionary urges to eat when not hungry. When trying to choose good foods, we have to try to imagine the process the particular food underwent to transform it into the product it's become.

It's in the evening as people unwind from their busy days and settle in front of the television that the majority of mindless eating takes place. That period is when people really need to dig deep and find the self-control to resist the temptation to binge. For some reason, relaxing to watch movies tends to stir up a desire to nibble on popcorn and eat chips or any other junk food. This happens whether there are commercials advertising food or not.

This is exactly the time when many people create problems for themselves in keeping a healthy weight. Food is to nourish the body and give it energy. It's not required when we are about to retire to bed. Sleeping burns only so many calories. Having a substantial dinner helps avoid snacking at night. There are some who say it's better to have your largest meal at breakfast or lunch. However, if you are prone to snacking in the evenings, ensuring you eat a balanced, healthy dinner helps kick that habit.

Restraint enforced here pays off big. This is all part of developing healthy eating habits. I've experienced this myself. If I start snacking in the evenings, I put on weight. I've tested this theory more than once. If you simply choose to snack at night, make it a small portion of something healthy. It's exactly for weight control reasons you need to curb this habit.

When we learn to appreciate food and what it's intended for, there comes a realization there's so much more going on than just feeding our hunger by filling up the stomach. Food is intended to deliver energy, not zap it. With discriminating choosing, distinguishing what foods give you power becomes top priority.

Once you stop reactive eating, you'll be able to differentiate how certain foods make you feel. There's a good chance you'll find out you're sensitive to some. If you are, you'll need to abstain from these foods until your body is able to tolerate them. The body lets you know how it feels when you begin to gradually reintroduce them into your diet. Many problems resolve themselves when you're eating sufficient real foods.

Because more and more people have given up the basics of food preparation, there's a great possibility much will be lost as convenience replaces value. One valuable cooking art missing from our present modern-day lifestyle is homemade soup. Preparing soups from scratch by boiling bones, meats, or vegetables for broth or stock packs so much wholesome goodness; it's a real shame to let this practice fade away.

Beware of packaged soup broths boasting lower sodium values. Often monosodium glutamate (MSG) has taken its place at the top of the list of ingredients in order to compensate for taste. Comparing between the light and regular versions of a popular manufactured chicken stock, I saw that, in the light version, MSG was listed as the fourth ingredient on a label of twelve ingredients. Sodium content came in at 680 mg per cup. In the regular version, MSG is still incorporated. It appeared as the last ingredient on the list of twelve ingredients, but sodium was higher, at 970 mg per cup.

Again and again, thinking we are making a better food choice, we're fooled. With MSG included in both types and sodium between half to the maximum daily allowance, the stock doesn't make for a smart food choice either way. Do not be deceived by the size of flavor cubes for soups. They are not any better; they can pack as much as 1,780 mg per cube.

Soup, an occasional indulgence, became a regular staple in my diet after being introduced to Vietnamese pho soup many years ago. For the beef noodle pho, the stock preparation involves boiling beef bones with chuck beef meat with various spices and then simmering for at least three hours. After straining, the liquid is chilled to let the fat harden for easy removal from the top. Other variations of pho include chicken, seafood, and vegetable phos. They can easily be prepared at home and personalized by adding steamed vegetables such as broccoli, Chinese cabbage, carrots, and bok choy just prior to serving. The gelatins and important nutrients delivered from making your own broths cannot be equaled in any processed soups.

It's in keeping with the basics that we can ensure we're getting the most value from the foods we eat, avoiding the ill effects of preservatives, additives, and excess flavorings. There are people who are of the mindset that it's cheaper to buy foods already prepared than it is to make them at home. Shoppers choose boneless meat, as they do not want to have to pay for bones, not realizing the presented boneless option is usually higher priced. We think it's practical to choose convenience when it's cheaper. Doing so not only takes away from the taste; the whole nutrient composition is lost.

To add flavor, the practice of injecting sodium in cuts of meats, known as meat plumping, has been used since the 1970s. If manufactured foods make up the bulk of someone's diet, manifestations of digestive distress in one form or another will be felt. Consequently, the food choices made (based on those foods being cheaper and easier) not only become intolerances but also end up causing health issues that cost money to treat down the line. When choosing foods, cutting corners for convenience is simply not worth it in the long run.

Meal planning is a good way to maximize time, not only in the preparation of food but also when shopping for food. Knowing what foods you need to buy and putting them on a shopping list before you venture out to the food markets helps minimize impulsive buying. Having all items readily at hand when you need them makes preparing meals not only easier and faster but also more enjoyable.

Responsible people keep within their budgets when shopping. We need to stick to our list and not deviate by going up and down the aisles looking for items to add to our baskets. Avoiding this walk not only helps keep our focus on making healthier choices, it also saves time. Just as it was with everything else we needed to learn, choosing only real foods eventually becomes the only way of eating we know.

Food: Friend or Foe

The average size of the human stomach is the size of our clenched fist. It can hold up to one quart or close to one liter of substances, if it is not distended from overeating. The supersize portions we are accustomed to have distorted our views on what is the right amount of food we need to eat to feed our bodies. Instead of satisfying our need for food when we eat in those quantities, we stress our bodies' digestion system.

Depending on what and how much we choose to eat, we could be tipping scales in more ways than one. Making conservative portion sizes part of our conscientious healthier food choices goes a long way toward relieving the burden on our digestive system, keeping a healthy weight, and potentially fending off diseases.

Meat grown in laboratories from cattle stem cells has been developed to help satisfy the world's meat appetite. This hunger is expected to double by 2050. The first ever lab burger was unveiled back in 2013. Much work is underway in this domain, with hopes of helping feed the world and reducing the carbon footprint of meat production. This does look a bit more promising than genetically modified organisms. The chances of an

90

unforeseen environmental catastrophe related to meats grown in labs are very limited. How this food is integrated in our bodies and affects our health over the long run is a mystery.

As citizens and custodians of this great planet, we must do our part by not adding to the environmental damage and helping to alleviate animal suffering by curbing our appetites. Unless you're loading up on vegetables or know what the recommended serving sizes are, measuring foods until you're familiar with what a serving looks like should be practiced. An adequate amount of meat is the size of our fist, while a handful of nuts is sufficient to avoid excess calories.

It is cultures that do not overeat whose people are said to live the longest and healthiest lives. They've learned to treat their bodies with respect and appreciate food for its value in health. Those who satiate their need for food without overeating by leaving a bit of room for digestion seem to fair better at controlling their weight. The requirement for food between a professional athlete and an office worker is very different. The laborer who exerts him or herself physically for numerous hours on a daily basis requires and uses greater caloric amounts than does the bus driver or taxi driver who sits for the greatest portion of the day. Daily food requirements vary depending on physical activity, size, age, and disease presence.

I've been privy to observing, through close personal friendships, different cultures' diet lifestyles. I noticed that cultures who eat meat minimally have more control over their weight. They do not use meat as the prime ingredient in meal preparations. Meat is used sparingly to provide protein and enhance dishes. Whether or not this lifestyle was in part adopted because of the necessity to conserving due to limited meat resources, the end result is more balanced.

This style of eating is now being recognized in our necks of the woods. We are encouraged to build our meals around vegetables rather than meat. Doing so takes some adjustments at first, but it is more than equally satisfying by far. Choose vegetables you enjoy and add sprinkles of nuts and seeds if you want to add extra protein.

The Mediterranean diet is claimed to be a healthy way of eating. According to the Mayo clinic, the Mediterranean diet is a heart-healthy choice and reduces the incidents of cancer, Parkinson's, and Alzheimer diseases. It doesn't come as a surprise that the majority of the foods consumed come from plant-based sources. Real foods such as fruits, vegetables, legumes, nuts, and grains are what make up the bulk of this diet. Fish and seafood, along with poultry, are consumed a couple times a week. Red meat is limited to a few times a month. Herbs and spices are integral and used regularly for flavoring.

Instead of spreading butter or margarine on their bread, people following the Mediterranean diet dip it in olive oil. They get their fats, good fats, from nuts and olive oil. Some include canola oil when they talk about the Mediterranean diet; I prefer not to. Canola oil has not been an established part of the diet for as long as olive oil has. An appealing part of the diet for many is the inclusion of a daily glass of red wine. The real difference might be that, as part of their lifestyles, those groups of people choose to walk rather than drive.

As we gave up natural fats used for generations and replaced them with so-called healthier options, such as those of seeds and other polyunsaturated oils, unhealthy balances of acids developed in our bodies—possibly not entirely as a result of but as a part of the fundamental dietary changes made to our entire manufactured food production system. The overemphasis on polyunsaturated fats delivering linoleic acids may play a role in the development of some diseases—for example, macular degeneration. Without protective oils, available through regular fish consumption or supplementation, the unbalance created by overconsumption of polyunsaturated fats is believed to lead to the condition. It promises to be interesting if this proves true. This disease affects so many as they age.

Here is an example of one of many dangerous deceptions out in the marketplace. A healthy spice with increasingly proven health benefits is commonly substituted with another member of its family, which doesn't have the same beneficial qualities. The cheaper, potentially harmful *Cinnamomum cassia* is the variety distributed in mass. For simplicity I will call it cassia from now on. True *Cinnamomum zeylanicum*, shortened to Ceylon cinnamon or called *Cinnamomum verum*, is the one we want to consume. This is the spice used for centuries, proven as an effective remedy for numerous ailments, including *Candida albincans*. It's not found in the usual stock of spices at the supermarkets. Even if cassia is just as tasty, its coumarin content is harmful. Ceylon, on the other hand, has little of the naturally occurring coumarin.

This very popular spice used to flavor foods and beverages can deliver toxic amounts of coumarin, causing liver and kidney damage in sensitive people. Prepared foods such as cinnamon buns and breads, mulled wines, and other drinks are made using cassia for economic reasons. If you find two varieties listed in an ingredients list, you can bet the cheapest, cassia, is more plentiful. For taste, many prepared products are loaded with excess cassia. In those substantial quantities, the spice is toxic depending on overall amounts consumed and frequency.

Coumarin, which occurs naturally in other foods, was banned as a food additive. It's still found in artificial vanilla flavoring, in pipe tobacco, and in some alcoholic beverages. It's coumarin that is concentrated and present in rodenticide. If you haven't gone out of your way to find it, the powdered cinnamon you are using is probably *Cinnamomum cassia*.

The identifying variety name is usually not displayed on spice packages. Companies will argue that it is cinnamon; there is no need to disclose the variety. The cinnamon sticks to look for are lighter than the deep orange color we associate cinnamon sticks with. They appear to have layers when looking at them from the ends—as if numerous thinner sheets were rolled up instead of one thick sheet.

The reference books failed to reveal the toxicity potential of the cinnamon popularly used in this part of the world. I don't know what variety is consumed in other parts of the world. Here, the healing cinnamon is more expensive and is not regularly stocked at the grocery store. Specialty health food stores should carry it. Who knew that, when choosing cinnamon, we were potentially exposing ourselves to a harmful substance?

Digestion

Digestion processes convert the food we eat into chemicals so it can be delivered through our blood and used by the body. Enzymes are used in the processes of breaking down proteins, starches, and fats. All foods are not digested equally. There are many processes involved in digestion, and the first of these begins as soon as we contemplate putting something in our mouths. There are some basic rules to digestion some claim are helpful for digestion and optimum nutrient absorption. Others say digestion happens regardless of what and how we eat. As far as we know this is true, since no one has ballooned up and burst. Yet, we are witness to a rise in digestion problems.

Oxidation happens when energy is released from the foods we eat. Since chewing helps break down food before it enters the stomach, it is helpful to spend enough time chewing. This not only assists with digestion, it also minimizes gas. The stomach further breaks down the food and separates the different macronutrients, carbohydrates, proteins, and fats so they can be further processed depending on the need.

Some recommend proteins be included every time we eat. The digestion process for proteins takes longer than that for foods from the other food groups. In that sense, proteins satisfy one's hunger longer. All proteins are not created equal. Some proteins are not complete. Those that are complete provide all the essential amino acids our bodies require on a daily basis. Typically, people associate complete proteins with animals and their byproducts, such as milk and cheese. Plants sources of complete protein include soy, hemp, quinoa, and amaranth.

The protein of choice for athletes is whey protein. Derived from milk, it's a complete, fast-acting protein taken before or after exercise. It has vitamins and minerals and contains the highest branched-chain amino acids—leucine, isoleucine, and valine. Whey protein of the most un-denatured state available had been part of my daily food supplementation for many years. I believe it helped me maintain a certain level of energy.

Nowadays, many people are indulging in an overabundance of foods possibly containing man-made chemicals and then washing everything down with sugary drinks. There are repercussions to such modern-day overindulgences—repercussions felt in our digestive systems. Is it simply that we're consuming foods in too great amounts? Or is there more to it? Is there relevance to the rules some are presenting on food combinations? You be the judge.

As strange as this may be for many people, for the sake of argument, and in case this helps anyone, following is what I learned on this subject thus far. Interestingly, it is as if much of our modern-day diet goes against these guidelines.

- First, gastric digestion occurs in the stomach and is the process used for the digestion of **proteins**. The hydrochloric acid (HCl) necessary for the breakdown of proteins is in the stomach's gastric juices.
- Second, salivary digestion begins in the mouth by chewing and releasing enzymes from our salivary glands. This is the process used for digesting **starches**. The enzyme, ptyalin, secreted in our saliva is essential for digestion of starches. Important to note is this enzyme is not delivered if sugar is ingested. There's virtually no protein or fat digestion occurring in the mouth.

- These two processes are said to work better independently of each other. It's best to eat each separate from the other. Either combines well with vegetables.

- Third, fruits should be eaten by themselves, preferably half an hour apart from other foods. Fruits require little digestion and pass through the stomach rather quickly. If combined with other foods, fruits are left to linger in the stomach as the other food is digested. This causes fermentation, which creates upset.

Melons, which are mostly water, are best eaten separately from other fruits. The rapid speed at which melons decompose make them harmful to consume with other foods requiring a greater amount of time to digest. Acidic fruits are not to be eaten with sweet fruits.

Maybe our diets of beef patties on buns, pasta with meat sauces, crackers with cheese, cereals with milk, jam on toasts, and so forth have set us up for digestive distress.

The list of digestive disorders and medications to treat them keeps on growing. Many, including younger people, probably get away eating whatever without much more than an upset stomach. However, if you suffer from digestive issues, try practicing one or a couple of these basic rules to see if you find any relief.

It might be useful to try to imagine how our ancestors ate. When recreating in our minds the conditions of ancient times, it's easy to conclude only one or two food groups were consumed at once. Unless you were wealthy or party to the gluttony feasts or the likes of such as those in ancient Roman times, you were, in all possibility, restricted in the types of foods available at any one given time.

Cooking food, whether it is baking, broiling, steaming, or frying, destroys some of the nutrients and essential living enzymes. In other cases, cooking produces better assimilation and nutrition. Cooked tomatoes deliver higher lycopene levels than raw tomatoes. There are even raw diets people swear by to have improved health dramatically. I'm not familiar with taking this extreme of a position with regards to diet, so I cannot say at this juncture.

Regardless, there are good reasons why raw foods should be part of the everyday diet. The enzymes delivered from eating certain fresh vegetables and fruits are abundant when these foods are eaten raw. If you don't already include raw in your diet, do try it for some time and see if you can feel a difference. I know I do—I feel better with some raw.

One Size Does Not Fit All

The start of a new year has just passed, and the health resolutions people make abound on the Internet. A food recommendation in a particular article had put peanuts on the list of foods people need to remove from their diets. The reason given was peanuts are prone to mold. The recommendation was to eat other nuts and nut butters.

Taking this information with a grain of salt, as we all should with these types of suggestions, I decided to explore this a bit further, given that peanut butter was part of my diet. Have I been lucky? That is, by never having bitten into a peanut and experiencing the gross taste of mold. I have had this experience when biting into nuts on more than one occasion. So I beg to differ with the recommendation for more reasons than one.

The first thing we need to realize is that peanuts are not nuts. As the name implies, they are in the same category as peas. In fact, they're from the *Arachis hypogaea* legume family. For those with nut allergies, peanuts can be a healthy alternative; they do provide some important nutrients. When choosing peanut butter, it's best to find one containing only peanuts.

Many brands have added sugar and sodium, meaning they aren't a healthy choice. The nutritional value of peanuts comes in the forms of potassium, iron, and fiber. Yes there are other foods that deliver these same nutrients. This food has a good ratio for fats. Monounsaturated fats make up the bulk of fats with only 20 percent saturated. So far as we know monounsaturated fat is a good fat.

Let's compare the difference between two unsalted butters, one from the supernut of all nuts, almonds to peanut butter. If we use the charts provided by the USDA National Nutritional Database to compare the two butters, we find they're very similar in nutritional values. They both consist of the same nutrients in different concentrations. There's an equal amount of protein in each, at 3.35 grams per tablespoon. Fiber is almost the same, with almond butter providing an extra .3 grams.

The major differences between the two, in favor of almond butter, is its mineral content. They're almost double for all, except for potassium, which is basically equal, with only 1 mg difference. Zinc is slightly more by .8 mg in almond butter. It's calcium that stands out in almond butter. It is eight times more abundant, at 56 mg per tablespoon, and riboflavin in almond butter is also over eight times greater.

The amount of vitamin E is over three times greater in almond butter. What is extra in peanut butter is niacin, at over five times more, and thiamin, a bit better than over double. Vitamin B_6 is double in peanut butter. There are many in the health community who believe people are consuming too much B_6. It's still an important vitamin to have in our diets. Peanut butter is an economical way to get some important nutrients.

Another important benefit of peanuts is that they enable the body to produce uric acid. Similar to amino acids, uric acid is categorized as an antioxidant. It occurs as a result of the body breaking down purines. Purines are available in anchovies, dried beans and peas, mackerel, mushrooms, organ meats, and beer. Since dry peanuts fall into the category of dry peas and legumes, they deliver purines. Elevated levels of uric acid are uncommon in healthy individuals. Levels could become high as a result of acidosis, alcoholism, chemotherapy, diabetes, diuretic pills, gout, hypothyroidism, immune-suppressing drugs, obesity, purine-rich diets, and renal failure. Uric acid dissolves in the blood and travels to the kidneys to be released in the urine.

Too much uric acid is called hyperuricemia, and although this is harmful in the majority of people, it offers some benefits for those of us afflicted with MS. Low serum uric acid is seen in people with MS. This theory was tested with very promising results. Uric acid was successfully used in both preventing and providing treatment of the animal model with MS. Treatment approaches based on the elevation of serum uric acid might prove beneficial for some MS patients.

Hopefully I didn't lose any of you. I felt it important to bring this up. This does correlate to something beneficial I have eaten all along but wasn't aware of until now. As stated above, uric acid occurs when the body breaks down purines present in dried peas and legumes. The purines from peanuts are much lower than those derived from the other legumes.

A concept that is given more credibility within the alternative medicine community is the alkaline and acid profiles of food. If you've practiced or read up on the subject, you know it is widespread knowledge in the alternative medicine field. An acidic body is unhealthy and susceptible to disease.

Most of us have heard of the absolute necessity of maintaining an ideal pH level in fish tanks and swimming pools. It's the same for our bodies. Our bodies perform at their best when we are in an alkaline state. Foods either alkalize or acidify our bodies. The best way to maintain balance is eating a ratio of 80 percent alkaline-producing foods to 20 percent acid-producing foods. If our bodies become too acidic, health problems ensue.

If you've never heard of this or the concept eludes you and you don't care to give it much thought, keep in mind the foods producing the most acidifying reactions in the body are red meat and sugar. It comes as no surprise then these are the exact substances associated with the development of the deadliest of diseases—cancer and cardiovascular diseases.

Urine pH is simply a reflection of what the body is no longer requiring and is disposing of. Blood pH levels are stabilized and regulated in the body. Because of this, many argue that there is no such thing as alkalizing and acidifying foods, and the body is capable of keeping things balanced.

Just because something has not been accepted by the mainstream does not mean it's without merit.

At the other end of the spectrum, we have some diets encouraging the consumption of large amounts of meat to reach a ketosis metabolic state. Basically, ketosis is when the body burns fat for energy instead of carbohydrates. When the liver has exhausted its reserve of glycogen, elevated levels of ketones are made. To recap, glycogen is glucose stored by the liver when it is not needed anywhere else in the body.

Ketosis can be detected by measuring ketone levels in the blood. Urine strips can also be used but are not as accurate. Experts do not agree on whether ketosis is harmless in healthy people. Individuals on high protein diets reach a state of ketosis in their bodies. Are we right to think that, throughout human evolution, the body must have experienced ketosis on a fairly regular basis? Nevertheless, this extreme is definitely no better than any other extreme for any length of time.

If it looks like I am contradicting myself here, since I do believe in eating meat sparingly, I apologize. I will reiterate. There are people who may benefit from a ketogenic diet as a type of reboot. It is worth considering for a period of time until the body relearns to use fat for fuel instead of sugar. As always, it is best to check with a professional before starting any diet. As of now, I know of no other option to facilitate reestablishment of this natural process. I strongly believe giving up sugar cancels any need for a ketogenic diet.

It's easy to automatically assume citrus fruits, because of their acidic taste, would acidify our bodies. Actually these fruits have an alkaline effect in the body. As stated earlier, red meat has the highest acidifying effect. This fact alone should encourage us to eat smaller amounts of it to keep to the ratio of 20 percent acid-producing food. I will take the risk of repeating myself here—sugar, no surprise, has an acidifying effect.

There are varying degrees in either category on the effects of different foods. Fruits have a mildly acidifying effect because of their fructose content, whereas meat has a highly acidifying effect. Vegetables have an alkaline effect. Fruit juices with added sugar are highly acidifying to the body. Milk is listed as somewhat acidifying. Herbs are alkalizing, as are most seeds. If this concept interests you, there are many websites with detailed lists of the different foods and their effects in the body.

Macho Micronutrients

Proper nutrition comes in very minute forms in vitamins, minerals, and enzymes that not only keep us alive but also keep our bodies functioning well, our minds alert, and our senses keen. I feel it's interesting and important to understand how some of these work in the body. Without getting too technical, I will spend some time on this. It is an important aspect of our overall well-being. I aim to keep this discussion as simple as possible yet helpful for an easy reference.

Hopefully you are eating a well-balanced diet and are able to get all the nutrients you need from food. However, many of us are not. If such is the case, it's appropriate to consider supplementation. Some of these powerhouse substances need to be replenished daily for optimal health. As a precaution it's always advisable to consult a health professional before taking any nutritional supplements. Ideally, it's better to get proper nutrition from the foods we eat.

There are times when adding some supplements is helpful and recommended. Women are prescribed prenatal vitamins as soon as pregnancies are confirmed. A 400-mcg supplement of folic acid is also advised for women intending on getting pregnant. This is regardless of the amount they're getting in their diets. This proactive approach emphasizes the role of nutrition in health. Proper nutrition helps keep us in best physical health longer and wards off diseases.

It seems dated that the only nutritional question asked to patients during routine physical examinations is if they have an appetite. There's no further discussion about nutrition unless results demand attention, patients inquire, or apparent signs of imbalances are observed. Sometimes just a little tweak here and there makes a huge difference in how a person feels, whether it's in the form of adding certain foods to the diet or with supplements.

As it is with much of the health advice and recommendations given to the general public, contradictory information regarding supplementation and what is safe, effective, and necessary gets disseminated. While it's long been thought of as helpful to up the dosages of vitamin C when suffering from colds or flus, we're now told too much of a type of this vitamin leads to kidney stones.

Another antioxidant, vitamin E, once touted as the one essential vitamin for heart health got its fair share of negative reviews. To this date, the positives outweigh the negatives for supplementation. The tolerable upper intake level (UL) of 1,000 mg daily is attained with about 1,500 IU of natural vitamin E or 1,100 IU of synthetic vitamin E. That is the established reasonable amount to take.

A BCC Research report released the figures on the global market for nutraceuticals encompassing foods, beverages, and supplements at a worth of $160.6 billion in 2013, with increase to $171.9 billion in 2014. The research projected annual compound growth rate of 7 percent would up this figure to $241.1 billion by 2019. A newer version of the report confirming their forecasted growth for this market was expected out in March 2017. Elsewhere the projected compound annual growth rate is slightly higher, at 7.5 percent, with Morden Intelligence's valuation of global nutraceuticals for 2016 at $250 billion to reach $385 billion by 2021.

As we can see from these figures, the market for vitamins and supplements is ever increasing as more and more people take proactive measures to achieve and maintain physical health through nutrition. Despite the mainstream downplaying this factor in nutrition—as in the recently published results of a study disproving the role of supplementation in health—many people believe otherwise. With such a huge market, we are right in assuming not all supplements are created equal and not all are beneficial or up to standards.

Upon recommendation from my neurologist, I did take evening primrose oil (EPO) since my diagnosis for almost twenty years. A couple of years later, he recommended I take vitamin D, and I had since then. After suffering from dry eyes—because EPO is an omega-6 supplement and I never compensated by adding omega-3s, I decided to shelve EPO for now. It's my feeling I need more 3s at this time.

Those were two supplements I took on a daily basis for many years. At various times, I did take a multivitamin depending on the state of my diet. Additionally, I supplemented with a whey protein for a few years. For the most part, I try to get the nutrition I need from the foods I eat.

On the occasions when we choose to supplement, particularly if it's for any long duration, it is wise to monitor levels. As easy as we feel it is to treat ourselves with just taking one supplement or the other, there could be ramifications. There are known interactions between some compounds we may not be aware of. Some work well together, and some don't. Others need to be taken separately if at all. And others are detrimental in too large of doses. There are many aspects to consider, such as lifestyle, age, and overall physical and mental conditions, along with general diet.

We get most of our nutrients from the carbohydrates, proteins, and fats in the foods we eat and others from the water and beverages we drink. Vitamins and minerals are classified as micronutrients essential to health. They're not always available in the foods we consume. Diminished values in the foods we eat make for a lack, and preservatives and the like overburden. There are many reasons additional nutritional requirements are necessary.

Life Hackers' survey of users on the top five best food and nutrition tracking tools came up with (1) My Fitness Pal, (2) Lose It, (3) CRON-o-Meter, (4) Spark People, and (5) Fat Secret. Please check out the list for a description of each at http://lifehacker.com/

five-best-food-and-nutrition-tracking-tools-1084103754. There are nifty tech gadgets coming out for those who can afford them. Hopefully as these become more common, they'll be affordable for the majority.

TellSpec builds sensors that, when passed over a food item, scans and provides details on the food macronutrient contents, including sugars and their glycemic index ranking. It lets you know of the presence of any allergens or contaminants and reports on the integrity of the food. It tells you if the food has been altered by use of cheaper substitutions.

One more worth mentioning, fairly lower in price, is the HAPIfork made by HAPILABS. It doesn't give the nutritional information like the others. It brings awareness to how fast we eat. The fork vibrates to let users know if they're eating too fast, keeps count of how many forkfuls were eaten, and records how much time it took to eat the food.

In trying to keep with mainly the natural contents of food, dairy products have not been included for the most part. There are too many variables and factors to consider in order to arrive at an accurate figure in each category.

Following is an overview of the different vitamins and minerals. I encourage everyone to further research these. The Internet is a great tool, offering many informative nutritional websites. Keeping a journal of the foods we eat fits in well with tracking how we feel with what we feed our bodies, along with vitamin and mineral contents. Because we are not properly screened for these levels with regular blood and urine tests, identification of problem areas might be possible if we do our own monitoring.

Here is the breakdown of individual vitamins with their daily recommendations for healthy adults age nineteen and older. Each includes the range from the recommended daily allowance (RDA) to the maximum, or upper tolerable level (UL), if available. The RDA is the average amount of daily intake needed to meet nutrient requirements in the majority of healthy adults. Alternate recommendations are provided in lieu—if no RDA has been determined.

A. Vitamins

There are only three of the essential vitamins the body is able to produce—vitamin D, vitamin B_7/biotin, and B_5/pantothenic acid. When exposed to the sun, our skin is able to produce vitamin D, and we get the Bs from intestinal bacteria. All other vitamins must be obtained from our diets, either through animal and plant sources and supplements.

If we are not eating a wide variety of nutritious foods on a daily basis, we are lacking in some vitamins. We can fall short of some occasionally, or we're deficient in one due to excess consumption of another. It is worth taking a look at how our diets fare in providing us with the vitamins our bodies need to function properly. A few vitamins have synergistic qualities when taken with other compounds—vitamin C helps iron absorption.

There are natural and synthetic vitamins available in different supplement formulas. Natural vitamins are made from food sources while synthetic vitamins are prepared in laboratories with chemicals to mimic the natural form. An exception can be made; it's still beneficial for people who are not able to get it from the sun to take vitamin D_3.

There are various additives incorporated in the making of synthetic vitamins such as artificial colorings, additives, sugars, starches, and chemicals that are harmful. Choosing natural varieties is preferable. If the list of nonmedicinal ingredients far exceeds the actual therapeutic agents, it's probably wiser to pass on that brand.

The water-soluble vitamins, C and B-complex, must be consumed daily; they cannot be stored in the body. The fat-soluble or oil-soluble vitamins, A, D, E, and K, are stored in the liver and fatty tissue. The oil-soluble vitamins need fat to be absorbed. These are best taken with meals for proper assimilation. Water-soluble vitamins can be taken without food. Should stomach upset be experienced, taking these with a snack or a meal will help. When taking a multivitamin, it's recommended that it be taken with the largest meal of the day for better absorption.

The vitamin descriptions mention (a) some of their roles in various body functions, (b) their synergy with other vitamins and nutrients, (c) their contents in some of the foods they occur in, (d) what a deficiency looks like, (e) how too much manifests, and (f) any cautions indicated.

If taking more than one type of vitamin supplement, it's important to add the total of the particular vitamin(s) if present in more than one supplement. It would be wise to figure out if the foods we eat contain them too, providing us with ample amounts of one or the other. Excesses of certain vitamins are harmful.

The vitamins classed as antioxidants prevent free radicals from attaching and damaging cells and tissue. The processes of converting food to energy give us free radicals. Furthermore we're exposed to myriads of toxins that only a diet rich in antioxidants can suppress.

Vitamin A

RDA for females is 700 mcg or 2,333 IU to UL of 3,000 mcg or 10,000 IU.

For males, RDA is 900 mcg or 3,000 IU to UL of 3,000 mcg or 10,000 IU.

This vitamin falls in the class of antioxidant. It has a role in the health of our cells, eyes, immune and vascular systems, skin, and mucous membranes.

It can be found in animal livers, fish liver oils, and in green and yellow fruits and vegetables. The bright oranges and yellows provide the body with high amounts of beta-carotene—a precursor to vitamin A. These help our bodies' defenses against free radical damage.

A deficiency in vitamin A shows up as poor night vision; as dry eyes, hair, and skin; or in a reduced capacity to fight infection, such as in pneumonia, due to loss of cells lining lungs to fight bacteria.

Excesses could prove toxic to the liver and body. It's nearly impossible to overdose on vitamin A from a regular diet. Caution is advised for those who regularly consume animal livers. Some of these contain way over the maximum daily allowance for vitamin A. It is equally prudent to monitor when someone is taking a multivitamin with vitamin A or cod liver oil, which can pack 1,382 mcg per teaspoon. Pregnant women are advised to limit their food intake of liver to once every two weeks.

The following examples of the different vitamin A contents show the 3,000-mcg maximum daily limit is more than met in a diet that includes animal livers.

Vitamin A in animal livers	Approximate values
beef, cooked liver	75 g (2 1/2 oz) = 5,808–7,082 mcg
chicken, cooked	75 g (2 1/2 oz) = 3,222 mcg
lamb, cooked	75 g (2 1/2 oz) = 5,618–5,836 mcg
pork, cooked	75 g (2 1/2 oz) = 4,054 mcg
turkey, cooked	75 g (2 1/2 oz) = 16,950 mcg
veal, cooked	75 g (2 1/2 oz) = 15,052-15,859 mcg

Foods to help meet daily requirements of vitamin A follow.

Vitamin A in foods	Approximate values
Fruits	
apricot, dried	1/4 cup = 191 mcg
cantaloupe, raw	1/2 cup = 143 mcg
cantaloupe, 1/8	1 medium = 5,986 IU
mangoes, sliced	1 cup = 1,785 IU
papaya	1 small = 1,444 IU
peach	1 medium = 489 IU
Herbs and spices	
dandelion greens	1 cup = 5,589 IU

Vitamin A in foods	Approximate values
marjoram	100 g = 8,068 IU
paprika	1 tbsp = 3,448 IU
purslane	100 g = 1,320 IU/44% RDA
Vegetables	
bok choy, cooked	½ cup = 190 mcg
carrot juice	½ cup = 966 mcg
carrots, cooked	½ cup = 653–709 mcg
carrot, raw	1 medium (61 g) = 509 mcg
collards, cooked	½ cup = 406–516 mcg
kale, fresh, frozen, cooked	½ cup = 468–505 mcg
lettuce, red leaf, raw	1 cup = 218 mcg
lettuce, romaine, raw	1 cup = 258 mcg
pumpkin, canned	1/2 cup = 953 mcg
spinach, cooked	1/2 cup = 498 mcg
squash, butternut	1/2 cup = 604 mcg
sweet potato, baked	1 medium = 1,098 mcg
Swiss chard, cooked	1/2 cup = 566 mcg
tomato	1 medium = 1,025 IU
turnip greens	1/2 cup = 290–466 mcg

Other significant food sources to help meet daily requirements of vitamin A are found in fish. See the following list for specific amounts.

Fish and seafood	Approximate values
eel, cooked	75 g (2.5 oz) = 853 mcg
herring, pickled	75 g (2.5 oz) = 194 mcg
mackerel, cooked	75 g (2.5 oz) = 189 mcg

tuna, bluefin, raw, cooked	75 g (2.5 oz) = 491–568 mcg
Additional sources	
eggs	2 large = 190–252 mcg

Vitamin B-complex

The vitamin B is complex in that there are many different forms classified in the B category. These micronutrients fall in the class of coenzyme—they help in enzyme chemical reactions to other substances and provide energy. The Bs play a role in the health of our brain, eyes, gastrointestinal tract, hair, liver, mouth, muscle tone, nerves, and skin.

Bs' deficiencies are more common in older populations since they become harder to absorb with age.

The Bs are naturally found in brown rice, egg yolks, fish, legumes, liver, peas, peanuts, poultry, whole germs, and grains.

Following are the different Bs with some of the foods they occur in.

- **B_1/thiamine**
  RDA for females is 1.1 mg, and it's 1.2 mg for males. Significant food sources of natural thiamin follow.

B_1/thiamine in foods	**Approximate values**
Legumes (cooked)	
adzuki, black, kidney, lima,	
navy, pinto, roman, and	
soy beans	3/4 cup = 0.18–0.32 mg
edamame	1/2 cup = 0.25 mg
soybean sprouts	1/2 cup = 0.26 mg
tempeh	3/4 cup/150 g = 0.5 mg
Grains	
wheat germ, raw	1/4 cup/30 g = 0.50 mg

B$_1$/thiamine in foods	Approximate values
Nuts and seeds	
seeds, sunflower, shelled	1/4 cup = 0.54 mg
Others	
soybean burger	2.5 oz = 2.00 mg

- **B$_2$/riboflavin**

  RDA for females is 1.1 mg, and that for males is 1.3 mg.

  Significant natural food sources other than dairy products follow.

B$_2$/riboflavin in foods	Approximate values
Fish and seafood	
cuttlefish, cooked	2.5 oz (75 g) = 1.3 mg
mackerel, cooked	2.5 oz (75 g) = 0.3–0.4 mg
salmon, cooked	2.5 oz (75 g) = 0.4 mg
squid, cooked	2.5 oz (75 g) = 0.3 mg
trout, cooked	2.5 oz (75 g) = 0.3 mg
Nuts and seeds	
almonds	1/4 cup = 0.1–0.4 mg

- **B$_3$/niacin/nicotinic acid/niacinamide**

  RDA is 14 mg for females and 16 mg for males to UL of 35 mg for both.

  Many processed foods, such as cereals, pastas, and the like, have been fortified with niacin.

  Foods to help meet daily requirements for vitamin B$_3$/niacin follow.

B$_3$/niacin in foods	Approximate values
Fish and seafood	
anchovies, canned	2.5 oz (75 g) = 19 mg
haddock, cooked	75 g = 7 mg
herring, cooked	75 g = 7 mg
mackerel, cooked	75 g = 7–12 mg
rainbow trout, cooked	75 g = 8–10 mg
salmon, cooked or canned	75 g = 11–17 mg
sardines, canned in oil	75 g = 7 g
tuna, cooked or canned	75 g = 12–18 mg
Grains	
bread, whole wheat	1 slice = 2 mg
oatmeal, instant cooked	175 ml = 3–5 mg
wheat germ, toasted	1/4 cup (30 g) = 4 mg
Legumes	
beans, black, cooked	1 cup (172 g) = 0.87 mg
beans, kidney, cooked	1 cup (177 g) = 1.02 mg
beans, navy, cooked	1 cup (182 g) = 1.18 mg
beans, pinto, cooked	1 cup (171 g) = 0.54 mg
lentils, cooked	1 cup (198 g) = 2–4 mg
peanuts, without shells	1/4 cup = 6–7 mg
peas, split, cooked	1 cup (196 g) = 1.74 mg
Meats (cooked)	
Various cuts,	
beef, lamb, pork	2.5 oz (75 g) = 6–14 mg
chicken, various cuts	2.5 oz (75 g) = 8–15 mg
liver (beef, chicken, pork,	
and turkey)	2.5 oz (75 g) = 10–17 mg

B$_3$/niacin in foods	Approximate values
turkey, various cuts	2.5 oz (75 g) = 6–9 mg
Nuts and seeds	
almonds	1/4 cup = 3 mg
pumpkin seeds, no shells	1/4 cup = 8 mg
soy, nuts	1/4 cup = 3 mg
seeds, squash, no shells	1/4 cup = 8 mg
seeds, sunflower, no shells	1/4 cup = 3–4 mg
Others	
eggs, cooked	2 large = 3–4 mg
soy products:	
tempeh, cooked	150 g = 8 mg
tofu, cooked	150 g = 3–4 mg
Vegetables	
mushrooms, portabella	1/2 cup = 6 mg
potatoes, cooked	1 medium = 3–4 mg

- **B$_5$/pantothenic acid**
  RDA for both females and males is 5–10 mg. No UL determined.

    Integral to coenzyme CoA for metabolism, B5 is involved in cholesterol manufacturing for hormone and vitamin D production. It works with choline for signal molecule acetylcholine production.

    As B5 is abundantly found naturally in all food groups, deficiency is observable only in the severely malnourished. Toxicity is not a known issue.

- **B$_6$/pyridoxine**
  RDA for females is 1.3 mg, and that for males is 1.5 mg up to UL of 100 mg for both.

    B$_6$ is needed in enzyme activation, protein utilization, nervous system function, glycogen and hydrochloric acid productions, and hemoglobin formation. It works with B_{12} in immune system functioning and antibody production.

Contrary to what many people believe, it's not vitamin B12 people are lacking but vitamin B6.

Deficiency found in ADHD, anemia, asthma, carpal tunnel syndrome, convulsions, depression, epilepsy, fibrocystic breasts, headaches, high homocysteine, nausea, premenstrual syndrome, skin dermatitis, sore tongue, and water retention.

Toxicity with prolonged use of over 1,000 mg daily can cause nerve damage and/or poor coordination.

B6 is naturally found in the following foods.

B_6/pyridoxine in foods	Approximate values
Fish and seafood	
cod	4 oz = 0.15 mg
salmon	4 oz = 0.64 mg
sea vegetables	1 tbsp = 0.05 mg
shrimp	4 oz = 0.27 mg
tuna	4 oz = 1.18 mg
Fruits	
avocado	1 cup = 0.39 mg
banana	1 medium = 0.43 mg
cantaloupe	1 cup = 0.12 mg
figs	1 medium = 0.06 mg
pineapple	1 cup = 0.18 mg
strawberries	1 cup = 0.07 mg
watermelon	1 cup = 0.07 mg
Herbs and spices	

B$_6$/pyridoxine in foods	Approximate values
asparagus	1 cup = 0.14 mg
chili peppers	2 tsp = 0.11 mg
garlic	6 cloves = 0.22 mg
turmeric	2 tsp = 0.08 mg
Legumes	
beans, lima	1 cup = 0.30 mg
beams, pinto	1 cup = 0.39 mg
lentils	1 cup = 0.35 mg
Meats	
beef	4 oz = 0.74 mg
chicken	4 oz = 0.68 mg
turkey	4 oz = 0.92 mg
Nuts and seeds	
seeds, sunflower	1/4 cup = 0.47 mg
Vegetables	
beans, green	1 cup = 0.07 mg
beets, green	1 cup = 0.19 mg
beets	1 cup = 0.11 mg
bell peppers	1 cup = 0.27 mg
bok choy	1 cup = 0.28 mg
broccoli	1 cup = 0.31 mg
Brussels sprouts	1 cup = 0.28 mg
cabbage	1 cup = 0.34 mg
carrots	1 cup = 0.17 mg
cauliflower	1 cup = 0.21 mg
celery	1 cup = 0.07 mg
collard greens	1 cup = 0.24 mg

B₆/pyridoxine in foods	Approximate values
corn	1 each = 0.11 mg
eggplant	1 cup = 0.09 mg
kale	1 cup = 0.18 mg
leeks	1 cup = 0.12 mg
lettuce, romaine	2 cups = 0.07 mg
mushrooms, crimini	1 cup = 0.08 mg
mushrooms, shiitake	1/2 cup = 0.12 mg
mustard greens	1 cup = 0.14 mg
onions	1 cup = 0.27 mg
potatoes	1 cup = 0.54 mg
spinach	1 cup = 0.44 mg
squash, summer	1 cup = 0.12 mg
squash, winter	1 cup = 0.33 mg
sweet potatoes	1 cup = 0.57 mg
Swiss chard	1 cup = 0.15 mg
tomatoes	1 cup = 0.14 mg
turnip greens	1 cup = 0.26 mg

- **B₇/biotin, vitamin H, or Coenzyme R**

  No RDA or UL have been determined. Unofficially, 30 mcg to 100 mcg for both females and males is the normal recommended intake.

  B7 is needed for cell growth; breakdown of fats, proteins, and carbohydrates; fatty acid production; and utilization of other Bs.

  Deficiency is indicated in anemia; anorexia; baldness; depression; dry and inflamed, pale skin; hallucinations; infant cradle cap; inherited carboxylase deficiency; insomnia; listlessness;

muscular pain; nausea; poor appetite; sore tongue; and tingling in arms and legs.

Smokers are at risk of deficiency, as are those who consume large amounts of egg whites. Fats and oils exposed to heat or air for too long inhibit biotin absorption, as do antibiotics, sulfa drugs, and saccharin.

Toxicity is rare, as B7 is produced by the body in the intestines. Biotin/ B7 is natural in the following foods.

B₇/biotin in foods	Approximate values
Fish and seafood	
salmon	4 oz = 4.54 mcg
Fruits	
banana	1 medium = 3.07 mcg
grapefruit	1/2 medium = 1.28 mcg
raspberries	1 cup = 2.34 mcg
strawberries	1 cup = 1.58 mcg
watermelon	1 cup = 1.52 mcg
Grains	
oatmeal	100 g = 22–31 mcg
oats	1/4 cup = 7.80 mcg
Legumes	
peanuts	1/4 cup = 6.40 mcg
Meats	
chicken, liver	100 g = 170–200 mcg
Nuts and seeds	
almonds	1/4 cup = 14.72 mcg
walnuts	1/4 cup = 5.70 mcg
Others	

B₇/biotin in foods	Approximate values
brewer's yeast	100 g = 200 mcg
eggs	1 each = 8 mcg
eggs, yolk	100 g = 60 mcg
milk, cow's	4 oz = 2.32 mcg
yogurt	1 cup = 3.92 mcg
Vegetables	
carrots	1 cup = 6.10 mcg
cauliflower	1 cup = 1.61 mcg
cucumber	1 cup = 0.94 mcg
lettuce, romaine	2 cups = 1.79 mcg
onions	1 cup = 7.98 mcg
sweet potatoes	1 cup = 8.60 mcg
tomatoes	1 cup = 7.20 mcg

- **B_8/inositol**

    No RDA or UL have been determined.

    No official recommendations are available. However, supplementation is deemed safe at 250 mg for adults.

    B_8 is needed for healthy cell formation, CNS, neurotransmission, liver fat processing, calcium mobilization, and hair growth.

    Deficiency is rare, as B_8 is manufactured in the body. Impairment is possible as a result of smoking or drinking excess caffeine and alcohol. A lack of B_8 is found in obsessive compulsive, anxiety, and panic disorders; depression; constipation; eczema; gastritis; high cholesterol; and hypertension.

    Toxicity results in dizziness, fatigue, nausea, and headaches.

    Supplemental form with added phosphorus is phytic acid. It's commonly found in fortified cereals.

    Some foods with natural inositol, aka myo-inositol, follow.

Myo-Inositol in foods	Approximate values
Fruits	
apples, yellow	1 each (80 g) = 19.2 mg
cantaloupe, fresh	1/4 each (100 g) = 355 mg
cherries, red	5 medium (75 g) = 10.5 mg
cranberries, fresh	1 cup (100 g) = 16 mg
dates, dried	2 each (20 g) = 30.4 mg
grapefruit, fresh	1/2 each (100 g) = 199 mg
grapefruit, juice	8 oz = 468 mg
grapes, green, fresh	20 each (100g) = 16 mg
kiwi, fresh	1/2 cup (100 g) = 136 mg
lime, fresh	1 each (100 g) = 194 mg
mango, fresh	1/2 each (100 g) = 0.99 mg
nectarine, fresh	1 each (100 g) = 118 mg
orange, fresh	1 each (100 g) = 307 mg
pear, fresh	1 each (100 g) = 73 mg
pineapple, fresh	1/2 cup (100 g) = 33 mg
plums, purple	2 medium (100 g) = 11 mg
plums, red	2 medium (100 g) = 30 mg
prunes, dried	2 medium (20 g) = 94 mg
strawberries, fresh	3/4 cup (150 g) = 19.5 mg
Herbs and spices	
asparagus, fresh	1/2 cup (100 g) = 29 mg
Legumes	
beans, green, fresh	1/2 cup (100 g) = 193 mg
beans, green, frozen	1/2 cup (100 g) = 55 mg
beans, lima	100 g = 44 mg
beans, navy	100 g = 65 mg

Myo-Inositol in foods	Approximate values
peanuts, raw and cooked	12 each (15 g) = 20 mg
Nuts and seeds	
almonds	8 each (15 g) = 41.7 mg
cashews	5 each (15 g) = 12.2 mg
coconut, grated	1 tbsp (14 g) = 4.6 mg
seeds, sunflower	1 1/2 tbsp (20 g) = 2.4 mg
walnuts	5 each (10 g) = 19.8 mg
Vegetables	
artichoke	200 g = 120 mg
broccoli, fresh	1/2 cup (100 g) = 30 mg
Brussels sprouts	200 g = 80.4 mg
cabbage, Chinese	1/2 cup (100 g) = 27 mg
cabbage, white, fresh	1/2 cup (100 g) = 21 mg
collard greens, fresh	1/2 cup (100 g) = 64 mg
cucumber, fresh	1/2 cup (100 g) = 15 mg
lettuce, endive	1/4 head (100 g) = 70 mg
lettuce, romaine	1/2 cup (100 g) = 17 mg
okra, fresh	1/2 cup (100 g) = 33 mg
radish, red, fresh	1/2 cup (100 g) = 10 mg
sweet potatoes, baked	1/4 cup (50 g) = 46 mg
tomatoes, fresh	1/2 cup (100 g) = 54 mg
tomatoes, cherry, fresh	1/2 cup (100 g) = 41 mg
zucchini, fresh	1/2 cup (100 g) = 53 mg

- **B_9/folate/folacin/folic acid**

   RDA for both females and males is 400 mcg to UL of 1,000 mcg.

   B_9 plays a role in fetal neural development, energy production, red and white blood cells, and homocysteine regulation. It also works with B_{12} and iron.

Deficiency leads to anemia, digestive disturbances, fatigue, hair and skin color changes, heart palpitations, memory difficulties, paranoia, shortness of breath, and sores on or redness of tongue.

Toxicity though rare, as B_9 is water soluble (expected to be excreted in the urine), nevertheless has been observed in masking the symptoms of pernicious anemia, which is a vitamin B_{12} deficiency.

Folate food fortification is common in manufactured foods.

A list of some natural food sources of B_9/folate follows.

B_9/folate in foods	Approximate values
Fruits	
avocado	1 cup = 90 mcg
grapefruit	1 each = 30 mcg
orange	1 each = 50 mcg
papaya	1 each = 115 mcg
strawberries	1 cup = 25 mcg
raspberries	1 cup = 14 mcg
Herbs and spices	
asparagus, boiled	1 cup = 262 mcg
Legumes	
beans, black	1 cup = 256 mcg
beans, garbanzo	1 cup = 282 mcg
beans, green	1 cup = 42 mcg
beans, kidney	1 cup = 229 mcg
beans, lima	1 cup = 156 mcg
beans, navy	1 cup = 254 mcg

B$_9$/folate in foods	Approximate values
beans, pinto	1 cup = 294 mcg
lentils	1 cup = 358 mcg
peanuts	1/4 cup = 88 mcg
peas, green	1 cup = 101 mcg
peas, split	1 cup = 127 mcg
Nuts and seeds	
almonds	1 cup = 46 mcg
seeds, flax	2 tbsp = 54 mcg
seeds, sunflower	1/4 cup = 82 mcg
Vegetables	
beets, roots, boiled	1 cup = 136 mcg
broccoli	1 cup = 96 mcg
Brussels sprouts	1 cup = 100 mcg
cauliflower	1 cup = 55 mcg
celery, raw	1 cup = 34 mcg
corn, cooked	1 cup = 76 mcg
okra, cooked	1 cup = 37 mcg
spinach	1 cup = 263 mcg
squash, summer	1 cup = 36 mcg
squash, winter	1 cup = 57 mcg

- **B$_{12}$/methylcobalamin**

  RDA for both females and males is 2.4 mcg. No UL has been determined.

  B$_{12}$ plays a role in absorption and digestion, cardiovascular function, cell longevity and development, iron utilization, and metabolism. It promotes normal growth and development and protein synthesis; helps folic acid in red blood cell formation; and protects nerves.

Deficiency of B_{12} due to malabsorption can be seen in people with digestive disorders. In addition, older people are vulnerable to deficiencies because of medications they may be taking such as antigout medication and anticoagulants. They're also at risk if taking potassium supplements or if they have type 1 diabetes. A B_{12} deficiency can occur in people who drink alcohol regularly.

Symptoms of a deficiency are many and include abnormal gait, bone loss, difficulty breathing, digestive disorders, dizziness and drowsiness, enlargement of the liver, extended fatigue, eye disorders, headaches, heart palpitations, impaired memory, mood disorders, nervous tension, neurological damage, ringing in the ears, and spinal cord degeneration. A type of anemia, pernicious anemia, is another symptom of low B_{12}, leaving the body unable to produce sufficient healthy red blood cells. An intrinsic factor protein, which assists our intestines in absorbing B_{12} and is present in the cells of the stomach, is attacked by the body's immune system. At a time when no treatments were available, pernicious anemia proved fatal. Nowadays, early detection can reverse the onset. However, if permanent damage has incurred, treatment can only halt progression.

B_{12} is rare in vegetables, other than sea vegetables, so supplementation is often recommended for people who are vegetarians. Dairy foods and cereals are usually fortified with B_{12}.

Foods with naturally occurring B_{12} follow.

B_{12}/methylcobalamin in foods	Approximate values
Fish and seafood	
clams	3 oz = 84.06 mcg
cod	4 oz = 2.62 mcg

B$_{12}$/methylcobalamin in foods	Approximate values
crab	100 g = 6.59 mcg
mussels	3 oz = 20.4 mcg
oysters	3 oz = 29.77 mcg
salmon	4 oz = 5.67 mcg
sardines	3.20 oz = 8.11 mcg
scallops	4 oz = 2.44 mcg
shrimp	4 oz = 1.88 mcg
tuna	4 oz = 2.66 mcg
Meats	
beef	4 oz = 1.44 mcg
chicken	4 oz = 0.39 mcg
lamb	4 oz = 2.51 mcg
liver, turkey	100 g = 49.4 mcg
turkey	4 oz = 0.42 mcg
Others	
eggs, poached	1 each (100 g) = 0.71 mcg

- **Choline**

  RDA for females is 425 mg and for males is 550 mg to UL of 3,500 mg for both.

  Choline was recently added to lists of vitamins because of its crucial role in CNS, neurotransmitter acetylcholine, cardiovascular and intestinal systems, fetal development, metabolism, and muscle contraction.

  Deficiency results in concentration difficulty, slower learning and processing, poor memory, fatty liver, and kidney necrosis.

  Toxicity produces dizziness, fishy body odor, low blood pressure, sweating, and vomiting.

Some foods with naturally occurring choline follow.

Choline in foods	Approximate values
Fish and seafood	
cod	3 oz = 248 mg
salmon	4 oz = 81 mg
sardines	3.2 oz = 68 mg
scallops	4 oz = 125 mg
shrimp	4 oz = 153 mg
tuna	4 oz = 88 mg
Herbs and spices	
asparagus	1 cup = 47 mg
Legumes	
beans, green	1 cup = 21 mg
peas, green	1 cup = 41 mg
Meats	
beef	4 oz = 74 mg
beef, liver	2.4 oz = 290 mg
beef, various cuts	100 g = 126-139 mg
chicken	4 oz = 97 mg
chicken, liver	2.4 oz = 222 mg
lamb, lean	100 g = 129 mg
pork, ham, bone-in	100 g = 127 mg
turkey	4 oz = 94 mg
veal, loin	100 g = 125 mg
Others	
eggs, fried	100 g = 317 mg
eggs, hard-boiled	100 g = 294 mg

Choline in foods	Approximate values
eggs, poached	100 g = 234 mg
eggs, raw	100 g = 294 mg
eggs, yolk, raw	100 g = 820 mg
miso	1 tbsp = 12 mg
Vegetables	
bok choy	1 cup = 20 mg
broccoli	1/2 cup = 31.3 mg
Brussels sprouts	1 cup = 63 mg
cabbage	1 cup = 32 mg
cauliflower	1/2 cup = 24.2 mg
collard greens	1 cup = 73 mg
mushrooms, crimini	1 cup = 16 mg
mushrooms, shiitake	1/2 cup = 27 mg
mushrooms, shiitake, dried	100 g = 202 mg
spinach	1 cup = 35 mg
squash, summer	1 cup = 14 mg
Swiss chard	1 cup = 50 mg
tomatoes	1 cup = 12 mg

Vitamin C/ascorbic acid

For females, the RDA for vitamin C is 75 mg, and for males it's 90 mg to UL of 2,000 mg for both.

Vitamin C is another powerful antioxidant required for adrenal glands, collagen, gums, immune system and its protein interferon, and iron absorption, along with tissue growth and repair.

Deficiency results in bruising easily, dry hair and skin, fatigue, frequent infections, irritability, joint pain, prolonged healing time, and periodontal disease. Deficiencies can occur with consumption of alcohol, analgesics, anticoagulants, oral contraceptives, steroids, and smoking.

Excesses could potentially affect other vitamin levels, such as those of calcium, copper, and zinc. Vitamin C works synergistically with vitamin E and beta-carotene.

As is true with all supplements and even more important when taking this vitamin with any medication, check with your health care provider. Many prescription drugs lose their efficacies with vitamin C.

It is preferable and easy to meet our daily requirements when we have a diet rich in fruits and vegetables, as loss occurs during processing. Vitamin C is abundantly present in berries, citrus fruits, green vegetables, sweet peppers, and tomatoes.

Foods with naturally occurring vitamin C follow.

Vitamin C in foods	Approximate values
Fruits	
apples, raw with skin	1 cup (125 g) = 5.7 mg
avocado, raw	1 cup (150 g) = 15 mg
blueberries, raw	1 cup (148 g) = 14.4 mg
cantaloupe, medium size	1/4 each = 47 mg
cranberries, raw	1 cup (110 g) = 14.6 mg
grapefruit, juice	3/4 cup = 50–70 mg
guava, raw	1/2 cup = 188 mg
kiwi, medium	1 each = 70 mg
lemon, juice, fresh	1 cup (244 g) = 112 mg
lime, juice, fresh	1 cup (242 g) = 72.6 mg
mango	½ cup = 23 mg
orange, juice	¾ cup = 61–93 mg
orange, raw, medium	1 each = 70 mg

Vitamin C in foods	Approximate values
papaya, raw, medium	1/4 each = 47 mg
pineapple, raw	1/2 cup = 28 mg
strawberries, raw	1/2 cup = 49 mg
raspberries, raw	1 cup (123 g) = 32.2 mg
Herbs and spices	
asparagus, cooked	1 cup (180 g) = 13.86 mg
asparagus, raw	100 g = 5.6 mg
cilantro, dried	1 tbsp = 9.9 mg
dandelion, greens, raw	1 cup (55 g) = 19.3 mg
purslane, raw	1 cup (43 g) = 9 mg
rose hips, wild	1 oz (28 g) = 119 mg
Vegetables	
bell pepper, green, cooked	1/2 cup = 51 mg
bell pepper, green, raw	1/2 cup = 60 mg
bell pepper, red, cooked	1/2 cup = 116 mg
bell pepper, red, raw	1/2 cup = 142 mg
broccoli, cooked	1/2 cup = 37 mg
broccoli, raw	1/2 cup = 39 mg
Brussels sprouts, cooked	1/2 cup = 48 mg
cauliflower, cooked	1/2 cup = 28 mg
collard greens, boiled	1 cup (190 g) = 34.6 mg
collard greens, raw	1 cup (36 g) = 12.7 mg
kale, cooked	1/2 cup = 27 mg
kohlrabi, cooked	1/2 cup = 45 mg
mustard greens, boiled	1 cup (140 g) = 35.4 mg
mustard greens, raw	1 cup (56 g) = 39.2 mg
onions, cooked	1 cup (210 g) = 10.92 mg

Vitamin C in foods	Approximate values
peas, edible pod, cooked	1/2 cup = 38 mg
peppers, green	1/2 cup = 60 mg
peppers, red, cooked	1/2 cup = 116 mg
peppers, red, raw	1/2 cup = 130 mg
persimmons, Japanese, raw	1 each (168 g) = 12.6 mg
persimmons, native, raw	1 each (25 g) = 16.5 mg
radishes, icicles, raw	1/2 cup (50 g) = 14.5 mg
radishes, raw, slices	1 cup (116 g) = 17.2 mg
sweet potato, canned	1/2 cup = 34 mg
Swiss chard, boiled	1 cup (175 g) = 31.5 mg
Swiss chard, raw	1 cup (36 g) = 10.8 mg
tomato, juice	3/4 cup = 33 mg
tomato, plum, raw	1 each (62 g) = 7.9 mg
tomatoes, cherry, raw	1 cup (149 g) = 18.9 mg
tomatoes, green, raw	1 cup (180 g) = 42.1 mg
tomatoes, red, cooked	1 cup (240 g) = 54.7 mg
tomatoes, red, raw	1 cup (180 g) = 22.9 mg
turnip greens, boiled	1 cup (144 g) = 39.5 mg
turnip greens, raw	1 cup (55 g) = 33 mg
watercress, raw	1 cup (34 g) = 14.6 mg

Vitamin D

RDA for all healthy adults with minimal sun exposure is 15 mcg to UL of 100 mcg or 600 IU to UL of 4,000 IU.

Vitamin D is like a hormone; it interacts with 10 percent of our genes. It's necessary for bones and teeth, calcium and phosphorus absorption, heartbeat regulation, the immune system, and thyroid function. Important to note is increasing research shows it's a cancer preventative.

Serious consideration for supplementing with D_3, being as close to what our skin would absorb from the sun, is beneficial for the majority of people who don't get sun exposure on a daily basis. People who use sunscreen or live in the northern hemisphere, where radiation from sunlight is insufficient in winter months, along with those who don't drink milk need to supplement.

Deficiency is a major factor in fourteen types of cancer, diabetes, heart disease, osteoporosis, and MS.

Vitamin D is naturally found in egg yolks, flesh of fatty saltwater mackerel, salmon, tuna, and fish liver oils. The only vegetable delivering this vitamin naturally is the mushroom if grown under UV light. In mushrooms, it is the precursor to vitamin D, in the form of the plant sterol ergosterol, that converts to vitamin D_2 under ultraviolet light.

Vitamin D is added, and mostly consumed in synthetic form, in fortified products such as milk, orange juice, and cereals. It's listed as vitamin D, making it difficult to determine if it is D_3.

Some people only support getting vitamin D_3 from the sun, in the form of D_3 sulfate and propose supplementation with any other form is useless. Research is very much ongoing when it comes to vitamin D. Whether the fact so many people supplementing with D_3 has affected the outcome of diseases and much more will be revealed with time.

Vitamin E

RDA is 15 mg or 22.4 IU to UL of 1,000 mg or 1,500 IU for both females and males.

This popular vitamin stirred a bit of controversy some time ago. Its benefits are still being questioned, while its supplementation rate is never declining. Vitamin E is comprised of eight antioxidant compounds, four tocopherols and four tocotrienols, each having alpha, beta, gamma, and delta branches.

Alpha-tocopherols have the most presence in the body and may be the most beneficial. The gamma-tocopherols found in vegetable oils have been linked to lung problems. Vitamin E is an antioxidant inhibiting oxidization and formation of free radicals.

A deficiency in this vitamin may cause oxidation of red blood cells and destruction of nerves.

It's important for people who suffer from diabetes, rheumatic heart disease, or with an overactive thyroid to not exceed the recommended doses. People on anticoagulant medications should keep at a maximum of 200 IU daily. For those with high blood pressure who start taking vitamin E, upping dosages gradually to the desired level is best.

Found in foods such as dairy products and meats, vitamin E occurs naturally in many foods, including the following.

Vitamin E in foods	Approximate values
Fruits	
avocado	1/2 each (150 g) = 3.2 mg
blackberries	100 g = 3.5 mg
currants, black	50 g = 1.0 mg
kiwi, medium	1 each = 1.1 mg
mango	1/2 cup = 0.7 mg
raisins, sultana, dried	15 g = 0.7 mg
Herbs and spices	
asparagus	5 each (100 g) = 1.3 mg
parsley	2 sprigs (5 g) = 1.8 mg
Grains	
rice, brown cooked	1 cup = 0.6 mg
wheat germ, oil	1 tbsp = 20.3 mg

Vitamin E in foods	Approximate values
Legumes	
peanut butter	2 tbsp = 2.9 mg
peanuts, dry roasted	1 oz = 2.2 mg
peanuts, raw in shells	25 g = 5.6 mg
Nuts and seeds	
almonds, dry roasted	1 oz = 6.8 mg
Brazil nuts	20 g = 6.5 mg
hazelnuts, dry roasted	1 oz = 4.3 mg
seeds, safflower, oil	1 tbsp = 4.6 mg
seeds, sunflower, oil	1 tbsp = 5.6 mg
seeds, sunflower	1 oz = 7.4 mg
walnuts	20 g = 0.8 mg
Others	
eggs	1 large = 0.5 mg
Vegetables	
broccoli, boiled	1/2 cup = 1.2 mg
Brussels sprouts, boiled	70 g = 0.9 mg
corn, oil	1 tbsp = 1.9 mg
olive, oil	1 tbsp = 1.94 mg
peppers, green, raw	1/4 each (15 g) = 0.8 mg
peppers, green, boiled	50 g = 0.8 mg
spinach, boiled	1/2 cup = 1.9 mg
spinach, raw	1 cup = 0.6 mg
sweet potato, baked	1 cup = 1.42 mg
tomatoes, canned	120 g = 1.2 mg
tomato, juice	120 g = 1.2 mg
tomato, raw, medium	1 each = 0.7 mg

Vitamin K

No official RDA or UL has been determined. Adequate intake for females is 90 mcg, and for males it's 120 mcg.

There are three types of vitamin K. The first, vitamin K_1/phylloquinone or phytonadione, comes from plants. The second K_2, comprised of menaquinones, is made by intestinal bacteria and is found in butter, cow livers, chickens, egg yolks, fermented soybean products, and some cheeses. The third, K_3/menadione, is synthetic.

Vitamin K is necessary for blood clotting, bones, intestines, heart health, and the liver.

A deficiency causes abnormal and/or internal bleeding. Those at risk of deficiency are people who suffer from Crohn's disease, ulcerative colitis, or liver disease. Others at risk are people who take anticoagulants, antibiotics, aspirins, cholesterol-lowering medication, mineral oil, or are on a restrictive or poor diet.

K_1 can be found abundantly and naturally, as it's in vegetables. It is, however, K_2 that appears to play a big role in cardiovascular health. It is K vitamin recommended to heart patients. Some fermented foods deliver K_2, as do some animals and their byproducts, such as butter and cheese. It will only be available from grass-fed animals.

Fermented foods deliver probiotics. These help the body manufacture K_2, so it is worth adding these into our diets.

There's no exact ratio recommended between the Ks. Were our bodies ever able to convert K_1 into K_2? Are our diets leaving our body bacteria out of balance, making it necessary to consume each separately? I am no expert, so I cannot say.

Some foods with natural K_1 follow.

K₁ in foods	Daily values %
Herbs	
asparagus, cooked	1/2 cup = 57%
asparagus, frozen	1 cup = 180%
basil, dried	1 tbsp = 43%
basil, fresh	1 tbsp = 107%
chives, fresh	1 tbsp = 18%
coriander (dry cilantro)	1 tbsp = 34%
dandelion greens	1 cup = 1071%
marjoram, dried	1 tbsp = 16%
parsley, dried	1 tbsp = 34%
sage, dried	1 tbsp = 43%
Vegetables	
beet greens, cooked	1 cup = 871%
broccoli, cooked	1 cup = 276%
Brussels sprouts, cooked	1/2 cup = 137%
cabbage, red	1 cup = 90%
celery	1 cup = 37%
collards, cooked	1 cup = 966%
cucumber	1 cup = 22%
endive	1 cup = 144%
kale, cooked	1 cup = 1328%
kale, frozen	1 cup = 1433%
kale, raw	1 cup = 684%
lettuce, green	1 cup = 57%
lettuce, romaine	1 cup = 60%
lettuce, red	1 cup = 49 %
okra, cooked	1 cup = 80%

K₁ in foods	Daily values %
olive oil	1 tbsp = 11%
radicchio	1 cup = 138%
spinach, cooked	1 cup = 1111%
spinach, frozen	1 cup = 1284%
Swiss chard, cooked	1 cup = 716%
turnip greens, cooked	1 cup = 662%

A list of foods with natural vitamin K2 follows.

K₂ in foods	Approximate values
beef liver	1 cup = 5 mcg
chicken liver	1 cup = 3 mcg
cream cheese	100 g = 19.7 mcg
duck	1 cup = 6 mcg
lamb	1 cup = 6 mcg
mayonnaise, whole eggs	1 cup = 197 mcg
miso	1 cup = 10–30 mcg
nattō	3.5 oz = 1,000 mcg
turkey, dark meat	1 cup = 5 mcg

Vitamin P/flavonoids/bioflavonoids

No RDA or UL have been determined.

Bioflavonoids are antioxidants that were once called vitamin P. There are no official recommendations on dosages. They've become popular in nutritional guidelines issued under different circumstances. These are plant based, and, they, along with carotenoids, contribute to the vibrant colors of plant food.

There are approximately four thousand to six thousand types of flavonoids, classified according to the following six categories:

1) **Anthocyanidins** are cyanidin, delphinidin, malvidin, petunidin, kaempferol, pelargonidin, and peonidin, to name a few.

2) **Flavanols** are catechin, epicatechin, epigallocatechin, and others.

3) **Flavones** are apigenin, tangeritin, luteolin, and more.

4) **Flavonols** include the popular quercetin, along with kaempferol, myricetin, and isohamnetin, and there are others.

5) **Flavonones** are hesperitin, naringenin, homoeriodictyol, and eriodictyol, among others.

6) **Isoflavones** are genistein, daidzein, glycitein, and others.

Flavonoids support blood vessels, enhance the power of vitamin C, protect cells from oxygen damage, and reduce inflammation. They are widely used in supplementation for their role in capillary and circulatory health and in fighting oxidation and free radicals, as well as for their anti-inflammatory properties.

A deficiency is seen in diets low in fruits and vegetables. Deficiency presents as frequent colds and infections, nosebleeds, and easy bruising.

No actual numbers are available on the natural content of these nutrients in food. Adult North Americans get limited varieties of flavonoids. They get the majority as catechins from what they drink.

Some foods with the types of flavonoids they deliver are listed.

Beverages

- Tea, black, green, and red provide the flavanols catechin and epigallocatechin.

- Wine provides many flavonoids, and these vary depending on different factors including the grapes.

Chocolate
- All chocolates provide catechin flavanols, but dark chocolate has more.

Fruits
- Apples, apricots, peaches, pears, and plums provide the flavanols catechin and epicatechin.
- Bananas provide anthocyanidins.
- Blackberries and black grapes provide the flavanols catechin and epicatechin.
- Blueberries and cranberries provide the flavonols quercetin and myricetin.
- Cherries, raspberries, and red grapes provide the anthocyanidin cyanidin.
- Citrus fruits provide the flavonones hesperitin, naringenin, and eriodictyol.
- Grapes and grape juice provide anthocyanidins and the flavonols quercetin and myricetin.

Herbs
- Dill provides flavonols quercetin and isorhamnetin.
- Parsley provides flavonols quercetin and isorhamnetin and the flavone apigenin.
- Thyme provides the flavone luteolin.

Legumes
- Black and kidney beans provide the anthocyanidins delphinidin, malvidin, and petunidin and the flavonols kaempferol.
- Soybeans provide the flavanols catechin and isoflavones geinstein and daidzein.

Nuts and seeds

- Pecans and walnuts provide anthocyanidins.
- Pistachios provide the flavanols catechin.

Vegetables

- Artichokes provide the flavones apigenin and luteolin.
- Broccoli provides the flavonols quercetin, kaempferol, and myricetin.
- Celery provides the flavones apigenin and luteolin.
- Eggplants provide the flavonols quercetin and the flavones luteolin.
- Kale provides flavonols quercetin and kaempferol.
- Okra provides flavonols quercetin, kaempferol and myricetin.
- Onions red and green provide flavonols quercetin.
- Peppers provide flavonols quercetin and flavones luteolin.
- Snap peas provide flavonols quercetin, kaempferol, and myricetin.
- Tomatoes provide flavonols quercetin and flavones luteolin.

Coenzyme Q10

No RDA or UL have been determined.

Not recognized as an official vitamin by some, CoQ_{10}, called ubiquinone and vitamin Q, is still used in the treatment of medical conditions such as heart disease. CoQ_{10} contains antioxidant properties and is much like the other oil-soluble vitamins, especially vitamin E. The two are often found together in supplement forms.

CoQ_{10} is easily made and dispersed in the body. It is in higher concentration where energy is required, in the heart, liver, kidneys, and pancreas. CoQ_{10} plays a crucial role in cell energy production, circulation, and the immune system. Noteworthy is its ability to counter histamine, so it might prove useful for people suffering from allergies, asthma, and other respiratory diseases.

Deficiencies are seen in people with cancer, diabetes, fibromyalgia, heart disease, PD, periodontal disease, muscular dystrophy, fatigue, and seizures. Statin medication places people at risk of CoQ_{10} deficiency. These drugs interfere with the body's ability to produce this vitamin. Levels decline in people over fifty and are lower in those with high cholesterol.

Some foods with natural CoQ_{10}/ubiquinone follow.

CoQ_{10} in foods	Approximate values
Fruits	
avocado	200 g = 2 mg
Legumes	
peanuts	100 g = 7 mg 1 lb = 30 mg
Meats	
beef, organic, grass-fed	6 oz = 5 mg
chicken, organic	6 oz = 3 mg
Oils	
canola	1 tbsp = 1 mg
grapeseed	1 tbsp = 1–2 mg
olive	4 tbsp = 2.5–3.5 mg
soybean	1 tbsp = 3.9 mg
Nuts and seeds	
seeds, sesame	4 oz = 1.8-2.5 mg
Vegetables	
spinach	1 cup = 1.3 mg

The omegas

No RDA or UL have been determined.

The omegas are another class of nutrients without official intake recommendations; however, some dieticians and doctors do recommend adding these essential fatty acids to diets. The average recommendation made for adults, nineteen years and older is 1.6 grams for males and 1.1 grams for females.

As some of these are considered essential because they must be obtained from food sources—they are called essential fatty acids. Omega-3 fatty acids have become popular for their anti-inflammatory properties and supportive role in brain, cardiovascular, and eye health. They show promising results in helping those who suffer with diabetes and arthritis.

Omega-3s deliver three types of polyunsaturated fatty acids—alpha-linolenic acid (ALA); docosahexaenoic acid (DHA); and elcosapentaenoic acid (EPA). The ALAs need to be consumed in plant food. Our bodies are then able to use them to produce DHA and EPA. The consensus seems to be this conversion capacity is limited in people—hence the recommendations to eat foods rich in DHA and EPA, specifically fish.

Did our bodies always have difficulty making this conversion? Of importance to consider in trying to answer this question are the results of one large study. It showed plasma levels of DHA and EPA in vegans were almost the same as those of their fish-eating counterparts. This would indicate that, in people who do not consume meats including fish, the body compensates by revving up its ALA conversion.

The majority of people are getting their omega-3s from the oceans, but there are excellent plant-based sources that should be explored. Flax seeds are rich in ALAs and are the most notably recognized alternative to fish supplements. Other seeds and nuts offer good amounts of omega-3s, and some beans and vegetables deliver moderate amounts. In this category, the pièce de résistance from the plant kingdom comes to us from the herb purslane, *Portulaca oleracea,* as you'll see in the list below. Not only does it pack an incredible amount of omega-3s and vitamin A—it delivers plenty of minerals.

Omega-6 fatty acids, too, come only from the foods we eat. It is estimated that most North Americans' diets, consisting of too many oils and meats, have an excess of omega-6s and a lack omega-3s. I will not provide a list of omega-6s for this reason. Animal meats deliver substantially more omega-6s than omega-3s. These fatty acid are found abundantly in nuts at a much higher ratio than the 3s. Vegetable oils can pack high amounts of the 6s. One in particular, linoleic acid, is converted in the body to gamma-linolenic acid, believed to reduce inflammation. The fact we've become a society addicted to fried and manufactured foods could have greatly contributed to the unbalance.

A bit lesser known are the omega-9s. They are sometimes in combination with the previous two in supplemental forms. These are not classified as essential. The body is able to make them using unsaturated fats. Two of the most common are called oleic acid, found in animal fats and vegetable oils, and stearic acid. Omega-9s are in many of the foods with Omega-6s.

By far lesser known are the omega-7s under various forms. One exception making a lot of waves at the moment is palmitoleic acid. The omega-7s operate a bit differently than the other omegas; they are not involved in anti-inflammatory responses. Their major role is in the metabolic processes of energy production and storage.

Palmitoleic acid facilitates communication between fat and muscle tissue. These omegas are reported to have beneficial effects in the treatment of insulin resistance and help lower C-reactive protein, glucose levels, and bad cholesterol levels. Omega-7s are naturally in grass-fed animal meats, their full-fat byproducts, wild salmon, macadamia nuts, and sea buckthorn berries.

Even more obscure are the omega-5 fatty acids, classed as nonessential— our bodies are able to produce them. They not only function much like the other omegas by assisting in cardiovascular and immune health but also increase cell regeneration and enhance our bodies' resilience to toxins and stress.

Omega-5s have a rare occurrence in plants. The greatest source comes from pomegranate seeds and their oils. It is natural in animal meats and their byproducts, again, if the animals were grass-fed. Other foods with natural omega-5s are coconut and palm oils, wild salmon, macadamia nuts, and the herb saw palmetto.

Most of the natural foods listed contain both omega-3s and omega-6s. Some have a better ratio of one or the other. There are questions as to the correct balance for health. Rather than get too bogged down with ratios, let's trust they're what they are for a reason.

Perhaps if we ate better in the first place there would be no need for such considerations. Manufacturers advertise they've fortified many foods, such as cereals, dairy products, juices, and more, with omega-3s. Analyses of fortified juices revealed insignificant amounts are obtained from such sources.

Some foods with natural sources of omega-3s follow.

Plant sources of omegas-3s (ALAs)	Approximate values
Fruits	
acerola	100 g = 44 mg
avocado	100 g = 110 mg
blackberries	100 g = 94 mg
blueberries	1 cup = 174 mg
cantaloupe	100 g = 46 mg
cherries, sour red	100 g = 44 mg
currants, European and black	100 g = 72 mg
elderberries	100 g = 85 mg
guava, common	100 g = 112 mg
guava, strawberry	100 g = 65 mg
gooseberries	100 g = 46 mg

Plant sources of omegas-3s (ALAs)	Approximate values
kiwi	100 g = 42 mg
kumquats	100 g = 47 mg
mangoes	1 each = 77 mg
melon, honeydew	1 cup = 58 mg
raspberries	100 g = 126 mg
Herbs and spices	
cloves	2 g = 86 mg
marjoram	2 g = 49 mg
oregano	2 g = 73 mg
purslane	1 g = 8.5 mg
tarragon	2 g = 44 mg
Grains	
wild rice, cooked	1 cup = 157 mg
Legumes (cooked)	
beans, navy	3/4 cup = 0.17–0.24 g
beans, pinto	3/4 cup = 0.17–0.24 g
beans, soy, edamame	1/2 cup = 0.29–0.34mg
beans, soy, mature	3/4 cup = 0.76 g
peas, black-eyed	3/4 cup = 0.11 g
Nuts and seeds	
almonds, blanched and roasted	1/4 cup = 0.15 g
hemp	1 tbsp = 0.19 g
hickory nuts	1/4 cup = 0.32 g
pecans	1/4 cup = 0.25-0.29 g
pumpkin, no shells	1/4 cup = 0.06 g

Plant sources of omegas-3s (ALAs)	Approximate values
seeds, chia	1 tbsp – 1.9 g
seeds, flax, ground	1 tbsp = 2.43 g
soy nuts	1/4 cup = 0.42 g
walnuts, black	1/4 cup = 0.85 g
walnuts, English, Persian	1/4 cup = 2.30 g
Oils	
canola	1 tsp = 0.42 g
flax seed	1 tsp = 2.58 g
mustard	1 tbsp = 0.85 g
soybean	1 tsp = 0.31 g
walnut	1 tsp = 0.48 g
Vegetables (cooked)	
bok choy	1 cup = 0.07 g
broccoli	1 cup = 0.19 g
Brussels sprouts	1 cup = 0.27 g
cauliflower	1 cup = 0.21 g
collard greens	1 cup = 0.18 g
kale	1 cup = 0.13 g
lettuce, romaine, raw	2 cups = 0.11 g
seaweed, spirulina	1 tbsp = 0.58 g
spinach	1 cup = 0.17 g
squash, butternut, cubed	1 cup = 49.2 mg
squash, winter and acorn	1 cup = 53.9 mg
turnip greens	1 cup = 0.09 g

Foods with DHAs & EPAs	Approximate values
Fish cooked (canned)	
anchovies, with oil	2.5 oz = 1,540 mg
mackerel (jack)	3 oz = 1,000-1,500 mg
salmon (pink, sockeye and chum)	3 oz = 1,000–1,500 mg
tuna. light	3 oz = 200–500 mg
tuna, white albacore	3 oz = 500–1,000 mg
tuna, canned	3 oz = 500–1,000 mg
sardines, canned	3 oz = 500–1,000 mg
Fish, farmed and cooked	
catfish	3 oz = 200 mg
salmon, Atlantic	3 oz = 1,500 mg
tilapia	3 oz = 200 mg
trout, rainbow	3 oz = 500–1,000 mg
Fish, wild and cooked	
cod	3 oz = 200 mg
grouper	3 oz = 200–500 mg
haddock	3 oz = 200 mg
halibut, Pacific and Atlantic	3 oz = 200–500 mg
herring, Atlantic and Pacific	3 oz = 1,500 mg
mackerel, Pacific and jack	3 oz = 1,500 mg
mahi-mahi	3 oz = 200 mg
ocean perch	3 oz = 200–500 mg
orange roughy	3 oz = 200 mg
pollock, Alaskan	3 oz = 200–500 mg
rockfish, Pacific	3 oz = 200–500 mg

Foods with DHAs & EPAs	Approximate values
salmon (chum, coho, pink and sockeye)	3 oz = 500–1,000 mg
salmon, king	3 oz = 1,500 mg
snapper	3 oz = 200–500 mg
swordfish	3 oz = 500–1,000 mg
tuna, bluefin	3 oz = 1,000–1,500 mg
tuna, skipjack	3 oz = 200–500 mg
tuna, yellowfin	3 oz = 200 mg
Seafood (cooked)	
clams, wild and farmed	3 oz = 200-500 mg
crab, wild, Dungeness, king, and snow	3 oz = 500–1,000 mg
crab, wild, blue	3 oz = 200 mg
lobster, wild, northern	3 oz = 200 mg
mussels, wild and farmed	3 oz = 500–1,000 mg
oysters, wild and farmed	3 oz = 500–1,000 mg
scallops, wild	3 oz = 200 mg
shrimp, wild and farmed	3 oz = 200 mg
squid, wild, fried	3 oz = 200–500 mg

B. Minerals

There are bulk/macrominerals and trace/microminerals needed by the body. The bulk minerals are needed in greater amounts. They are calcium, magnesium, sodium, potassium, and phosphorus. Minerals can only be obtained from our diets; the body is unable to produce any of them. Minerals are mostly stored in bones and muscle tissue. They all play important roles in those structures, as well as being vital for energy production, our organs, and our immune system.

Calcium supplementation is an area where contradictions abound as to what is safe to take. While trying to compile an accurate list of minerals and their dosages, I came across mixed messages regarding calcium supplementation. Since this is one bulk mineral many of us are being advised to take as a supplement, I will try my best to clarify the reasons behind differing recommendations.

There have been numerous studies causing alarm about the possible role high intakes of calcium supplements may play in cardiovascular disease. High levels of calcium have been linked to kidney stones. Due to the many controversies surrounding calcium supplementation, it might be prudent to try to get our calcium requirements from food.

Several types of medication are known to negatively interact with calcium. Please check under the calcium subsection for further details on these. As always, it is important to discuss any supplement intake with a qualified health professional. Furthermore, it's worth noting there are researchers who believe the present RDAs for calcium are too high.

It is a bit surprising that some research material now advises taking calcium apart from magnesium. Since the opposite has been the norm for many years now, this definitely warranted further investigation. Most agree magnesium is required with calcium for proper assimilation and have followed this advice for decades. However, there are now sources who say that, not only do the two cancel each other out, calcium inhibits magnesium absorption. This is where it really gets confusing, until you dig a bit deeper for a better understanding. This is by no means completely understood or the end of the discussion.

These two bulk minerals work together in many bodily functions, including regulating heartbeat, nerve conduction, and muscle contraction and tone. At times, they compete at the same sites in the body. While it's true they cannot function without each other, if supplementing, it might be preferable to take them separately. Perhaps if both are in the body at adequate levels, each should become available when needed, either by the other or other nutrients. Since magnesium is a muscle relaxant, nighttime is sometimes recommended as the best time to take this supplement. Calcium would then be taken during the day.

It is revealing to observe that it's in the developed world, where calcium is abundantly available from dairy foods, supplements, and food fortification that the rates of osteoporosis and bone fractures are at their highest. In cultures who do not consume dairy foods or supplement with calcium, diseases of the bones are insignificant. Additionally, there is growing research pointing to increased calcium loss from animal proteins, caffeine, phosphorus, sodium, tobacco, and low physical activity.

While calcium from dairy foods is easily absorbed by the body, it does not appear to offer the same protection nondairy food sources provide. This is due, in part, to the metabolism of dairy proteins increasing urinary excretion of calcium. Perhaps it's the populations who get their calcium from food sources other than dairy who are able to accumulate more calcium in their bodies to prevent bone loss. It could be their plant-based diets provide more silica—another important mineral for bone health.

Returning to the subject of the possible role of calcium supplementation in cardiovascular disease, reports show heart disease patients have lower magnesium levels. There are other sources who say that, just as excessive calcium levels are harmful, they are even more so the lower the magnesium levels are. We should also take into account supplements of calcium that include magnesium will come with a ratio of two to one in favor of calcium. This could further aggravate conditions related to imbalances of these two minerals. Alcoholic beverages; antibiotics; some diuretics and other medications; thiamine, vitamin B$_6$, D, and selenium deficiencies; gastrointestinal disturbances; and diabetes mellitus all contribute to hypomagnesemia (low magnesium) in one way or another.

A further concern regarding calcium in our diets needing to be acknowledged is the amount of calcium carbonate we ingest unknowingly. This abrasive binding agent easily assimilates in our bloodstream, as it's used in the making of toothpaste. Unfortunately for those of us looking for more holistic brands, it's sometimes used in those preparations as well. So whether we know it or not, we are supplementing with calcium already, simply by brushing our teeth with toothpaste.

Calcium carbonate is used in manufactured foods and other products, including antacids, baking powder, prepared dry dessert and dough mixes, hand lotions, supplements, wines, and more. This more economical type of calcium is the one commonly utilized for calcium supplements. Calcium carbonate is also used in many industrial applications—making of mortar and chalk.

Just as a magnesium deficiency hinders proper chemical reactions helping put calcium into our bones, new evidence indicates that having adequate blood levels of vitamin D is crucial for calcium absorption. More on calcium follows the section on boron.

Following is the breakdown of individual minerals with amounts required for 19+ healthy adults. Again, if taking more than one supplement, it's important to add up the total of particular mineral(s). Noting its/their presence(s) in our foods is just as important.

It's essential for mineral supplementation to come from food sources. In many mineral supplements—natural often means natural rock. Check the labels carefully. Humans are not designed to ingest or digest rocks.

Boron

No RDAs have been determined. The UL is 20 mg for both females and males.

This is a trace mineral necessary for the body's metabolism of calcium, phosphorus, and magnesium; energy; the production of natural steroid compounds; antioxidant utilization; and alertness.

Deficiency results in decreased bone density, especially in postmenopausal women; diarrhea; improper calcium-magnesium balance; and poor coordination and mental alertness.

Toxicity leads to anemia; B$_2$ and B$_6$ vitamin deficiencies; cold-like symptoms; dermatitis; diarrhea; fatigue; gastrointestinal disturbances; nausea; ovarian, skeletal, and testicular abnormalities; seizures; and vomiting.

Even if supplementation shows great promise in the treatment of arthritis and osteoporosis, boron supplementation should be done under the supervision of a health care practitioner. It can be toxic if daily doses exceed 15 milligrams. There's evidence of possible hair loss resulting from diets that include multivitamin supplements containing boron.

In Canada, boron is a restricted cosmetic ingredient, whereas, if used in supplement products, manufacturers are only required to market them as a drug or prove their safety. With no regulations of natural health products, some oral products do include boron in their multivitamin preparations. However, there are no allowances for any specific health claims to be made regarding its use. Caution is strongly advised for anyone consuming these on a daily basis; there is no accounting for the amount people are getting from the foods they are eating. The UL could easily be surpassed. Some mouthwash solutions contain boron.

Boron is added to many foods, including enriched and fortified breads, pastas, and cereals. It richly occurs in dried fruits and is found naturally in the following foods.

Boron in foods	Approximate values
Fruits	
apples	100 g = 0.32 mg
apricots, dried	100 g = 2.12 mg
banana	1 each = 2.5 mg
currants	100 g = 1.73 mg
dates	100 g = 1.09 mg
grapes, dried	100 g = 4.47 mg

Boron in foods	Approximate values
grapes, red	100 g = 0.50 mg
kiwis	100 g = 0.26 mg
oranges	100 g = 0.25 mg
pears	100 g = 0.32 mg
peaches, dried	100 g = 3.24 mg
pears	150 g = 0.48 mg
plums	100 g = 0.45 mg
plums, dried	100 g = 1.88 mg
raisins	100 g = 4.5 mg
Herbs and spices	
honey	100 g = 0.51 mg
Legumes	
beans	100 g = 1.40 mg
beans, red kidney	130 g = 1.82 mg
chickpeas	130 g = 0.92 mg
lentils	100 g = 0.71 mg
peanuts, butter	100 g = 1.9 mg
Nuts	
almonds	100 g = 2.8 mg
Brazil nuts	20 g = 0.34 mg
hazelnuts	100 g = 2.72 mg
Vegetables	
broccoli	1 cup = 385.51 mcg
olives	100 g = 0.35 mg
potatoes	1 cup = 215.82 mcg

Calcium

The RDA for calcium is 1,000 mg to UL of 2,500 mg for females. At age fifty-one and older, the RDA is 1,200 mg to UL of 2,000 mg, and at seventy-one plus, the RDA is 1,200 mg.

The RDA for males is 1,000 mg to UL of 2,500 mg. At age fifty-one and older RDA is1.000 mg to UL of 2,000 mg, and at seventy-one plus, the RDA is 1,200 mg.

This bulk mineral is essential for blood clotting; bones, teeth, and gums; cardiovascular health; inhibition of lead absorption; lowering cholesterol; proper cell membrane permeability maintenance; muscle growth and contractions; the regulation of heartbeat; skin; some enzyme activation; and transmission of nerve impulses.

If you choose to supplement with calcium it's recommended that you split your dosages throughout the day, at about 500 milligrams at a time. Given all the controversy surrounding calcium supplementation, it is sensible to supplement only up to the amount we are lacking from our diets. The quality of the calcium in supplements varies depending on what form is used for delivery. As discussed earlier, calcium carbonate is a lower grade.

Deficiency results in aching joints, brittle nails, cognitive impairment, convulsions, depression, eczema, heart palpitations, high cholesterol, hypertension, insomnia, muscle cramps, nervousness, numbness in arms and legs, rheumatoid arthritis, rickets, and tooth decay. Excessive amounts of phosphorus such as those in carbonated soft drinks and processed and junk food interfere with calcium absorption.

Toxicity leads to abdominal and bone pain, coma, confusion, constipation, dehydration, depression, diarrhea, headache, hypercalcemia, hyperparathyroidism, irregular heartbeat, kidney stones, lethargy, mental imbalance, migraines, muscle spasms and twitching, nausea, weakness, and vomiting.

Anticonvulsant and steroid medications interfere with bone metabolism, and calcium can affect the effectiveness of these and others, including calcium channel blocker, tetracycline, and thyroid hormones.

Following is a list of foods with naturally occurring calcium. Don't forget to include all foods fortified with calcium, cereals, juices, and so on, when adding up your total daily intake.

Calcium in foods	Approximate values
Dairy products	
cheese	1 oz = 224 mg
milk, 2% or skim	1 cup = 285–305 mg
yogurt low-fat	8 oz = 345 mg
Fish and seafood	
salmon, canned with bones	3 oz = 181 mg
sardines, canned with bones	4 oz = 325 mg
Fruits	
figs, dried	5 each = 135 mg
orange juice (fortified)	1 cup = 300 mg
oranges	1 cup = 72 mg
Herbs and spices	
asparagus	100 g = 24 mg
dandelion leaves, raw	100 g = 187 mg/ 1 cup = 102.8 mg
garlic	3 cloves = 16.3 mg
oat straw	100 g = 59 mg
Legumes	
baked beans, canned	1 cup = 154 mg
black-eyed peas, boiled	1 cup = 211 mg
Nuts and seeds	

Calcium in foods	Approximate values
almonds	1 oz = 70 mg/100 g = 266 mg
Brazil nuts	3.5 oz = 176 mg
hazelnuts	3.5 oz = 188 mg
seeds, chia	100 g = 631 mg
seeds, sesame	1 cup = 1,404 mg
Others	
blackstrap molasses	1 tbsp = 172 mg
eggs, boiled	1 large = 25 mg
eggs, fried	1 large = 28.5 mg
eggs, poached	1 large = 28 mg
rice milk (fortified)	1 cup = 300 mg
soy milk (fortified)	1 cup = 300 mg
tempeh	1 cup = 340 mg
tofu, firm	1/2 cup = 204 mg
Vegetables	
bok choy, cooked	1 cup = 230 mg
broccoli	1 cup = 42.8 mg
cabbage	100 g = 40 mg
cabbage, Chinese, raw	1 cup = 74 mg
collard greens, boiled	1 cup = 357 mg
kale, cooked	1 cup = 180 mg
mustard greens	100 g = 115 mg
nori	1/2 cup = 600 mg
spinach, cooked	1 cup = 245 mg
turnip greens, cooked	1 cup = 230 mg
wakame	1/2 cup = 1,700 mg
watercress	100 g = 120 mg

Chromium

Adequate intake for females is 25 mcg and, at fifty plus years of age, 20 mcg. No UL has been determined.

For males, adequate intake is 35 mcg, with a decrease at age 50 plus to 30 mcg. No UL has been determined.

This trace mineral is essential in stabilizing blood sugar levels. The body does not easily absorb food sources of chromium, and most provide only tiny amounts. Chromium supplements come in various forms and are popular among some people for performance enhancement and weight loss.

Deficiency renders the body unable to use glucose for energy. Research into supplementing with chromium to treat diabetes is ongoing and inconclusive. Regardless, it could have a role in reducing fat accumulation and weight gain for those on diabetes medications. Urine excretion of chromium increased in people with high amounts of refined sugars in their diets. The elderly are at risk of lower levels.

Caution is advised for people suffering with diabetes, kidney ailments, liver disease, and psychiatric conditions and for those taking insulin or nonsteroidal anti-inflammatory drugs.

Exceeding acceptable levels can be damaging to renal function. Chromium makes it harder for the body to use iron. Vitamin C seems to help with absorption. However, taking zinc with chromium may decrease absorption of both.

The mineral chromium is naturally found in the following foods.

Chromium in foods	Approximate values
Fish and seafood	
herring	100 g = 2 mcg
mussels	3 oz = 110 mcg
oysters	3 oz = 49 mcg

Chromium in foods	Approximate values
Fruits	
apple with peel	1 medium = 36 mcg
banana	1 medium = 1 mcg
dates, dried	100 g = 29 mcg
oranges	100 g = 5 mcg
pear	1 small = 40 mcg
Grains	
barley	1/3 cup = 8.16 mcg
maize, whole grain	100 g = 9 mcg
oats	1/4 cup = 5.38 mcg
rice, brown	1 cup = 0.78 mcg
wheat, whole bread	2 slices = 2 mcg
wheat, whole, English muffin	1 each = 4 mcg
wheat, whole flour	100 g = 21 mcg
Herbs and spices	
basil, dried	1 tbsp = 2 mcg
garlic, dried	1 tsp = 3 mcg
pepper, black	2 tsp = 0.93 mcg
Meats	
beef, cubed	3 oz = 2 mcg
pork, chops	3 oz = 8.5 mcg
turkey breast	3 oz = 2 mcg
Nuts and seeds	
Brazil nuts	6 each = 28 mcg
hazelnuts	100 g = 12 mcg

Chromium in foods	Approximate values
Others	
brewer's yeast*	100 g = 112 mcg
eggs, organic	1 medium = 26 mcg
wine, red	5 oz = 1-13 mcg
Vegetables	
beans, green	1 cup = 2.04 mcg
broccoli	1/2 cup = 11 mcg
corn on the cob	1 each = 52 mcg
lettuce, romaine	2 cups = 1.25 mcg
mushrooms	100 g = 17 mcg
potatoes, mashed	1 cup = 3 mcg
potatoes, new	100 g = 21 mcg
potatoes, old	100 g = 27 mcg
spinach	100 g = 10 mcg
sweet potatoes	1 medium = 36 mcg
tomato	1 medium = 25 mcg

*Included in alcoholic beverages. Minimal information available on actual chromium content in beer.

Copper

Copper RDA for both females and males is 900 mcg to UL of 1,000 mcg or 10 mg.

Copper is trace mineral whose level is controlled by the liver. It is implicated in bone formation; fatty acid and iron metabolisms; the healing process and the immune system; hair, nerve, and joint health; hemoglobin and red blood cells. With zinc, is involved in production of proteins necessary for skin elastin and collagen.

Deficiency results in anemia, diarrhea, decreased ability to fight infections, elevated blood fat levels, bone and connective tissue abnormalities, weakness, skin eruptions, neurological disorders, and osteoporosis. High sulfur intake decreases level.

Elevated levels can be toxic and are often involved in common conditions. They're seen in some types of anemia, B_3/niacin deficiency, CNS damage, cirrhosis of the liver, diarrhea, eczema, high blood pressure, kidney disease, leukemia, mental and emotional disorders, nausea, premenstrual syndrome, and stomach pain.

Oral contraceptives and tobacco use raise copper level. Oxidation from toxicity can destroy eye tissue when in excess. People with eye problems need to maintain balance with iron, zinc, and calcium. An imbalance with zinc leads to thyroid problems.

Unsuspected sources where excess amounts accumulate to elevate blood levels include copper cookware and plumbing, herbicides and insecticides use, pasteurized milk, permanent wave hair products, and swimming pool chemicals.

Copper is found naturally in most foods, including the following.

Copper in foods	Approximate values
Fish and seafood	
crab, cooked	3 oz = 1.0 mg
lobster, cooked	3 oz = 1.3 mg
oysters, cooked	6 each = 2.4 mg
sardines	3.20 oz = 0.17 mg
shrimp	4 oz = 0.29 mg
Fruits	
apricots, dried	1/2 cup = 0.98 mg
avocado	1 each = 0.38 mg
banana	1 medium = 0.09 mg
currants, dried	1/2 cup = 0.98 mg

Copper in foods	Approximate values
dates	2 each = 0.17 mg
figs, dried	1/2 cup = 0.26 mg
grapes	1 cup = 0.19 mg
pear	1 medium = 0.15 mg
pineapple	1 cup = 0.18 mg
raisins, dried	1/2 cup = 0.86 mg
raspberries	1 cup = 0.11 mg
Grains	
barley	1/3 cup = 0.31 mg
buckwheat, roasted	1 cup = 1.22 mg
millet	1 cup = 0.28 mg
oats	1/4 cup = 0.24 mg
quinoa	3/4 cup = 0.36 mg
rice, brown	1 cup = 0.19 mg
Herbs and spices	
asparagus	1 cup = 0.30 mg
basil	1/2 cup = 0.08 mg
garlic	100 g = 0.3 mg
ginger, ground	1 tbsp = 0.024 mg
paprika	1 tbsp = 0.042 mg
pepper, black	2 tsp = 0.08 mg
Legumes	
adzuki beans, cooked	1 cup = 0.67 mg
beans, black	1 cup = 0.36 mg
beans, garbanzo	1 cup = 0.58 mg
beans, kidney	1 cup = 0.51 mg
beans, lima	1 cup = 0.44 mg

Copper in foods	Approximate values
beans, navy	1 cup = 0.38 mg
beans, pinto	1 cup = 0.37 mg
beans, soy, cooked	1 cup = 0.69 mg
chickpeas, cooked	1/2 cup = 0.29 mg
lentils	1 cup = 0.50 mg
peanuts	1/4 cup = 0.42 mg
peas, dried	1 cup = 0.35 mg
peas, green	1 cup – 0.24 mg
white beans, cooked	1 cup = 0.51 mg
Meats	
beef, various cuts, cooked	100 g = 0.15–0.21 mg
chicken, breast, cooked	100 g = 0.316 mg
chicken, dark meat	100 g = 0.144 mg
chicken, liver, cooked	100 g = 0.535 mg
quail, cooked	1 oz = 0.2 mg/1 lb = 2.7 mg
turkey, liver, cooked	100 g = 1.05 mg
Nuts and seeds	
almonds	1 oz = 0.34 mg
Brazil nuts	1 oz = 0.58 mg
cashews	1 cup = 3.04 mg/1 oz = 0.62 mg
cocoa, unsweetened powder	2 tbsp = 0.41 mg
flax seeds	1 oz = 0.41 mg
pecans	1 oz = 0.41 mg
pine nuts	1 oz = 0.46 mg
pistachio nuts	1 oz = 0.43 mg
seeds, pumpkin	1 oz = 0.46 mg
seeds, sesame	1 oz = 1.14 mg

Copper in foods	Approximate values
seeds, sunflower	1 oz = 0.62 mg
walnuts	1 oz = 0.53 mg
Others	
molasses	1 tbsp = 0.1 mg/1 cup = 1.64 mg
miso	1 tbsp = 0.07 mg
tofu	4 oz = 0.43 mg
Vegetables	
beets	1 cup = 0.13 mg
beets, greens	1 cup = 0.36 mg
Brussels sprouts	1 cup = 0.13 mg
cabbage	1 cup = 0.08 mg
collard greens	1 cup = 0.10 mg
kale, cooked	1 cup = 0.2 mg
kale, raw	1 cup = 0.24 mg
mushrooms, brown Italian, raw	1 cup = 0.43 mg
mushrooms, crimini	1 cup = 0.36 mg
mushrooms, morel, raw	1 cup = 0.50 mg
mushrooms, shiitake, cooked	1 cup = 1.3 mg
mushrooms, white, cooked	1 cup = 0.94 mg
mustard greens	1 cup = 0.20 mg
onions	1 cup = 0.14 mg
potatoes	1 cup = 0.20 mg
radicchio, shredded	1 cup = 0.1 mg
spinach	1 cup = 0.31 mg
spirulina	1 tbsp = 0.4 mg/1 cup = 6.8 mg
squash, winter	1 cup = 0.17 mg

Copper in foods	Approximate values
sweet potatoes	1 cup = 0.32 mg
Swiss chard	1 cup = 0.29 mg

Iodine

The RDA for both females and males is 150 mcg to UL of 1,100 mcg.

Iodine is a trace element needed to metabolize excess fat and for mental and physical development, protein synthesis, thyroid gland functioning, enzymatic activity, metabolism, and nerve and muscle functions.

Deficiency is found in breast cancer, depression, fatigue, hypothyroidism, gastrointestinal and skin problems, goiter, high cholesterol, mental retardation, neurological anomalies, rapid heartbeat, weakness, and weight gain.

Excessive levels lead to diarrhea and vomiting, inhibited thyroid hormone secretion, mouth sores or metallic taste, and swollen salivary glands.

A few raw foods eaten in large amounts block iodine absorption. Therefore, limited consumption is advisable for people with underactive thyroid. These include Brussels sprouts, cabbage, cauliflower, kale, peaches, pears, spinach, and turnips.

Bromine, in the form of bromide salts, found in some anticonvulsant medications and in numerous commercial applications, such as water purification, gasoline, pesticides, and swimming pool maintenance, to name a few, competes with the body for iodine, as does chloride and fluoride.

Caution is advised for people on antithyroid and high blood pressure medications.

Iodine is found naturally in sea salt and in the following foods.

Iodine in foods	Approximate values
Dairy	
yogurt, plain*	1 cup = 75 mcg
Fish and seafood	
cod, cooked	2.5 oz = 87 mcg
haddock, cooked	2.5 oz = 87 mcg
lobster	100 g = 100 mcg
salmon	4 oz = 32 mcg
sardines	4 oz = 36 mcg
shrimp	3 oz = 35 mcg
tuna, canned	2.5 oz = 15 mcg
Fruits	
banana	1 medium = 3 mcg
cranberries	4 oz = 400 mcg
prunes, dried	5 each = 15 mcg
strawberries	1 cup = 13 mcg
Legumes	
beans, green	1/2 cup = 3 mcg
beans, lima	1/2 cup = 8 mcg
beans, navy	1/2 cup = 32 mcg
peas, green, boiled	1/2 cup = 3 mcg
Meats*	
beef, liver, cooked	2.5 oz = 32 mcg
beef, various cuts, cooked	2.5 oz = 11–14 mcg
chicken, cooked	2.5 oz = 11–13 mcg
lamb chop, cooked	2.5 oz = 8 mcg
pork, various cuts, cooked	2.5 oz. = 5–9 mcg
turkey, light meat, cooked	2.5 oz. = 30 mcg

Iodine in foods	Approximate values
Others	
eggs	2 large = 48–52 mcg
Himalayan salt	1/2 g = 250 mcg
Vegetables	
arame	1 tbsp = 730 mcg
potatoes	1 medium = 60 mcg
seaweed, dried	.25 oz = 4,500 mcg
seaweed, sheet	1 g = 16–2,984 mcg
wakame	1 tbsp = 80 mcg

*Exact amounts depend on animal feed.

Iron

The iron RDA for females, ages nineteen to fifty is 18 mg and, at age fifty plus is 8 mg. The UL is 45 mg.

The RDA for males is 8 mg up to UL of 45 mg.

Iron is another trace mineral needed for oxygenation of red blood cells, energy production, enzymes, growth, and the immune system.

Iron is classified according to the source from which it is delivered. Iron from animals is attached to the heme protein and, hence, is called heme iron. Nonheme iron is obtained from plant sources.

Supplement only under professional advice; iron supplementation is usually reserved for anemic individuals or women with heavy menstrual cycles. Calcium inhibits iron absorption, while vitamin C increases it. The phytates in some foods, along with tannic acid in tea, coffee, nuts, and some fruits and vegetables could interfere with absorption.

Iron deficiency, known as anemia, is the most common nutritional deficiency in the United States; food fortification with this nutrient is relatively common in manufactured foods. Individuals who suffer from celiac and Crohn's disease or IBS and those who take antacids beyond the recommended dosages are at a greater risk of deficiency due to malabsorption.

Symptoms of deficiency include hair loss, fatigue, and weakness that interfere negatively with day-to-day activities; headaches; decreased concentration; brittle, chipping nails; fluctuating body temperature; and increased susceptibility to infections due to diminished immune function.

Toxicity symptoms are similar to those of deficiency. It is highly advised that levels be measured before starting any supplementation.

Iron is naturally found in the following foods.

Iron in foods	Approximate values
Fish and seafood	
clams, canned	3 oz = 23.8 mg
oysters	100 g = 7.7 mg
sardines, canned in oil, drained	3 oz = 2.5 mg
shrimp, canned	3 oz = 2.3 mg
Fruits	
prunes, juice	3/4 cup = 2.3 mg
Herbs and spices	
asparagus	1 cup = 1.64 mg
basil	1/2 cup = 0.67 mg
cloves	2 tsp = 0.50 mg
cumin	2 tsp = 2.79 mg
oregano	2 tsp = 0.74 mg
parsley	1/2 cup = 1.88 mg
pepper, black	2 tsp = 0.56 mg
thyme	2 tbsp = 0.84 mg
turmeric	2 tsp = 1.82 mg

Iron in foods	Approximate values
Legumes	
beans, kidney, cooked	1/2 cup = 2.6 mg
beans, lima, cooked	1/2 cup = 2.2 mg
beans, navy, cooked	1/2 cup = 2.1 mg
beans, refried	1/2 cup = 2.1 mg
beans, soy, green, cooked	1/2 cup = 2.2 mg
beans, soy, cooked	1/2 cup = 4.4 mg
beans, white, canned	1/2 cup = 3.9 mg
chickpeas, cooked	1/2 cup = 2.4 mg
cowpeas, cooked	1/2 cup = 2.2 mg
lentils, cooked	1/2 cup = 3.3 mg
Meats	
beef, chuck, blade, roast cooked	3 oz = 3.1 mg
beef, ground, 15% fat, cooked	3 oz = 2.2 mg
beef, round, cooked	3 oz = 2.8 mg
beef, rib, cooked	3 oz = 3.4 mg
beef, top sirloin, cooked	3 oz = 2.0 mg
duck, roasted	3 oz = 2.3 mg
lamb, shoulder, cooked	3 oz = 2.3 mg
organ meats (liver, giblets, cooked)	3 oz = 5.2-9.9 mg
Nuts and seeds	
almonds	100 g = 3.7 mg
seeds, pumpkin and squash, roasted	1 oz = 4.2 mg
seeds, sesame	100 g = 14.5 mg

Iron in foods	Approximate values
Others	
blackstrap molasses	1 tbsp = 3.5 mg
eggs	1 each = 1 mg
tofu	4 oz = 3.02 mg
Vegetables	
beets	1 cup = 1.34 mg
beets, greens	1 cup = 2.74 mg
bok choy	1 cup = 1.77 mg
broccoli	1 cup = 1.15 mg
Brussels sprouts	1 cup = 1.87 mg
cabbage	1 cup = 0.99 mg
collards green	1 cup = 2.15 mg
fennel	1 cup = 0.64 mg
kale	1 cup = 1.17 mg
leeks	1 cup = 1.14 mg
lettuce, romaine	2 cups = 0.93 mg
mustard greens	1 cup = 1.22 mg
olives	1 cup = 4.44 mg
sea vegetables	1 tbsp = 0.56 mg
spinach, cooked	1/2 cup = 3.2 mg
squash, summer	1 cup = 0.65 mg
Swiss chard	1 cup = 3.96 mg
tomato, paste	1/4 cup = 2.2 mg
tomato, puree	1/2 cup = 2.0 mg
tomatoes	1 cup = 0.49 mg
turnip greens	1 cup = 1.15 mg

Magnesium

For magnesium, the RDA for females is 310 mg. For females thirty-one years and older, it's 320 mg. No UL has been determined.

The RDA for males is 400 mg. At thirty-one years and older, it's 420 mg. No UL has been determined.

This bulk mineral is essential to enzyme activities, especially energy production, blood pressure regulation, bone formation, and carbohydrate and mineral metabolisms.

Deficiency is found in alcoholism, asthma, cardiovascular disease, chronic fatigue, diabetes, eye twitches, facial tics, fibromyalgia, gastrointestinal and renal disorders, irritability, and muscle spasms. Absorption decreases in the older population.

Toxicity symptoms include breathing difficulties, diarrhea or laxative effects, muscle weakness, heart problems, and irregular heartbeat.

Alcohol consumption, diuretics, and high levels of zinc and vitamin D increase the need for magnesium. Individuals who are diabetic and those with kidney problems or heart disease need to consult with their physicians before supplementing with magnesium.

Magnesium is found naturally in many foods including the following.

Magnesium in foods	Approximate values
Fish and seafood	
crab, snow	2.5 oz = 47 mg
halibut	2.5 oz = 21 mg
mackerel, Atlantic	2.5 oz = 73 mg
pollock, Atlantic	2.5 oz = 64 mg
salmon, Chinook	2.5 oz = 92 mg
scallops	4 oz = 41.9 mg
tuna	4 oz = 47.6 mg

Magnesium in foods	Approximate values
Fruits	
apple	1 medium = 9.1 mg
apple, without skin	1 medium = 6.44 mg
apricots	100 g = 10 mg
apricots, dried	100 g = 32 mg
avocados, pureed	1 cup = 66.7 mg
banana	1 medium = 32 mg
cantaloupe	1 medium = 66 mg
grapefruit	1 medium = 20–22 mg
figs, dried	1 cup = 101 mg
lemon, with peel	1 small = 13 mg
lemon, without peel	1 small = 4.64 mg
orange	1 each = 13.1 mg
papaya	1 medium = 57.9 mg
peaches	1 cup = 33.5 mg
pear, Bartlett	1 large = 13.6 mg
raspberries	1 cup = 27.1 mg
strawberries	1 cup = 18.7 mg
watermelon	1 cup = 15.2 mg
Grains	
barley	1/3 cup = 81.6 mg
buckwheat	1 cup = 85.7 mg
millet	1 cup = 76.6 mg
oats	1/4 cup = 69.0 mg
quinoa	3/4 cup = 118.4 mg
rice, brown	1 cup = 83.8 mg
rye	1/3 cup = 69.3 mg

Magnesium in foods	Approximate values
wheat	1 cup = 58.2 mg
Herbs and spices	
asparagus	1 cup = 25.2 mg
basil	1/2 cup = 13.6 mg
cloves, dried	2 tsp = 10.9 mg
cumin	2 tsp = 15.4 mg
mustard seeds	2 tsp = 14.8 mg
parsley	1/2 cup = 15.2 mg
Legumes	
beans, black	1 cup = 120.4 mg
beans, green	1 cup = 22.5 mg
beans, kidney	1 cup = 74.3 mg
beans, lima	1 cup = 80.8 mg
beans, navy	1 cup = 96.5 mg
beans, pinto	1 cup = 85.5 mg
beans, soy	1 cup = 147.9 mg
edamame	1/2 cup = 52 mg
lentils	3/4 cup = 52 mg
peanuts	1/4 cup = 65.0 mg
peas, black-eyed	3/4 cup = 52 mg
peas, split	1/4 cup = 52 mg
Nuts and seeds	
almonds	1/4 cup = 61.6 mg
Brazil nuts	1/4 cup = 133.0 mg
cashews	1/4 cup = 116.8 mg
chestnuts, Chinese	1/4 cup = 54.0 mg
hazelnuts	1/4 cup = 52-66 mg

Magnesium in foods	Approximate values
pine nuts	1/4 cup = 70–86 mg
seeds, flax	2 tbsp = 54.9 mg
seeds, pumpkin	1/4 cup = 190.9 mg
seeds, sesame	1/4 cup = 126.4 mg
seeds, sunflower	1/4 cup = 113.7 mg
Others	
tempeh	4 oz. = 87.3 mg
tofu	4 oz. = 65.8 mg
Vegetables	
beets	1 cup = 39.1 mg
beets, greens	1 cup = 97.9 mg
bell peppers	1 cup = 11.0 mg
bok choy	1 cup = 18.7 mg
broccoli	1 cup = 32.8 mg
Brussels sprouts	1 cup = 31.2 mg
cabbage	1 cup = 25.5 mg
cauliflower	1 cup = 11.2 mg
celery	1 cup = 11.1 mg
collard greens	1 cup = 39.9 mg
cucumber	1 cup = 13.5 mg
fennel	1 cup = 14.8 mg
kale	1 cup = 23.4 mg
leeks	1 cup = 14.6 mg
lettuce, romaine	2 cups = 13.2 mg
mustard greens	1 cup = 18.2 mg
okra, cooked	1/2 cup = 50 mg

Magnesium in foods	Approximate values
potato with skin, cooked	1 medium = 44–55 mg
spinach	1 cup = 156.6 mg
squash, summer	1 cup = 43.2 mg
squash, winter	1 cup = 26.6 mg
Swiss chard	1 cup = 150.5 mg
tomatoes	1 cup = 19.8 mg
tamarind	1/2 cup = 58 mg
turnip, greens	1 cup = 31.7 mg

Manganese

The RDA for both females and males is 2 mg. No UL has been determined.

This trace mineral is required in tiny amounts for blood sugar regulation, bone and cartilage formation, enzymes, glucose production, metabolism, mitochondria maintenance, health of nerves and the immune system, the urea cycle, utilization of vitamins B1 and E, and wound healing.

Manganese supplementation is required for those with iron-deficiency anemia.

Deficiencies are rare but could lead to atherosclerosis, hypertension and heart disorders, confusion, convulsions, eye and hearing problems, excess perspiration, high cholesterol, irritability, memory loss, muscle contractions, pancreatic damage, teeth grinding, and tremors.

Toxic levels due to environmental manganese observed in people living near or working in mining and some factories and in welders. Symptoms mimic those of PD—its possible implication along with copper and lead in the disease are investigated, reports the National Parkinson Foundation. Toxicity results in aggressiveness, concentration and memory difficulties, hallucinations, increased susceptibility to bronchitis and pneumonia, irritability, liver disease, and neurological and respiratory problems.

Following are foods with naturally occurring manganese.

Manganese in foods	Approximate values
Fish and seafood	
bass, cooked	3 oz = 1.0 mg
clams, cooked	3 oz = 0.86 mg
crayfish, cooked	3 oz = 0.44 mg
mussels, cooked	3 oz = 5.8 mg
perch	3 oz = 0.8 mg
pike	3 oz = 0.9 mg
trout	3 oz = 0.9 mg
Fruits	
banana	1 medium = 0.32 mg
blueberries	1 cup = 0.50 mg
cranberries	1 cup = 0.36 mg
pineapples	1 cup = 1.53 mg
raspberries	1 cup = 0.82 mg
strawberries	1 cup = 0.56 mg
Grains	
barley	1/3 cup = 1.19 mg
buckwheat, cooked	1 cup = 0.7 mg
millet	1 cup = 0.77 mg
oats	1/4 cup = 0.92 mg
quinoa, cooked	1 cup = 1.1 mg
rice, brown	1/2 cup = 1.1 mg
rye	1/3 cup = 1.44 mg
wheat, whole, bread	2 slices = 1.4 mg

Manganese in foods	Approximate values
Herbs and spices	
asparagus	1 cup = 0.28 mg
cinnamon	2 tsp = 0.91 mg
cloves	2 tsp = 2.53 mg
garlic, cloves	3 each = 0.15 mg
pepper, black	2 tsp = 0.74 mg
turmeric	2 tsp = 0.34 mg
Legumes	
beans, adzuki	1 cup = 1.3 mg
beans, black	1 cup = 0.76 mg
beans, kidney	1 cup = 0.8 mg
beans, lima	1/2 cup = 1.1 mg
beans, soy	1 cup = 1.42 mg
beans, white	1 cup = 1.1 mg
chickpeas	1 cup = 1.7 mg
lentils	1 cup = 0.98 mg
peanuts	1/4 cup = 0.71 mg
peas, black-eyed	1 cup = 0.9 mg
peas, dried	1 cup = 0.78 mg
peas, green	1 cup = 0.72 mg
Nuts and seeds	
almonds	1 oz = 0.64 mg
cashews	1/4 cup = 0.66 mg
hazelnuts	1 oz = 1.6 mg/100 g = 5.6 mg
macadamia nuts	1 oz = 0.86 mg
pecans	1 oz = 1.1 mg
pistachios	1 oz = 0.34 mg

Manganese in foods	Approximate values
seeds, chia	1 oz = 0.76 mg
seeds, flax	1 oz = 0.70 mg
seeds, pumpkin	1 oz = 1.3 mg/100 g = 4.5 mg
seeds, sesame	1 oz = 0.70 mg
seeds, sunflower	1 oz = 0.60 mg
walnuts	1 oz = 0.96 mg
Others	
tempeh	½ cup = 1.08 mg
tofu, firm	½ cup = 1.4 mg
Vegetables	
broccoli	1 cup = 0.30 mg
beets	1 cup = 0.55 mg
beets, greens, cooked	1 cup = 0.7 mg
bok choy	1 cup = 0.24 mg
Brussels sprouts	1 cup = 0.35 mg
cabbage	1 cup = 0.33 mg
carrots	1 cup = 0.17 mg
cauliflower	1 cup = 0.16 mg
collard greens	1 cup = 0.97 mg
kale	1 cup = 0.54 mg
leeks	1 cup = 0.26 mg
mushrooms, shiitake	1/2 cup = 0.15 mg
mustard greens	1 cup = 0.38 mg
onions	1 cup = 0.32 mg
potatoes	1 cup = 0.38 mg
sea vegetables	1 tbsp = 0.31 mg
spinach, cooked	1/2 cup = 0.8 mg

Manganese in foods	Approximate values
squash, summer	1 cup = 0.38 mg
squash, winter	1 cup = 0.38 mg
sweet potatoes	1 cup = 0.99 mg
Swiss chard, cooked	1 cup = 0.6 mg
tomatoes	1 cup = 0.21 mg
turnip greens	1 cup = 0.49 mg

Molybdenum

The RDA for both females and males is 45 mcg to UL of 2,000 mcg.

Molybdenum is a trace mineral needed in nitrogen metabolism and involved in activation of some enzymes, normal cell function, bone growth, teeth strength, and the final stages of converting purines to uric acid.

Deficiency is found in cancer, gum disease, impotence, inability to produce uric acid, irregular heartbeat, and irritability. There is increased risk of molybdenum deficiency in people who eat highly refined and processed foods.

High-ferrous sulfate iron and sulfur intake can decrease molybdenum level. Too much molybdenum, more than 15 mg daily, can interfere with copper metabolism and may also lead to gout.

Foods with natural molybdenum include the following.

Molybdenum in foods	Approximate values
Fish and seafood	
cod	4 oz = 3.86 mcg
Grains	
barley	1/3 cup = 27 mcg
oats	1/4 cup = 28.8 mcg

Molybdenum in foods	Approximate values
Legumes	
beans, black	1 cup = 130 mcg
beans, garbanzo	1 cup = 123 mcg
beans, kidney	1 cup = 132 mcg
beans, lima	1 cup = 142 mcg
beans, navy	1 cup = 195 mcg
beans, pinto	1 cup = 128 mcg
beans, soy	1 cup = 129 mcg
lentils	1 cup = 148 mcg
peanuts	1 cup = 42.4 mcg
peas, black-eyed	1 cup = 180 mcg
peas, dried	1 cup = 147 mcg
peas, split	1 cup = 148 mcg
Meats	
veal, liver	3.5 oz = 8.9 mcg
Nuts and seeds	
almonds	1 cup = 46.4 mcg
cashews	1 cup = 0.38 mcg
chestnuts	1 cup = 42.4 mcg
Others	
eggs, cooked	1 cup = 9 mcg
yogurt	1 cup = 11.3 mcg
Vegetables	
carrots	1 cup = 6 mcg
celery	1 cup = 5 mcg
cucumber	1 cup = 5.2 mcg
fennel	1 cup = 4.35 mcg

Molybdenum in foods	Approximate values
lettuce, romaine	2 cups = 5.64 mcg
peppers, bell	1 cup = 4.6 mcg
tomatoes, fresh	1 cup = 9 mcg

Phosphorus

The RDA for both females and males is 700 mg to a UL of 4,000 mg.

This bulk mineral is required for blood clotting, bones and teeth, cell growth, energy production, heart muscle contraction and rhythm, and kidney function.

Phosphorus deficiencies are rare, as it is naturally found in many foods. Symptoms of deficiency include anxiety, bone pain, changes in breathing and weight, fatigue and weakness, irritability, numbness, skin sensitivities, and trembling. Too much calcium can interfere with phosphorus absorption.

Excessive amounts of this mineral from carbonated soft drinks and processed and junk food interferes with calcium absorption. Vitamin D increases phosphorus effectiveness.

Toxicity is seen in dysregulation of calcium metabolism, leading to bone loss or calcium deposits.

Following are foods with natural phosphorus.

Phosphorus in foods	Approximate values
Fish and seafood	
cod	4 oz = 391 mg
salmon	4 oz = 365 mg
sardines	3.2 oz = 444 mg
scallops	4 oz = 483 mg
shrimp	4 oz = 347 mg

Phosphorus in foods	Approximate values
tuna	4 oz = 377 mg
Fruits	
strawberries	1 cup = 34 mg
Grains	
barley	1/3 cup = 162 mg
buckwheat	1 cup = 118 mg
millet	1 cup = 174 mg
oats	1/4 cup = 204 mg
quinoa	3/4 cup = 281 mg
rice, brown	1 cup = 162 mg
rye	1/3 cup = 185 mg
Herbs and spices	
asparagus	1 cup = 97 mg
cumin	2 tsp = 21 mg
garlic, cloves	3 each = 14 mg
mustard seeds	2 tsp = 33 mg
parsley	1/2 cup = 18 mg
Legumes	
beans, black	1 cup = 240 mg
beans, garbanzo	1 cup = 275 mg
beans, green	1 cup = 36 mg
beans, kidney	1 cup = 244 mg
beans, lima	1 cup = 216 mg
beans, navy	1 cup = 262 mg
beans, pinto	1 cup = 251 mg
beans, soy	1 cup = 421 mg
lentils	1 cup = 356 mg

Phosphorus in foods	Approximate values
peanuts	1/4 cup = 137 mg
peas, black-eyed	1 cup = 180 mcg
peas, dried	1 cup = 194 mg
peas, green	1 cup = 161 mg
peas, split	1 cup = 148 mcg
Meats	
beef	4 oz = 240 mg
chicken	4 oz = 258 mg
lamb	4 oz = 204 mg
turkey	4 oz = 261 mg
Nuts and seeds	
almonds	1/4 cup = 111 mg
cashews	1/4 cup = 237 mg
seeds, flax	2 tbsp = 90 mg
seeds, pumpkin	1/4 cup = 398 mg
seeds, sesame	1/4 cup = 226 mg
seeds, sunflower	1/4 cup = 231 mg
Others	
eggs	1 each = 86 mg
milk, cow's	4 oz = 102 mg
miso	1 tbsp = 27 mg
tempeh	4 oz = 222 mg
tofu	4 oz = 215 mg
yogurt	1 cup = 233 mg
Vegetables	
beets	1 cup = 65 mg
beets, greens	1 cup = 59 mg

Phosphorus in foods	Approximate values
bok choy	1 cup = 49 mg
broccoli	1 cup = 104 mg
Brussels sprouts	1 cup = 87 mg
cabbage	1 cup = 49 mg
carrots	1 cup = 43 mg
cauliflower	1 cup = 40 mg
celery	1 cup = 24 mg
collard greens	1 cup = 60 mg
corn	1 cup = 59 mg
cucumber	1 cup = 25 mg
fennel	1 cup = 43 mg
kale	1 cup = 36 mg
lettuce, romaine	2 cups = 28 mg
mushrooms, crimini	1 cup = 86 mg
mustard greens	1 cup = 59 mg
onions	1 cup = 73 mg
peppers, bell	1 cup = 24 mg
potatoes	1 cup = 121 mg
sea vegetables	1 tbsp = 18 mg
spinach	1 cup = 101 mg
squash, summer	1 cup = 70 mg
sweet potatoes	1 cup = 108 mg
Swiss chard	1 cup = 58 mg
tomatoes	1 cup = 43 mg
turnip, greens	1 cup = 46 mg

Potassium

The RDA for both females and males is 4,700 mg. No UL has been determined.

Potassium is another bulk mineral needed for blood pressure stability, chemical reactions within cells, healthy immune system, hormone secretion, and regular heart rhythm.

Potassium works with sodium at maintaining water balance.

Deficiency results in acne and dry skin, chills, constipation or diarrhea, depression, slow reflexes, edema, high cholesterol, insomnia, labored respiration, low blood pressure, muscular fatigue and weakness, nausea and vomiting, nervousness, thirst, and salt retention.

Lethargy, circulatory damage, and weakness that come with age may be due to diminished regulatory transfer of nutrients through cell membranes. Diarrhea, using diuretics, and laxatives will upset potassium levels; caffeine and tobacco reduce its absorption; and stress increases the requirement.

Toxicity leads to cardiac arrhythmia, high blood pressure, kidney failure, muscle weakness, temporary paralysis, and tingling in extremities. There is a possible risk of toxicity for those taking anticoagulants, diuretics, high doses of potassium in supplements, nonsteroidal anti-inflammatories, and hypertensive drugs.

Potassium is natural in the following foods.

Potassium in foods	Approximate values
Dairy products	
milk, low-fat, nonfat,	
or whole	1/2 cup = 350–380 mg
yogurt	6 oz = 260–435 mg
Fish and seafood	
cod	4 oz = 328 mg

Potassium in foods	Approximate values
salmon, baked or broiled	3 oz = 319 mg
scallops	4 oz = 356 mg
tuna	4 oz = 598 mg
Fruits	
apple	1 small = 150 mg
apricots	1 each = 90 mg
avocado	1/4 medium = 245 mg
banana	1 medium = 425 mg
cantaloupe, cubed	1 each = 245 mg
fig	1 medium = 116 mg
grapefruit	1/2 medium = 178 mg
honeydew, melon, diced	1 each = 200 mg
kiwi	1 medium = 240 mg
mango	1 medium = 240 mg
orange	1 small = 240 mg
orange, juice	1/2 cup = 235 mg
papaya	1/2 each = 390 mg
peach	1 medium = 185 mg
prunes, juice	1/2 cup = 270 mg
raisins	1/4 cup = 270 mg
strawberries, fresh	1/2 cup = 125 mg
watermelon	1 cup = 170 mg
Herbs and spices	
asparagus	1/2 cup = 155 mg
chili peppers	2 tsp = 105 mg
parsley	1/2 cup = 168 mg
turmeric	2 tsp = 111 mg

Potassium in foods	Approximate values
Legumes	
beans, green, fresh	1/2 cup = 90 mg
beans, green, frozen	1/2 cup = 85 mg
beans, kidney	1 cup = 717 mg
beans, lima	1 cup = 955 mg
beans, pinto, cooked	1/2 cup = 400 mg
beans, soy	1 cup = 886 mg
lentils, cooked	1/2 cup = 265 mg
peanuts, roasted	15 g = 92 mg
peas, dried	1 cup = 709 mg
Meats	
beef, lean, cooked	3 oz = 224 mg
turkey, roasted, dark meat	3 oz = 250 mg
Nuts and seeds	
almonds	1 oz = 200 mg
cashews	1 oz = 200 mg
chestnuts, Chinese	60 g = 269 mg
coconut powder	10 g = 82 mg
pine nuts, raw	10 g = 73 mg
seeds, poppy	10 g = 70 mg
seeds, sesame	10 g = 40 mg
seeds, sunflower	1/2 cup = 241 mg
walnuts, roasted	10 g = 54 mg
Others	
chocolate	1.5 oz = 165 mg
molasses	1 tbsp = 295 mg
Vegetables	

Potassium in foods	Approximate values
beets	1 cup = 518 mg
beets, greens, boiled	1 cup = 1309 mg
broccoli	1/2 cup = 230 mg
Brussels sprouts, fresh	1/2 cup = 250 mg
carrots, fresh or cooked	1/2 cup = 180 mg
cauliflower, fresh	1/2 cup = 150 mg
collard greens	1 cup = 222 mg
corn	1/2 cup = 195 mg
cucumber	1/2 cup = 80 mg
lettuce, all types	1 cup = 100 mg
mushrooms	1/2 cup = 280 mg
mustard greens	1 cup = 227 mg
onions	1 cup = 348 mg
potatoes, baked with skin	1 medium = 925 mg
sea vegetables	1 tbsp = 111 mg
spinach	1 cup = 839 mg
squash, summer	1 cup = 346 mg
squash, winter, cooked	1/2 cup = 250 mg
sweet potatoes	1 cup = 950 mg
sweet potatoes, baked with skin	1 medium = 450 mg
Swiss chard	1 cup = 961 mg
tomatoes	1 cup = 426 mg
tomato, juice	1/2 cup = 275 mg
tomatoes, raw	1 medium = 290 mg
zucchini, cooked	1/2 cup = 220 mg

Selenium

The RDA for both females and males is 55 mcg to UL of 400 mcg.

This trace element is a vital antioxidant, which activates thyroid hormones, inhibits oxidation, assists pancreatic function, prevents free radicals, and is involved in tissue elasticity.

Selenium works with vitamin E in antibody production and maintaining heart and liver health. Combined with zinc and vitamin E, it provides relief from prostate enlargement.

Deficiency leads to exhaustion, high cholesterol, infections, liver and pancreatic impairments, and sterility and is linked to cancer and heart disease.

Supplement with caution, as excess levels appear in arthritis, brittle nails, gastrointestinal disorders, hair loss, irritability, kidney and liver impairment, metallic taste, paleness, skin eruptions, tooth loss, and yellowish skin.

Brazil nuts are very high in selenium and should be avoided if supplementing. However, for those suffering from low levels of selenium, eating these nuts could be effective in raising the levels.

Selenium is naturally present in the following foods.

Selenium in foods	Approximate values
Fish and seafood	
cod	4 oz = 32 mcg
crab, cooked	2.5 oz = 33–36 mcg
halibut	3 oz = 47 mcg
oysters, farmed, cooked	2.5 oz = 58 mcg
oysters, Pacific, cooked	2.5 oz = 116 mcg
pike	2.5 oz = 45 mcg
salmon	4 oz = 43 mcg

Selenium in foods	Approximate values
sardines	3.20 oz = 48 mcg
scallops	4 oz = 25 mcg
shrimp	4 oz = 56 mcg
tuna	4 oz = 123 mcg
various—bass, herring, mackerel, and orange roughy	2.5 oz = 12–66 mcg
Grains	
barley	1/3 cup = 23 mcg
couscous, cooked	1/2 cup = 23 mcg
oat bran	1/2 cup = 10 mcg
rice, brown	1 cup = 19 mcg
rice, white	1/2 cup = 8 mcg
Herbs and spices	
asparagus	1 cup = 11 mcg
garlic, cloves	3 each = 1.28 mcg
seeds, mustard	2 tsp = 8.32 mcg
Legumes	
beans, lima	1 cup = 10 mcg
beans, pinto	1 cup = 10 mcg
lentils	1 cup = 8 mcg
Meats	
beef	4 oz = 24 mcg
chicken	4 oz = 31 mcg
lamb	4 oz = 28 mcg
organ, liver, beef	3 oz = 28 mcg
organs, liver (chicken, lamb, pork, and turkey)	2.5 oz = 51–87 mcg

Selenium in foods	Approximate values
pork	2.5 oz = 20–34 mcg
turkey	4 oz = 34 mcg
Nuts and seeds	
Brazil nuts	1 each = 75 mcg .5 oz = 268 mcg
cashews	1 oz = 3 mcg
nuts, mixed, no shells	1/4 cup = 51–154 mcg
seeds, chia	1 oz = 15 mcg
seeds, flax	2 tsp = 4 mcg
seeds, sesame	1/4 cup = 12 mcg
seeds, sunflower	1/4 cup = 19 mcg
walnuts, roasted	10 g = 54 mg
Others	
eggs	1 each = 15 mcg
milk, cow's	4 oz = 4.5 mcg
tofu	4 oz = 20 mcg
Vegetables	
broccoli	1 cup = 2.5 mcg
cabbage	1 cup = 3.5 mcg
mushrooms, crimini	1 cup = 19 mcg
mushrooms, shiitake	1/2 cup = 18 mcg
spinach	1 cup = 3 mcg
Swiss chard	1 cup = 1.57 mcg

Silicon

No RDA or UL have been determined for silicon.

Neither are there any official recommendations on allowable dosages for the mineral. It's not recognized as an essential mineral. Alternatively, a safe recommendation for supplementing is between 10 to 20 milligrams.

This trace mineral, better known as silica, is needed for collagen; bones and tissues; flexible arteries; healthy hair, nails, and skin; and the immune system. Demand increases with age, as silica levels decrease as people get older.

Much of silica's availability in foods is lost during processing. If you're not eating your veggies or having any whole grains, chances are you are deficient. Boron, calcium, magnesium, manganese, and potassium are needed for utilization efficacy.

Deficiency results in brittle nails and dull hair; osteoporosis; premature aging; rough, itchy skin; and loss of tissue elasticity and volume.

Toxicity, as a result of long-term use of silica in supplemental forms and inhalation, leads to lung damage. Symptoms of toxicity include chest pains, chronic bronchitis, COPD (chronic obstructive pulmonary disease), emphysema, kidney disease, and shortness of breath. People with any kidney or heart issues should never supplement.

The herb horsetail, also known as *Equisetum,* is rich in silica. The exact content amounts are difficult to obtain and vary depending on the cultivar. Caution is strongly advised regarding supplementing with any type of silica.

Silica is found naturally and abundantly in unrefined grains and root vegetables and occurs in the following foods.

Silica in foods	Approximate values
Fruits	
banana	250 g = 13.6 mg
raisins, California, seedless	100 g = 8.25 mg
Grains	
barley	100 g = 233 mg
millet	100 g = 500 mg

Silica in foods	Approximate values
oats	100 g = 500 mg
rice, brown	200 g = 4.14 mg
rice, white	200 g = 2.48 mg
rye	100 g = 17 mg
whole wheat	100 g = 158 mg
Herbs and spices	
asparagus	100 g = 18 mg
Legumes	
beans, green, cooked	250 g = 6.10 mg
Vegetables	
artichoke, Jerusalem	100 g = 36 mg
beets	100 g = 21 mg
carrots, raw	200 g = 4.58 mg
corn	100 g = 19 mg
potatoes	100 g = 200 mg

Sodium

The RDA for both females and males is 1,500 mg. RDA for those age fifty plus is 1,300 mg and then, at seventy plus, 1,200 mg. UL is 2,300 mg.

Proper balance of potassium and sodium is required for good health. People who consume large amounts of sodium require more potassium. You'll notice the RDA for potassium is over three times the sodium recommendation. An imbalance between the two can lead to heart disease.

Deficiencies are rare but seen with abdominal cramps, anorexia, confusion, dehydration, depression, dizziness, fatigue, flatulence, headache, heart palpitations, low blood pressure, memory impairment, muscle weakness, nausea and vomiting, poor coordination, recurrent infections, and seizures.

Excessive levels result in edema, high blood pressure, potassium deficiency, and kidney and liver diseases.

Please refer back to the section entitled "Salt Is Not All Sodium" in chapter 3 for more detailed information.

Present in almost all foods—the most naturally occurring sodium in the following foods.

Sodium in foods	Approximate values:
Fish and seafood	
cod, baked	100 g = 340 mg
crab, boiled	150 g = 370 mg
oysters	12 or 100 g = 510 mg
prawns	6 or 120 g = 1,590 mg
sardines, canned	50 g = 540 mg
salmon	100 g = 570 mg
tuna, canned in oil	120 g = 420 mg
Herbs and spices	
dandelion greens, boiled	1 cup = 46.2 mg
dandelion greens, raw	1 cup = 76 mg
Legumes	
beans, garbanzo	60 g = 850 mg
beans, mung	100 g = 820 mg
Vegetables	
artichoke hearts	1/2 cup = 80 mg
beet	1 each = 65 mg
carrot	1 large = 50 mg
celery	1 medium stalk = 50 mg
collard greens, boiled	1 cup = 28.5 mg
collard greens, raw	1 cup = 6.1 mg

Sodium in foods	Approximate values:
mustard greens	1 cup = 11.2 mg
mustard greens, boiled	1 cup = 12.6 mg
spinach	1/2 cup = 80 mg
Swiss chard, raw	1 cup = 76.7 mg
Swiss chard, boiled	1 cup = 313.2 mg
turnip greens, cooked	1 cup = 41.76 mg

Sulfur

No RDA or UL have been determined for sulfur, or sulfate as it is called.

However there's no shortage of information regarding sulfate's essential role in our bodies. The consensus among many is that 800 to 1,000 milligrams is a safe and healthy amount to aim for.

This trace mineral disinfects the blood; promotes bile secretion; protects against pollution, radiation, and toxins; resists foreign bacteria; and is used in the synthesis of collagen and in carbohydrate metabolism.

Sulfate should not be confused with the sulfites used as preservatives in high concentration in dried fruits and some manufactured foods. These preservatives can cause distress to asthma sufferers, as well as severe allergic reactions, digestive problems, and other issues.

When listed in manufactured foods, the sulfite chemicals should have a number following the name such as sulfur dioxide (E220), sodium sulfite (E221), sodium bisulfite (E222), sodium metabisulfite (E223), potassium metabisulfite (E224), calcium sulfite (E226), and calcium bisulfite (E227)—to name a few. Some of these are hidden in the most inconspicuous of foods as mentioned earlier, including dried fruits, and it's also found in others, like fruit salads, garlic powder, and dried ginger.

Deficiency results in acne and other skin infections, diabetes, muscle and skeletal disorders, and obesity. Supplementation can help repair the damaged joint cartilage of arthritis and relieve the pain.

Methylsufolnylmethane (MSM) is an adequate form of sulfur to use as a supplement.

Toxicity results in bloating, diarrhea, flatulence, gas, and stomach burning. It also affects calcium, copper, and potassium absorption. People taking glucosamine sulfate or MSM regularly need to be mindful that such supplementation may worsen calcium and copper deficiencies' symptoms and/or disorders. In addition, those who take potassium medications may need to up their dosages.

Sulfur is naturally found in the following foods. In most cases, at higher levels in the raw, overcooking destroys sulfur.

Sulfur in foods	Approximate values
Fish and seafood	
cod, baked	100 g = 230 mg
cod, poached	100 g = 250 mg
cod, steamed	100 g = 210 mg
crab, boiled	150 g = 470 mg
haddock, fried	100 g = 290 mg
haddock, steamed	100 g = 300 mg
lobster, boiled	120 g = 510 mg
mussels, boiled	12 each (120 g) = 350 mg
oysters, raw	12 each (120 g) = 250 mg
prawns, boiled	6 each (120 g) = 370 mg
salmon, canned	100 g = 220 mg
sardines, canned	60 g = 260 mg
scallops, steamed	10 each (100 g) = 570 mg
Fruits	
apple, with skin	100 g = 5 mg
apricots, dried	25 g = 160 mg

Sulfur in foods	Approximate values
banana	100 g = 10 mg
blackberries	100 g = 10 mg
currants, black	90 g = 30 mg
currants, black, dried	15 g = 30 mg
currants, red	90 g = 30 mg
dates, dried	6 each (35 g) = 50 mg
figs	2 each (75 g) = 10 mg
figs, dried	2 each (40 g) = 80 mg
grapes, black	20 each (100 g) = 6 mg
grapefruit	200 g = 3 mg
lemons, slices	2 each (15 g) = 10 mg
olives, in brine	5 each (20 g) = 30 mg
oranges	130 g = 7 mg
passion fruit	30 g = 8 mg
peaches, dried	25 g = 240 mg
peaches, stewed	120 g = 90 mg
raisins, dried	20 g = 20 mg
raspberries	100 g = 20 mg
rhubarb, stewed	120 g = 7 mg
Grains	
barley, pearl, boiled	100 g = 35 mg
bran, wheat	8 g = 55 mg
rice, boiled	100 g = 30 mg
Herbs and spices	
asparagus, boiled	5 each or 100 g = 20 mg
garlic	Unavailable
pepper	100 g = 100 mg

Sulfur in foods	Approximate values
Legumes	
beans, kidney	100 g = 50 mg
beans, mung	100 g = 60 mg
chickpeas, cooked	60 g = 80 mg
lentils, split, boiled	100 g = 40 mg
peanuts, raw, in shells	5 each (25 g) = 260 mg
peanuts, roasted, salted	30 each (25 g) = 380 mg
peas, boiled	60 g = 40 mg
peas, split, boiled	60 g = 50 mg
Meats	
chicken, boiled	100 g = 300 mg
chicken, livers, fried	130 g = 250 mg
lamb, livers, fried	130 g = 270 mg
veal, cutlet, fried	110 g = 130 mg
Nuts and seeds	
almonds	10 each (15 g) = 150 mg
Brazil nuts	5 each (20 g) = 290 mg
chestnuts	4 each (20 g) = 30 mg
coconut, desiccated	15 g = 80 mg
hazelnuts	10 each (15 g) = 80 mg
walnuts	5 each (20 g) = 100 mg
Others	
eggs, boiled and poached	55 g = 180 mg
eggs, fried	60 g = 210 mg
eggs, raw	55 g = 180 mg
lard	100 g = 30 mg
Vegetables	

Sulfur in foods	Approximate values
artichoke, boiled	100 g = 10 mg
beet root, boiled	30 g = 20 mg
Brussels sprouts, boiled	70 g = 80 mg
cabbage, boiled	100 g = 30 mg
cabbage, raw	50 g = 90 mg
carrots, raw and boiled	50 g = 10 mg
celery, boiled	50 g = 10 mg
celery, raw	50 g = 20 mg
cucumber, slices	5 each (30 g) = 10 mg
endive, raw leaves	3 each (5 g) = 30 mg
leeks, boiled	100 g = 50 mg
mushrooms, fried	6 each (60 g) = 70 mg
mushrooms, raw	3 each (30 g) = 30 mg
onions, boiled	100 g = 20 mg
onions, fried	70 g = 90 mg
onions, raw	1/4 each (20 g) = 50 mg
onions, spring	4 each (20 g) = 50 mg
parsnip, boiled	1/2 each (60 g) = 20 mg
potato, baked, with skin	20 g = 30 mg
potatoes, boiled	120 g = 20 mg
potatoes, mashed	100 g = 20 mg
potatoes, roasted	120 g = 60 mg
pumpkin	100 g = 10 mg
radishes	2 each (20 g) = 40 mg
spinach, boiled	60 g = 90 mg
sweet potatoes, boiled	100 g = 20 mg
tomatoes, raw	120 g = 10 mg

Sulfur in foods	Approximate values
tomatoes, fried	120 g = 10 mg
turnips, boiled	80 g = 20 mg

Vanadium

No RDA has been determined for vanadium. The UL is 1.8 mg for both females and males.

This trace mineral is needed for bones and teeth, cellular metabolism, growth and reproduction, and insulin utilization.

Vanadium works with molybdenum at lowering elevated copper levels but decreases chromium levels. Using tobacco decreases vanadium intake.

Deficiency is found in cardiovascular and kidney diseases and reproduction difficulties.

Toxicity results in arthritis, fatigue, gastrointestinal problems, green tongue, and weakened immune system. Vanadium levels appear to be increasing, possibly due to consumption of manufactured foods prepared with vegetable oils and margarine.

Supplementation is advised only under medical supervision. Vanadium is present in some multivitamins.

Vanadium can be naturally found in the following foods.

Vanadium in foods	Approximate values
Fish and seafood	
cod	1 g = 28 mcg
lobster	1 g = 5 mcg
scallops	1 g = 22 mcg
tuna (canned)	1 g = 11 mcg
Fruits	
apple	1 g = 4 mcg

Vanadium in foods	Approximate values
banana	1 g = 3 mcg
Grains	
barley	1 g = 14 mcg
buckwheat	3.5 oz = 100 mcg
oatmeal	1 g = 6 mcg
Herbs and spices	
dill	100 g = 14 mcg
dill seeds	1 g = 431 mcg
parsley	3.5 oz = 80 mcg
pepper, black	1 g = 987 mcg
Legumes	
beans, navy	1 g = 14 mcg
beans, soy	3.5 oz = 70 mcg
beans, soy, oil	1 g = 1 mcg
peas	1 g = 7 mcg
rice, white	1 g = 21 mcg
Meats	
beef, ground	1 g = 1 mcg
beef, liver	1 g = 6 mcg
chicken, dark	1 g = 12 mcg
chicken, light	1 g = 22 mcg
pork, chops	1 g = 1 mcg
Others	
eggs, yolks	1 g = 21 mcg
Vegetables	
cabbage	1 g = 4 mcg
carrot	1 g = 1 mcg

Vanadium in foods	Approximate values
corn, oil	1 g = 1 mcg
lettuce	1 g = 4 mcg
radish	100 g = 79 mcg
squash	1 g = 4 mcg
tomatoes	1 g = 2 mcg

Zinc

The RDA for females is 8 mg, and that for males is 11 mg to a UL of 40 mg for both.

This last, but certainly not least, trace mineral increases the absorption of vitamins. Zinc is needed for collagen formation, healing wounds, the immune system, liver and prostate gland functions, and protein synthesis.

Deficiency can be seen in acne, fatigue, growth impairment, delayed sexual maturation, hair loss, high cholesterol, impotence, infertility, loss of senses of taste and smell, memory impairment, prostate problems, reduced night vision, skin lesions, susceptibility to infection, and white-spotted thin fingernails.

Typically, low levels are seen with cirrhosis of the liver, diarrhea, fiber consumption, kidney disease, and perspiration. Do not take with iron. As previously mentioned, chromium interferes with zinc absorption.

Toxicity results in abdominal pain, copper deficiency, dizziness, headaches, fatigue, lethargy, nausea, reduced immune and iron functions, and vomiting.

Exceeding 100 mg daily can depress the immune system rather than assist it.

Zinc is naturally found in the following foods.

Zinc in foods	Approximate values
Fish and seafood	
crabs, Alaska king	3 oz = 6.5 mg
flounder	3 oz = 0.3 mg
lobster	3 oz = 3.4 mg
oyster	1 each (1 oz) = 8–9 mg
shrimp	4 oz = 1.95 mg
sole	3 oz = 0.3 mg
Fruits	
avocado	1 medium = 1.3 mg
berries, Logan	1 cup = 0.5 mg
blackberries	1 cup = 0.8 mg
dates	1 cup = 0.4 mg
raspberries	1 cup = 0.5 mg
Grains	
quinoa	3/4 cup = 2.02 mg
oats	1/4 cup = 1.55 mg
wheat, germ	100 g = 17 mg
Herbs and spices	
asparagus	1 cup = 1.08 mg
chervil	100 g = 8.8 mg
parsley	1/2 cup = 0.33 mg
Legumes	
beans, garbanzo	1 cup = 2.51 mg
beans, green	1 cup = 1 mg
beans, kidney, cooked	1/2 cup = 0.9 mg
beans, lima	1 cup = 2 mg
beans, soy	1 cup = 9 mg

Zinc in foods	Approximate values
Brussels sprouts	1 cup = 0.5 mg
chickpeas, cooked	1/2 cup = 1.3 mg
lentils	1 cup = 2.51 mg
peanuts, roasted	100 g = 3.3 mg
peas	1 cup = 2 mg
Meats	
beef, chuck roast	3 oz = 7.0 mg
beef, grass-fed	1 oz = 1 mg
chicken, breast, skinless	1/2 each = 0.9 mg
chicken, dark meat	3 oz = 2.4 mg
lamb	4 oz = 3.87 mg
turkey	4 oz = 1.95 mg
veal	100 g = 7.4 mg
Nuts and seeds	
almonds, dry roasted	1 oz = 0.9 mg
cashews	1/4 cup = 2.31 mg
chocolate, dark, plain	100 g = 9.6 mg
cocoa powder	100 g = 6.8 mg
seeds, pumpkin	1/4 cup = 2.52 mg
seeds, pumpkin, raw	100 g = 10.3 mg
seeds, sesame	1/4 cup = 2.79 mg
seeds, sesame, tahini	100 g = 10.5 mg
seeds, squash	100 g = 10.3 mg
Others	
miso	1 tbsp = 0.44 mg
tofu	4 oz = 1.78 mg
yogurt	1 cup = 1.75 mg

Zinc in foods	Approximate values
Vegetables	
beet, greens	1 cup = 0.72 mg
bok choy	1 cup = 0.29 mg
broccoli	1 cup = 0.70 mg
Brussels sprouts	1 cup = 0.51 mg
corn	1 cup = 0.7 mg
hearts of palm	100 g = 3.7 mg
mushrooms, crimini	1 cup = 0.79 mg
mushrooms, shiitake	1 cup = 0.96 mg
potatoes	1 cup = 0.6 mg
pumpkin	1 cup = 0.6 mg
sea vegetable, kelp	100 g = 1.2 mg
sea vegetables	1 tbsp = 0.33 mg
spinach	1 cup = 1.37 mg
squash, summer	1 cup = 0.70 mg
Swiss chard	1 cup = 0.58 mg
tomatoes	1 cup = 0.31 mg

C. Enzymes

Enzymes are energized protein molecules necessary to activate and speed up almost all of the biochemical processes in the body. The body produces some enzymes; plus there are others we get from the foods we eat. Those of us who have heard of enzymes are mostly familiar with their role in assisting with digestion. They also repair tissues, organs, and cells. You can think of them as transformers; they break down to rebuild. Each enzyme has only one function.

There are two groups of enzymes at work in the body—digestive enzymes and metabolic enzymes. Digestive enzymes are in the gastrointestinal tract, where they break down foods for absorption of nutrients in the blood. Digestive enzymes fall under three major categories.

In the first category are amylase enzymes. They are in our saliva, intestinal juices, and the pancreas. Their job is to break down carbohydrates. Within this category, there are three distinct types of enzymes helping in the breakdown of sugars. The lactase break down milk sugars; the maltase, malt sugars; and the sucrase break down sucrose, such as beet and cane sugars.

The second category, protease enzymes, break down proteins. These enzymes are in our intestinal, pancreatic, and stomach juices.

The third category of digestive enzymes, lipase enzymes, assist in fat digestion and are located in the pancreatic and stomach juices and in food fats.

The metabolic enzymes are mainly produced in the pancreas. They are involved in producing energy, detoxifying cells, ensuring normal function of every body system and organ, and delivering nutrients and oxygen. An important metabolic enzyme that acts as an antioxidant, superoxide dismutase, attacks the free radical superoxide. Another metabolic enzyme of major significance is the catalase, which breaks down the metabolic waste product hydrogen peroxide to free oxygen for use in the body.

Consuming enzyme rich foods assists with all of our bodily functions. Enzymes rich foods include:

- alfalfa sprouts, barley grass, bee pollen, raw honey, royal jelly, and wheatgrass;
- fruits like avocados, bananas, dates, grapes, guava, kiwis, mangoes, papaya, and pineapple;
- olive oil (extra virgin) and some other raw oils; and
- vegetables including broccoli, Brussels sprouts, cabbage, olives, and raw onions.

Supplementation with enzymes is helpful for those who have sluggish digestion or absorption issues. Since enzyme production declines with age, supplementation might be beneficial in older populations to ensure proper nutrient assimilation.

Caution is advised for those who are pregnant or breastfeeding, hemophiliacs, or anyone on blood thinner medication.

Enzyme supplementation is ill advised for anyone awaiting surgery. Consulting with your doctor is always recommended before taking any supplements.

Of Earth's Garden

There are people who actively seek and produce medications made with natural ingredients. A good example of this is reported by Independent. co.uk. Every August, two gardeners provide loaded truckfuls with their clippings from a 33-foot-wide, 150-foot-long and 40-foot-tall yew hedge on the Bathurst estate. The three hundred-year-old wonder's clippings provide a key ingredient for the production of the cancer-fighting drug Docetaxel.

Friendship Estates Limited is always on the lookout for new yew hedges to collect clippings for pharmaceutical companies. The bark from the yew tree is used in the making of another cancer-fighting drug called Paclitaxel. There are numerous other examples along these lines we can find if interested. Many plants have been involved in healing for millennia—this is a good place to start when wanting to use natural and alternative therapies.

Herbs and spices are truly miraculous gifts of the earth for the taking. Some may be growing somewhere in the wild near you and perhaps in your yard if you have one. It was after I was given Bach Rescue remedy tincture and felt a calming effect instantaneously that my interest in the healing power of herbs really took off.

Herbs were the first things I studied when I took up gardening. These plants have withstood the test of time, are in keeping with the traditions of the ages and should be better incorporated into our lives for their supportive roles in our overall health. They definitely should not be merely reserved for culinary purposes. Many ancient civilizations used herbs and spices extensively for their beneficial and medicinal properties. To this day, many cultures regularly use herbs to heal.

A great number of herbs provide numerous nutritional values in the forms of amino acids, vitamins, minerals, trace elements, enzymes, and hormones. Herbs that can safely be consumed on a regular basis and in quantity include alfalfa, beet root, chamomile, dandelion, evening primrose, flax, ginger, hops, marshmallow, parsley, turmeric, and watercress. There are other herbs that are strictly restricted for medicinal purposes and, therefore, warrant thorough investigation before use.

It's really about choosing natural over synthetic and safety with a track record instead of gambling with too many unknowns. It is foolish and, more often than not, completely unnecessary to rely on modern-day drugs. Too many drugs come with long lists of side effects, whereas there are harmless and natural alternatives in the form of herbs available.

Natural remedies such as herbs are not only automatically and ignorantly, but most likely deliberately overlooked. New drugs keep being rolled out, and the race to mass-produce these more cheaply than the competition in order to gain more of the marketplace is never ending. The race is seldom about one being better than the other. They are all the same—they do not address the root causes of ailments.

Due to consumer demand, herbal medicinal alternatives are gradually becoming more conveniently available for us in the Western world. This is a good step in assisting consumers to make healthier choices for their health. Gone are the days when you had to go to a specific type of store to purchase herbal products. Providing easier access not only benefits the few who actually want natural treatments; it consequently attracts those buyers thinking about trying something new.

As with conventional medications, it's important we know how herbs react with other medications and if there are any contraindications to their use. Unless a combination has been prepared as such, medicinal herbs should be taken separate at about five hours apart. It's best to err on the side of caution before using some of the medicinal herbs—some contain very powerful compounds.

If contemplating medicating with herbs, it's advisable to consult a qualified practitioner, a naturopath doctor, an herbalist, or someone knowledgeable and trained in their uses. However, when searching for relief of common ailments, herbs should come to mind first. Many healing herbs can be effective alternatives to laboratory drugs that may harm in the long run. There are herbs to heal many of the day-to-day complaints and disturbances people experience.

The practice of isolating chemicals from herbs for medicinal uses dates far back and continues to reveal unknown benefits. It's from an herb once considered sacred, *Papaver somnuferum*, that we get opium and the painkillers codeine, morphine, and heroine. This herb is named after Hypros, the Greek god of sleep, known as Somnus to the Romans. Scientific investigations into the unique properties of herbs have increased in recent years. Let's hope this trend continues to grow—and leads to safer natural treatments down the road.

Myrrh, closely related to frankincense (resin of a tree), was an essential common medicine used by healers in ancient Egypt, Greece, Rome, and Persia. Myrrh was long used to fragrance incense, and experiments in London yielded very promising results proving its antifungal and anti-inflammatory properties. Its ability to relieve discomforts of asthma and lung infections is impressive. Furthermore, Italian researchers were able to show its pain-relieving qualities. Studies in India of species closely related to myrrh revealed their capacities to lower blood cholesterol levels.

If it was available, the drug of choice for treatment during the recent pandemic of H1N1 (swine flu) in 2009 was Tamiflu. This drug was developed by extracting the shikimic acid in the Chinese star anise spice.

Star anise is often used in traditional Chinese medicine and oriental cuisine.

Due to the high cost of extracting the compound, a better cost-effective synthetic version of shikimic acid is now in development. Now whether this is a good substitute for the real thing is another matter. Might we westerners soon see a day when conventional modern medicine is complemented with other traditional forms of healing such as herbs?

In and of themselves some herbs are supernutritious real foods deserving a substantial and regular place in our diets. If you're missing a particular vitamin and/or mineral, introducing herbs into your diet can provide the punch just where it is needed. If you suffer from headaches, as I was, and frequently take aspirins, risking peptic ulceration, a more natural approach for relief offered with the herbs elderberry, feverfew, and others is curative, not masking. Before reaching for pills, it's a good idea to find out what herbal alternatives are effective and try them. Relieving while providing healthful benefits, herbs will save us money spent on drugs.

With some herbs like dandelions, the entire plant, from the rhizome to the leaves, flowers, and stems, is valued for one use or another. In other herbs, only certain parts are good. The various therapeutic uses of herbs and spices include antiviral, antimicrobial, antihelminthic, anti-inflammatory, anticoagulant, antiseptic, and even antibiotic. The unique medicinal properties of different herbs can have synergistic effects in some combinations.

Not only do many herbs pack nutritive and/or healing properties, herbs are the easiest plants to grow. Given the right conditions (and these are by no means difficult to provide), many herbs thrive and reward with prolific growth once established. Most do well in full sun, although some like mint prefer shade. They easily grow in most soils and do not require fertilizer or an excessive amount of water to flourish. Their only requirement is good drainage. I did have difficulty growing herbs in clay soil. I had to regularly amend the soil.

Several types arouse the senses with their beauty and pleasing aromas. *Lavendula officinalis* or lavender, commonly known for its bluish-purple flower spikes gracing fields and gardens, produces a strong fragrance cherished and used by many and has therapeutic uses too. Herbs make up the bulk of natural vitamin supplements. There are prescription drugs containing natural or synthesized compounds of herbs.

Essential oils extracted from the flowers, leaves, roots, seeds, and stems of herbs have concentrated amounts of healing properties. The oils are used with massages, baths, inhalations, and perfumes. The healing art of aromatherapy makes use of diverse aromas to relax, improve mood, clear the mind, improve memory, and so on. It is an integrative part of medicine in some cultures.

Keep oils out of the reach of children and pets. It's important to remember that essential oils are extremely concentrated. If applied directly to the skin, they could cause a rash reaction or an interaction to conventional medication.

Weeds Some Are Not

Definitions of weeds vary greatly depending on who is describing them. To gardeners, they are plants that pop up where they are not wanted. To farmers they are nuisances competing with their crops and must be controlled at all costs. What some people call weeds are revered by others for their health benefits.

While North Americans are obsessed with eradicating the invasive dandelion, *Taranacum officiale*, from their manicured lawns, Europeans, Asians, and others pay no mind to this nutrient-rich, liver rejuvenating medicine. They let it be where it is. It has rightful mention in herb books and is listed in weed documentation. Once we realize all the nutrition this herb provides, it's hard to look at it as a weed.

Not only is dandelion trusted as an effective diuretic and laxative—in only one hundred grams it delivers six and half times the daily vitamin K requirement. Additionally, it provides over three times the recommended daily vitamin A, 58 percent of vitamin C, and 39 percent of daily iron recommendations. It gives 19 percent calcium and 20 percent of riboflavin daily allowances plus other beneficial nutrients and chemical compounds.

Back in 2012, researchers from University of Windsor, Ontario, applied to Health Canada for approval of a stage 1 clinical trial. They wanted to determine what dose of dandelion root extract is tolerated and effective in treating patients with an aggressive type of leukemia and other cancers. Previous lab results had shown the dandelion root extract caused leukemia cancer cells to die off.

Monies for continuing research were donated to the project by a philanthropist digital-age angel investor in 2014. The latest news out in February 2015 was that human clinical trials were set to begin. Furthermore, announcement was made of a new company started to sell a dandelion root extract for therapeutic development.

As you can see, it is well worth giving this one the respect it deserves, starting by dedicating a spot, even a confined one, in our gardens for growing this herb. It offers such a concentrated abundance of nutrition and is now proving to be a defensive opponent to cancer. It has made its way into some of the prepared salad mixes at the supermarkets—a good beginning for incorporating it into our diets. I expected it to have a greater representation in the health food stores by now.

Red clover, or *Trifolium pretense*, is another herb listed as a weed. It is so very rich in flavonoids—one in particular, quercetin. As we learned in the vitamins section, flavonoids are antioxidants, and quercetin is one of the major flavonoids found in the rinds and barks of a wide range of plants. It's worth being on the lookout for this one.

Its antihistamine properties are proving useful in controlling allergies and asthma. It has antiviral and anti-inflammatory properties as well. While lacking clinical evidence, early laboratory findings look promising for its use in the fight against cancer. Red clover is included in the popular herbal cancer tincture remedy Essiac.

Another plant with endless beneficial properties thought of as a weed in some parts of the world comes to us from the Urticaceae family, with over a thousand species worldwide. Some names include slender nettle, common nettle, tall nettle, big-sting nettle, and stinging nettle native to North America. This plant is equipped with self-defensive hairs that, with the slightest touch, break and pierce through the skin, leaving a substance that creates an itchy, burning sensation.

Its armor-like exterior transforms to a velvetlike texture after approximately twelve hours of being picked. This feature is what makes it easily identifiable—downy leaves garnished with hairs and square bristly stems. It grows two to seven feet tall and produces clusters of small, greenish flowers from July to September. It can be spotted along roadsides, wastelands, gardens, fences, and walls.

The leaves pack plenty of chlorophyll, the green of the vegetable world, along with iron, both crucial to red blood cells. It, too, like the dandelion, is a significant source of calcium. One cup of this nutrition-packed herb provides between 32.9 to 42.8 percent of the recommended daily requirement for calcium. It delivers big at 1,790 IU or three times our daily recommendation of vitamin A and 369 to 493 percent of our daily intake requirement for vitamin K. Minerals in nettle include magnesium, phosphorus, iron, and silicon. It gives vitamin C and almost all essential amino acids, except for leucine and lycine.

Not only is it useful for treatment in anemia, allergy relief, eczema, and circulatory and digestive system issues, it is able to bring down blood sugar levels. This could help diabetic patients reduce their antidiabetic medication dosages. The young leaves with a flavor similar to spinach can easily be incorporated into salads, pestos, and polentas. In some parts of Europe, nettles are used in a soup dish called under different names depending on the language. Just before the summer solstice the annual Stinging Nettle Eating Championship is held in Dorset, United Kingdom.

There is so much more to be discovered and studied about this powerhouse herb. As an important source of protein, its potential use to help feed and provide nutrition to the poor is feasible.

Those were a couple of examples of miraculous healing properties in the most unassuming plants. It is indeed fascinating to realize how plentiful and well designed the offerings of Mother Nature truly are.

For What Ails You

The range of medicinal uses of certain herbs is almost as wide as the range of plants we call herbs. Some of these act as analgesic, antibacterial, antiviral, anticoagulant, anticonvulsant, antifungal, antihistamine, anti-inflammatory, antimicrobial, antiparasitic, antiseptic, antispasmodic, antiviral, and so on, with some filling in more than one or two of these roles. For whatever ails you, there's probably an herb out there to help treat it.

Unfortunately, in this part of the world, the extent to which most people think of using herbs is for the treatment of indigestion. As a resurgence in interest grows for more natural curative methods of treatment, herbal options appeal. There are herbs that calm and soothe, others invigorate, and there are some to relieve pain. A little investigation in this department is worthwhile—helping avoid dependence on packaged products on the shelves of pharmacies.

The too common condition of hypertension is possibly treatable with the following herbs—black cohosh, chrysanthemum, dandelion, dong quai, evening primrose oil, hawthorn, mistletoe, and wood betony. More than likely, sufferers never think about taking a natural approach to treatment for this ailment once they are diagnosed and given a drug prescription by the doctor. People are stuck controlling their high blood pressure with pharmaceutical drugs. The fear of jeopardizing their health by going against the norm keeps them from trying anything natural. They are worried about what going off their meds will do to them. It's not advised to just forego your prescribed medication. A consultation with a naturopath doctor might be in order. Drugs do not cure; many only guarantee a lifetime dependency.

Other ways to use herbs and spices to benefit our health can include adding the leaves of chickweed, lovage, celery, dandelion, fennel, and hawthorn to salads. Using whole spices like star anise in a tea or using the seeds of anise, cardamom, caraway, and fennel are other easy ways of incorporating healing plants in our diets while tantalizing our taste buds. Herbs that help with digestion are chamomile, fennel, lemon balm, and mint.

There are a few herbs that are very supportive to our immune system. One such popular herb, called an immune system booster, is *Echinacea angustifolia.* Another lesser known is chaparral, *Larrea divericata,* which is described in *Heinerman's Encyclopedia of Healing Herbs & Spices* as one of "nature's most superb immune system strengtheners."

Turmeric is an herb that has been studied in great depth. It helps our adrenal glands produce a hormone that fights inflammation. Gingko biloba helps protect our bodies from damage by free radicals. Astragalus, a Chinese herb, stimulates the immune system and aids in adrenal gland function and digestion. Others you'll want to check out that assist our immune system are cat's claw, *Uncaria tomentosa,* ginger, and ginseng.

The high concentration of sulfur mineral compounds in garlic give it its pungent odor. It's in the raw that these bulbs best deliver their very beneficial compounds. This powerful herb, known as a blood thinner and classed as an antibiotic among other things, comes in over twenty varieties. Books have been written explicitly about garlic. Buying it locally, even if a bit more expensive, ensures the integrity of the bulbs is not compromised during the irradiation process some imported foods are subjected to.

The Forbidden

Marijuana, *Cannabis sativa*, became forbidden much like when alcohol was prohibited because of its mind-altering properties. It is encouraging to witness marijuana's benefits finally being investigated rather than ignored. Marijuana is not only useful as a natural alternative to laboratory drugs for many conditions only marijuana is able to relieve, it has proven to be lifesaving for patients with serious and life-threatening conditions.

The public has spoken and is demanding the freedom to choose with free access to this medicine. As more scientific proof becomes available, governments have no choice but to flow with the times and change their laws. In this day and age, it seems almost barbaric to deny people medicine that can alleviate their pain and suffering.

I will only say I was not using marijuana when I got MS. That being said, with the forthcoming legalization of this herb in my country, I feel the need to express some of my views on the subject. I do feel the legalization of it will benefit some of the most vulnerable in society. If only for this reason, yes, I am for its legalization.

However, I do believe it should fall under the same strict laws as those for alcohol consumption. As with booze, people may abuse marijuana. Unfortunately, by its legalization, the door opens wide for many to indulge who shouldn't. No doubt, legalization is sure to make it easier to overuse marijuana, especially by those with a propensity for addictions.

Marijuana needs to be respected as the healing herb it is. It has a place in treating physical and mental illnesses. I do not buy into the notion that it is addictive. It is addictive if used as an emotional crutch, in the same way that alcohol is now the legal choice as a de-stressor. There are no apparent physical withdrawal symptoms as those experienced with other addictive substances. It's never been proven otherwise, but there are always exceptions. I believe one of the persistent arguments against the use of marijuana is its alleged influence in leading users to dangerous chemical drugs. This is simply a misconception.

How many people have experimented to never become addicted? Or how many used it during a particular phase of their lives only to give it up and never look back? If it was as addictive as some make it out to be, it surely wouldn't be so easy to just stop. Yes, there are many people who quit addictive habits, such as tobacco, cold turkey. Unfortunately that is not the standard. Yet, in the case of marijuana, it appears to be. If we compare that to alcohol use, finding people who drank for some time and then never touched alcohol again is uncommon. Most of the time, drinking alcohol becomes a lifetime habit. It's not until they are forced that alcohol users give it up; usually for medical reasons, people put it away.

Hopefully, with its legalization, marijuana will become so mainstream that societies will view it as a normal part of treatment rather than seeing it used as a form of escapism as it is today. It should be kept in as natural a state as possible for medicine. Not unlike with other revenue-generating substances, alterations and deviations to marijuana could become par for the course—all in the name of efficacy and economical production.

People who abuse it believe they're operating normally and it is part of life, similar to when people drink and drive. I would ask them if they would be so accepting if perhaps their surgeon or airline pilot were under the influence of this herb. Would they readily place their lives in the hands of someone who was high?

Scientists have come a long way since *tetrahydrocannabinol* (THC), the chemical that gives marijuana its euphoric effect, was first identified. Numerous chemical compounds known as cannabinoids make up cannabis. The most abundant and potent, cannabidiol (CBD), effects anti-inflammatory responses in mice with MS-type disease and is a medicine for various conditions.

The article, "Chemicals in Marijuana 'Protect Nervous System' against MS," reports on a study out of Tel Aviv University following up a previous study from 2011. It was previously shown that CBD prevented immune cells from attacking spinal cord cells in mice with MS-like symptoms. The mice with the condition had partially paralyzed limbs; when injected with CBD, they regained mobility.

The conclusion of the recent study was that both CBD and THC not only restrained immune cells from producing inflammatory molecules; they also limited the ability of molecules to get to and damage the brain and spinal cord. This is significant because it means the inflammatory molecule interleukin-17 (IL-17) harmful to nerve cells and their protective covers—strongly implicated in MS—would be kept in check.

Again, it comes down to choosing what is natural over synthetically prepared substances. If you're taking synthetic medications for a disease or trying to alleviate distress of ailments such as headaches or lack of sleep, you might want to try this herb. It's also a good idea to investigate other herbs or types of natural remedies that do not entail altering your state of mind. In some instances, they're just as effective. Other healing modalities to consider include acupuncture, acupressure, massage, energy healing, relaxation techniques, and the like.

Mind Your Mind

Most people have heard of the mind-body connection or vice versa. I venture to guess that, in the near future, this will be brought more into focus in the Western world. There are many of us who already actively seek alternative therapies. Some people travel to other countries to receive treatments they cannot get in this part of the world. Spa retreat types of medical clinics promising healing and rejuvenation that treat the whole person are gaining in popularity.

A few years back, the results of an eighteen-year study that followed over 7,200 civil servants to track cases of heart diseases were released. The researchers wanted to find out what the perception of the effects of stress had on individuals. The study, published in June 2013 in the *European*

Heart Journal, showed researchers there was increased risk of the disease in those who believed stress was affecting their health.

What is believed in your mind is reflected in your body. Some cultures have always used an integrated system in their treatment of illness. Ayurvedic medicine, an ancient type of medicine, always made the connection between the mind and the body. Chinese medicine also bases a lot of its treatments on balancing energies of the body and the mind. Acupuncture is one such treatment.

It was the founder of medicine, Hippocrates—who lived around the late 400s BC and is believed to have lived for close to eighty years—who said, "Let food be your medicine and medicine be your food." Given that eighty is not far from today's life expectancy numbers, we can conclude that living nearly eighty years old was quite a feat for that era. Hippocrates's true age at his death is unknown; however, records of his accomplishments make it easy to envision such a number.

Hippocratic medicine practiced treating the patient, not just the disease. Another of Hippocrates's quotes, "Everything in excess is opposed to nature," rings very true. It's very reflective of where we find ourselves today with regards to our health. Excessive consumption of sugars, manufactured foods, synthetics, and chemicals has created an unbalance in our bodies. This unbalance has made us vulnerable to diseases and left us unable to maintain or regain our health.

It's best not to dwell on any diagnosis. As life changing as a diagnosis of illness is, it doesn't define you as a person. There's a lot more to any one person than a diagnosis. For myself, MS is something I try to ignore as best I can most of the time. I don't even like to speak the words. I have never participated in any group therapy for this reason. I've given it more attention writing this book than I ever intended or wanted to.

There are people who want and need to have support from others and cope better knowing they're not alone in their struggles. Support groups provide an important lifeline for many. Books have always been where I've turned for guidance and refuge. Not much of a fiction fan, I have found that my reading has always focused on self-help, non-fiction type books. My appetite for these books began in my early twenties with titles like *The Power of Positive Thinking* and has continued on to books on nutrition and health that I'm still reading to this day. Much of my outlook has been formed from the pages I have read in books. Everyone has his or her own specific needs insofar as ways to handle losing part of themselves—their health.

Kindly speak—you're listening

It is unfortunate that people do not hesitate when complaining about how bad they feel. It's not only when asked how they're doing that many people volunteer this information. Why is it that people only elaborate on how they feel physically in a negative way? You seldom hear someone speak out and say, "I feel particularly good today," or, "I feel extremely well today."

As it is expressed, it will be felt. I'm not talking about debilitating pain you really need to get to the bottom of. I mean the pain of common ailments. There are some pains that consume—I do know this all too well. I'm saying that people put way too much emphasis on everyday complaints. When someone says they have a headache or whatever else they're complaining about, they're placing too much focus on the particular problem.

Seemingly mindless, this chatter of complaint is only reaffirming the pain and bringing extra attention to it. It's not just the person expressing the words about not feeling well. The listener then places attention on the pain too. There's the saying, "Be careful what you wish for." I add one along the same lines, "Be careful what you speak of." If every time a person encounters another, he or she reiterates how bad he or she feels, how bad do you think the person will really feel at the end of the day?

Just as we can feel the music through our bodies when we hear it, we need to realize words also resonate in our bodies. When I have a headache, I prefer to say, "I feel good except for this headache." This way I am emphasizing that I feel good, instead of placing the attention on the headache itself.

This will seem crazy to some, but I have been reaffirming to myself for years that I am healthy. How can I say that when I have MS? Surely I feel better than the people who are constantly complaining who do not have any diseases. I am not a complainer. Always there are others who are worse off. I feel good at this moment—and every moment that I do feel good, yes, I feel healthy. There's no need to bring up you know what.

If you've ever been really upset by someone's spoken words directed at you, think back on how the words made you feel physically. You should be able to give credence to what it is I'm trying to bring across here. Think back to an occasion when upsetting words registered in your brain or, should I say, your heart. Remember how it felt when the rush of blood went to your face and then spread throughout your body as a reaction to spoken words. The words reverberated to reach the core of your being. Perhaps they impacted your physical being so much that you began shaking or trembling. It isn't far-fetched then to think words to yourself, or your thoughts, have as much impact on you as others' words.

Remaining upbeat no matter what is the only way to feel good. If you have ever met a chronic complainer, you should be able to relate to this. They, more often than not, suffer physical symptoms of one kind or another. For some of us, every day we're able to get up out of bed or to see and walk is experienced as a blessing.

It is sad that many people go through life without understanding there is joy to be experienced in even the most mundane of circumstances. It is important to live in the *now* of life. The past always stays with you, but it is behind you. As for the future, while it's okay to anticipate the best, in order to fully experience the wonderment of each moment, we must not dwell on it. *Now* is all we have at the present time, and then that too will be past.

It's when observing the fascination of nature that we learn to appreciate the little goings-on that are always happening and miss when we don't stop to look. Whether it's a bird taking flight, the distinctive shape of a cloud, or the stars in the night sky, there is a lot to take in. How we ourselves feel at a moment in time when we take time to observe is our own perception and no one else's.

When we're alone, presences and performances displayed in one moment feel even more personal. It's a bit empowering and brings a sense of connectedness to realize what we're seeing at a particular moment is witnessed by only us. This gives us the impression things were placed there for our exclusive enjoyment.

There are countless examples of people who have overcome their misfortunes and risen to extraordinary heights. Many who were afflicted with debilitating diseases, paralysis, abuse, neglect, or what have you are able to find inspiration within themselves or in others to feel a sense of appreciation for life itself. It really comes down to being present in the moment.

If there's anything I've learned it's for that tomorrow may not be as you hoped, and yesterday is a memory. Be thankful for the memory and the fact you are able to remember. Just don't go there too often or for too long. In some cases, do not go there at all if the memory is not a pleasant one. For myself, I find much comfort in feeling at this very moment that things are fairly normal. We need to make the conscious choice to accept things as they are. It doesn't mean they cannot get better. As sure as things can get worse, they can get better.

There is enough stuff life throws at us that's not in our control. We really need to take the reign on how we think, feel, react, and speak. It's too easy to get lost in others' intentions or feelings while ignoring our true source—our self. We are the directors of our thinking. No one is able to think for us. How we think is our choice. Although we can be influenced by many different things, the final judgment is ours to make. Even the most mundane of actions require some thought. It's important we stop and always choose wisely.

There may be times when we wonder how we ended up somewhere we didn't really want to be—becoming overweight or ending up sick. Unintentionally we must have drifted because surely we wouldn't have chosen those circumstances for ourselves. A good example of this is when we make food choices that make us feel bad after we eat them. Did we consciously choose to eat to become ill? I think not. We only ate what we wanted and didn't bother worrying about the aftereffects. On some level, we knew what was coming—we chose to ignore it.

In his book, *Evolve Your Brain*, Joe Dispenza tells us, "It is where we place our attention that maps out the very course of our state of being." What we are aware of we're thinking—if given too much attention is what we don't realize we're thinking—then becomes what we habitually think. You might have to read the last sentence again. This is important to remember if we find ourselves thinking negatively. What we place emphasis on is how we are neurologically wired. All thoughts send out biochemical reactions that become behaviors and patterns. We need to put in a bit of effort to bring our awareness to consciously realizing what unconscious script we're running.

As some of us go about our busy lives and tell ourselves we're just too busy to make time to incorporate some type of exercise, we eventually believe this without effort. Spare time is spent relaxing by watching some television. We don't think of doing any physical activity other than what we have to. It doesn't even cross our minds. We simply decided long ago that we didn't have time. For many, there's no time for even a simple walk. Much to our detriment down the road, we ignore the part of ourselves that benefits from these types of activities.

Our brains can regenerate new pathways through learning. A similar effect is mentally believing new things and imagining what we wish to experience. This possibly is one of the foremost important aspects of bringing about any change. Visualization techniques are an integral part of cancer treatments. Patients are led into meditation or just a quieting of the mind and guided to imagine a type of Pac-Man figure, or the like, on-site in their bodies ravaging the cancer cells.

If we add some feeling to what it is we want to accomplish, it greatly magnifies the process of envisioning the result we're shooting for. We need to feel what it is we are wanting to experience. When I became tired of the extra pounds I was carrying, I not only said I was thin in my mind—I let myself experience the feeling of being thin. It was buried somewhere in the distant past, but I found it and felt it.

It was a bit uncanny when writing this book. As I went along in search of the right evidence for a particular point I was trying to make, the answers appeared in plain view for my taking. It confirmed, once more, that when focus is applied to a particular outcome, the intended result is easier to achieve.

So if we reflect on our selection and see that change is needed, there are three steps to make anything happen. We have to go from thinking to doing to being—and being is best achieved with feeling.

As with most intentions requiring commitment, simply starting to take steps brings gratification. This in turn makes it enjoyable to continue with the objective. When the simple act of beginning is not applied, no reward is ever experienced to motivate. It's by giving some attention to health that we become responsive to the positive choices we make with regards to what we are putting on and into our bodies. Eventually we realize that, not only do we feel better, gradually the positive choices we implemented became a way of life.

In certain situations it is wise to seek out and get help if there are persistent feelings of not being up to par. I have gone through periods of deep depression in my life when everyday things seemed harder to deal with. During these times, I searched for hope in books and drew comfort from prayer—gradually things improved. If you're not the praying type, there are other avenues to help overcome ill feelings. There's no shame in participating in some type of therapy if it is available—either group or one-on-one.

Volunteering and helping those less fortunate is a good way to elevate one's spirit. Spending time in nature strengthens our connection to life. Learning new skills, if possible, creates more self-esteem. If money is an issue, check your community calendar. Sometimes you can find free programs offered, or an online search might come up with something that interests you.

There are times when sad feelings can be brought on by our diet or by nutritional deficiencies. Other times, our environment or negative thought patterns can play a role. In some instances, depression is the result of a brain chemical imbalance, which can only be treated with drugs. There are people who spend years on drugs under the care of psychiatrists.

If a chemical imbalance is not the case—although it will not feel like it at the time—for the most part, our feelings are entirely our creation. In the end, there's no one who can take away these feelings except our own self. It is helpful if you can speak with someone for encouragement or guidance. The real work, though, is still left to each individual. Whether it's in changing the way we feel and think or the way things are in our lives, at some point, there needs to be a conscious action taken to feel better.

There is a saying, "Prepare for the worst, but expect the best." I can think of no reason not to expect the best. I challenge anyone who implies otherwise, be it my doctor, the specialist, my family, or whomever. They have no clue how I really feel—they are not me. Just like I cannot possibly truly know how it feels to be them, they can't know how it feels to be me.

I have come to realize that thoughts create reactions to take action or turn into feelings. Thought patterns can be changed if need be. Apparently a good number of people need to make a change. How else can we explain why so many of us are medicating? In the majority of cases, wrong choices were made with wrong thoughts behind them. We get to how we feel with thought.

I do find a great release from negative feelings is achieved with exercise. I'm not implying adhering to an exercise regimen requiring an enormous amount of discipline for anyone, let alone someone suffering from depression. Simply a brisk walk or an invigorating dance to your favorite music can subside any negative feelings. If you can manage and are able and willing to engage in a more strenuous type of exercise, it could be even better for you.

It all depends on your particular circumstances and preferences. All I can say is, even if you can start small, make the commitment to give it a chance. Make some type of physical activity as regular as you can—you will like how it makes you feel. As you feel the difference, you can build on it or you can keep things at the same pace. I know and feel that incorporating exercise into my routine makes a big difference, not only to my physical health but also to my outlook on life.

I feel ever so blessed that I'm able to walk. I gladly choose to walk my dog almost daily. I remain eternally grateful to the little creature for showing me the benefits of walking. Some professional athletes have themselves admitted to suffering from depression. I would imagine the physical benefits gained from training and doing physical activities helped them overcome it. Our bodies function best when we're active— accordingly, our minds react positively.

Pleasure chemicals produced in the brain give off feel-good feelings when a person exerts him or herself physically for a period of time. One such chemical, the human growth hormone or HGH, has actually been synthesized in laboratories. Pills are popped by athletes to build up muscle mass and older people hoping to halt the aging process.

As we age, HGH production is reduced. This may be key in understanding why older people who exercise live longer and healthier lives than do their counterparts who don't exercise. The hormone is also produced when we sleep, proving on another level why lack of sleep is detrimental to our overall health. Not only is getting a good night's sleep keeping our minds sharp and alert—it also keeps us physically well.

Children are the lucky ones. They get to go jump around and play most of their spare time. As adults, we don't have that luxury. Responsibilities beckon, and leisure time is limited. Unless someone is involved in some type of sport or participates in regular exercises in some form or another, the flood of chemical euphoria experienced from such behaviors is unknown. I know I'm a bit harder to get along with when I'm prevented from walking outside for any length of time.

Adults need to worry when exercise or playtimes are reduced in school curriculums. It goes without saying that reducing time spent in these activities not only jeopardizes kids' health in more ways than one—it sends the wrong message about the importance of physical activity. It only reinforces the lazy mentality many people have adopted toward health. Instilling value and interest at this juncture is central if it is to be carried forward later into life.

Conclusion

We should not frown upon those who have differing points of views than our own. We need to open ourselves enough to consider practices that include nurturing the total environment—our mind, body, and spirit—with a more integrative, natural methodology. As intended natural nutrition and healing is replaced with manipulated substitutes and flawless versions of food—eventually—unintended negative repercussions will dramatically affect the whole. Temporary relief using medicines to mask symptoms brings the body further distress, creating additional symptoms, and the mind will be left to expect the worst.

Simply not understanding how something works doesn't make it not work, just as understanding how something works does not guarantee it will. What works for some may not work for others; this emphasizes the need for development and implementation of an individualized approach to treatment. In effect, the targeting of specific areas when administering certain therapies shows better results than the previous consensus of generalized applications.

If it's our bodies that have been running the show, with our bad habits bringing us to a state of unbalance leading to dis-ease, we must now learn to stop to think. We need to become conscious of the choices we make and understand why and how exactly we are making these choices. Once we begin to reflect on all our selections, seeing their effects not only on ourselves, but on the whole, we can begin to bring and demand change where it is needed. Change needs to start from the bottom up—it won't come from the top down.

By taking steps to better our health, we're acknowledging our true worth. We are then able to recognize and avoid the patterns and misrepresentations that don't serve us. We have to arrive at the point where this right is made available for all—taking back control from the select few who capitalize on the weaknesses of the vulnerable. Only then can we finally evolve past the dominance of fear to an inclusive and caring reality. Consider these words of Immanuel Kant:

> To secure one's own happiness is a duty, at least indirectly, for discontent with one's own condition, under a pressure of many anxieties and amidst unsatisfied wants, might easily become a great temptation to transgression of duty.

In some parts of the world, wisdom passed down through the generations is sought rather than dismissed because it is not well understood. It does not stand to reason how a large number of people instinctively search and gain spiritual knowledge from books written thousands of years ago yet won't entertain any thought of using natural remedies for healing.

Is it so unreasonable to think our ancestors might have had a deeper knowledge of health than we do? We have advanced to be able to genetically modify, but why do we still ignore the whole aspects of a person? The times are more complicated, but the basics remain.

References

Chapter 1: Diagnosis

AZoNano. "Introduction: What is Nanomedicine?" in *Nanotechnology in Implantable Medical Devices*. AZoNano (March 6, 2013). Accessed March 22, 2017. http://www.azonano.com/article.aspx?ArticleID=3207.

Carney, Scott, "Testing Drugs on India's Poor." *Wired* (December 19, 2005). Accessed March 22, 2017. http://www.wired.com/2005/12/testing-drugs-on-indias-poor/.

Eaton, Hillary, "Wearables Know When You're Sick Before You Do." *Livestrong* (January 17, 2017). Accessed March 22, 2017. http://www.livestrong.com/article/1012698-wearables-sick-before/?utm_source=newsletter&utm_medium=email&utm_campaign=0125_wed_ed_f.

Gladstone Institutes. "Gladstone Scientists Identify Key Biological Mechanism in Multiple Sclerosis." Gladstone Institutes (November 27, 2012). Accessed March 24, 2017. https://gladstone.org/about-us/press-releases/gladstone-scientists-identify-key-biological-mechanism-multiple%C2%A0sclerosis.

HealthDay. "Study Supports Link Between Obesity, Cavities in Homeless Kids." *US News* (November 19, 2012). Accessed March 22, 2017. http://health.usnews.com/health-news/news/articles/2012/11/19/study-supports-link-between-obesity-cavities-in-homeless-kids.

McPherson, Mark, Hong Ji, Jordan Hunt, Rob Ranger, and Gula Cheryl. "Medication Use among Canadian Seniors." CIHI Survey, *Healthcare Quarterly* 15(4) (Longwood, October 2012: 15-18. doi:10.12927/hcq2012.23192. http://www.longwoods.com/content/23192.

Chapter 2: Understanding Some Basics

Aarhus University. "Parkinson's Disease May Begin in the Gut: Parkinson's Disease Begins in the Gastrointestinal Tract, Large Study Indicates." Science Daily (June 23, 2015). Accessed March 22, 2017. www.sciencedaily.com/releases/2015/06/150623103609.htm.

Albert Einstein College of Medicine of Yeshiva University. "White blood cells found to play key role in controlling red blood cell levels." *Science Daily* (March 17, 2013). Accessed March 25, 2013, https://www.sciencedaily.com/releases/2013/03/130317154727.htm.

Anderson, Pauline. "Does Parkinson's Begin in the Gut?" *Medscape* (June 14, 2012). Medscape (765675). http://www.medscape.com/viewarticle/765675.

Associated Press. "India Launches Campaign for Deworming Millions of Children." *Mail Online* (February 10, 2016). Accessed March 26, 2017. http://www.dailymail.co.uk/wires/ap/article-3440236/India-launches-campaign-deworming-millions-children.html.

Bazian and NHS Choices, editor. "Could Young Blood 'Slow' Ageing?" *UK News* (May 6, 2014). Accessed March 22, 2017. http://www.nhs.uk/news/2014/05May/Pages/Vampire-treatment-with-blood-may-slow-ageing.aspx.

Berer, K. et al. "Commensal Microbiota and Myelin Autoantigen Cooperate to Trigger Autoimmune Demyelination." *Nature* (November 24, 2011). Accessed March 26, 2017. doi:10.1038/nature10554. http://www.nature.com/nature/journal/v479/n7374/full/nature10554.html.

Boyle, Rebecca. "Cancer Are Newly Evolved Parasitic Species, Biologist Argues," *Popular Science* (July 27, 2011). Accessed

March 22, 2017. http://www.popsci.com/science/article/2011-07/
cancers-are-newly-evolved-parasitic-species-biologist-argues.

Branswell, Karen. "Scientists on Lookout for Spread of Tapeworm." *The Canadian Press* (September 13, 2012). Accessed March 26, 2017. http://www.metronews.ca/news/canada/2012/09/13/scientists-on-lookout-for-spread-of-tapeworm.html.

Buzzle. "Vagus Nerve Damage." Buzzle.com. Accessed March 22, 2017. http://www.buzzle.com/articles/vagus-nerve-damage.html.

Chacon-Cruz, Enrique. "Intestinal Protozeal Disease Clinical Presentation." *Medscape* (updated May 2, 2014). Accessed March 22, 2017. http://emedicine.medscape.com/article/999282-clinical.

Davis, Larry E. "Unregulated Potions Still Cause Mercury Poisoning." *PubMed Central* 173(1) (July 2000). PMC (1090762). http://www.ncbi.nlm.nih.gov/pmc/articles/PMC1070962/.

Dixon, Bernard. *Power Unseen, How Microbes Rule the World*. New York: Bath Press, 1994.

Dr. Mercola. "Confirmed – Your Digestive System Dictates Whether You're Sick or Well." *Mercola* (January 2, 2013). Accessed March 22, 2017. http://articles.mercola.com/sites/articles/archive/2013/01/02/digestive-system-gut-flora.aspx.

Foulds, Penelope, David Mann, J. Douglas Mitchell, and David Allsop. "Development of A-Synuclein as a Potential Biomarker for Parkinson's Disease." November 20, 2014. Accessed March 22, 2017. https://www.researchgate.net/publication/251197951_Development_of_a-synuclein_as_a_potential_biomarker_for_Parkinson%27s_disease.

Hashimoto, H., S. M. Messerli, T. Sudo, and H. Maruta "Ivermectin Inactives the Kinase PAK1 and Blocks the PAK1-Dependent Growth of Human Ovarian Cancer and NF2 Tumor Cell Lines." *PubMed* 3(6) (December 2009): 243–466. PMID (22495656). http://www.ncbi.nlm.nih.gov/pubmed/22495656.

Hayes, Edward B. "Zika Virus outside Africa." *Infectious Diseases Journal* 15, no. 9 (September 2009). doi:10.3201/eid1509.090442. http://wwwnc.cdc.gov/eid/article/15/9/09-0442_article.htm.

Jaslow, Ryan. "Cyclospora Case Count Climbs to 353, Outbreak's Source Still Unknown." *CBS News* (July 29, 2013). Accessed March 22, 2017. http://www.cbsnews.com/8301-204_162-57595988/cyclospora-case-count-climbs-to-353 …

Johnson, Andy. "Parasites Found in Pre-Washed Packages of Lettuce: Health Canada," *CTV News* (March 5, 2013). Accessed March 26, 2017. http://www.ctvnews.ca/health/health-headlines/parasites-found-in-pre-washed-packages-of-lettuce-health-canada-1.1182977.

Khamsi, Roxanne. "How Studying Mummies Could Cure Modern Diseases." *Popular Science* (October 2, 2013). Accessed March 22, 2017. http://www.popsci.com/technology/article/2013-09/mummy-medicine.

London Drugs. Focus on Health & Wellness (Spring/Summer 2000).

Marsh, Beezy, "Secret Reports Reveals 18 Child Deaths Following Vaccinations." *The Telegraph* (February 13, 2006). Accessed March 22, 2017. http://www.telegraph.co.uk/news/uknews/3336455/Secret-report-reveals-18-child-deaths-following-vaccinations.html.

Matthews, Cate. "What Percentage of Our Brain Do We Actually Use? Popular Myth Debunked In Ted-Ed video." *The Huffington Post* (February 4, 2014). Accessed March 22, 2017. http://www.huffingtonpost.com/2014/02/04/ted-ed-percentage-brain-richard-cytowic_n_4719173.html.

Mortillaro, Nicole. "Researchers May Have Found the Cause of Crohn's Disease." *Global News* (September 28, 2016). Accessed March 22, 2017. http://globalnews.ca/news/2968985/researchers-may-have-found-the-cause-of-crohns-disease/.

Plotkin, Mark J. *Medicine Quest In Search of Nature's Healing Secrets*. New York: Penguin Group (USA) Inc., 2001.

Ramirez-Miranda, et al. "Parasites in Mexican Patients with Irritable Bowel Syndrome: A Case Controlled Study." *Parasites & Vectors* (October 13, 2010). Accessed March 27, 2017. https://parasitesandvectors. biomedcentral.com/articles/10.1186/1756-3305-3-96.

Reinberg, Steven. "Antibiotics Linked to Retinal Detachment Risk." *Health Day News* (April 3, 2012). Accessed March 22, 2017. https://consumer. healthday.com/infectious-disease-information-21/antibiotics-news-30/ antibiotics-linked-to-retinal-detachment-risk-663420.html.

Schmid, Jennifer. "Beautiful Black Poison." Weston A. Price Foundation (April 2, 2009). Accessed March 22, 2017. http://www.westonaprice. org/environmental-toxins/beautiful-black-poison.

"Serratiamarcescens." Serratiamarcescens.net.Accessed March 22, 2017. http://www.serratiamarcescens.net/.

Spalding, Kirsty L. et al, "Dynamics of Hippocampal Neurogenesis in Adult Humans." *Cell* 153, no. 6 (June 6, 2013): 1,219 –1,227. doi:10.1016/j.cell.2013.05.002.

Stark, D., et al. "Irritable Bowel Syndrome: A Review on the Role of Intestinal Protozoa and the Importance of their Detection and Diagnosis." *Science Direct* (September 2006). Accessed March 27, 2017. doi:10.1016/jpara.2006.09.009. http://www.sciencedirect.com/ science/article/pii/S0020751906003468.

Stovall, Sten. "Parasitic Worms May Offer Hope on MS." *Wall Street Journal* (June 28, 2011). Accessed March 26, 2017. https://www.wsj. com/news/articles/SB10001424052702304314404576413303666 083390.

"Vagus Nerve." In "Table 1. Cranial Nerves Summary." Meddean.luc. edu. Accessed March 22, 2017. http://www.meddean.luc.edu/lumen/ MedEd/GrossAnatomy/h_n/cn/cn1/cn10.htm.

Wikipedia. "Mercury(I) chloride." *Wikipedia: The Free Encyclopedia*. Accessed March 22, 2017. http://www.wikipedia.org/wiki/Calomel.

Winston, Mark L. *Nature Wars, People vs. Pests.* USA: First Harvard University Press, 1997.

Chapter 3: The Goods on Goods

Da Silva, Chantal. "Subway Agrees to End Use of a Controversial Chemical after Food Blogger Vani Hari's Protests." CBC News (February 8, 2014). Accessed March 23, 2017. http://www.cbc.ca/news/health/subway-agrees-to-end-use-of-controversial-chemical-after-food-blogger-vani-hari-s-protest-1.2525447.

Davis, William. "Wheat Belly." |*Wheat belly blog.* Accessed April 6, 2017. http://www.wheatbellyblog.com/books/.

Donnelly, Laura, "Juice Could No Longer Count towards 'Five' a Day." *The Telegraph* (June 26, 2014). Accessed March 22, 2017. http://www.telegraph.co.uk/news/health/news/10928992/Juice-could-no-longer-count-towards-five-a-day.html.

Goh, Su Ling. "Superbug Infections: Could Salt Be the Solution?" *Global News* (October 3, 2016). Accessed March 22, 2017. http://globalnews.ca/news/2980511/superbug-infections-could-salt-be-the-solution/.

Gowin, Joshua. "Your Brain on Alcohol. Is the Conventional Wisdom Wrong about Booze?" *Psychology Today.* Accessed March 28, 2017. https://www.psychologytoday.com/blog/you-illuminated/201006/your-brain-alcohol.

Hernandez, Amanda. "How Much Salt Is Naturally in Vegetables?" *SF Gate.* Accessed March 22, 2017. http://healthyeating.sfgate.com/much-salt-naturally-vegetables-8949.html.

Institute of Alcohol Studies. "Alcohol is a Class 1 Carcinogen, Warns Balance North East Ad." *Institute of Alcohol Studies* 20 (November 2013). Accessed April 9, 2017. http://www.ias.org.uk/News/2013/20-November-2013-Alcohol-is-a-Class-1-carcinogen-warns-Balance-North-East-ad.aspx.

Mientka, Matthew. "Vitamin E in Canola and Other Cooking Oils Linked to Asthma, Other Lung Problems." *Medical Daily* (May 25, 2014). Accessed March 23, 2017. http://www.medicaldaily.com/vitamin-e-canola-and-other-cooking-oils-linked-asthma-other-lung-problems-284524.

Millar, Heather. "The Truth About Sugar." *Prevention* (March 26, 2013). Accessed March 27, 2017. http://www.prevention.com/food/healthy-eating-tips/real-ways-eat-less-sugar.

National Health Research Institute. "- elements - 25: SODIUM." Apjcn. nhri.org. Accessed March 22, 2017. http://apjcn.nhri.org.tw/server/info/books-phds/books/foodfacts/html/data/data5a.html.

National Institutes of Health. "Alcohol Alert." *National Institute on Alcohol Abuse and Alcoholism* no. 47 (April 2000). Accessed March 22, 2017. http://pubs.niaaa.nih.gov/publications/aa47.htm.

O'Connell, Jeff. *Sugar Nation*. New York: Harper Collins, 2010.

Paddock, Catherine. "Repair of Multiple Sclerosis Damage May Be Possible." *Medical News Today* (November 2012). Accessed March 27, 2017. http://www.medicalnewstoday.com/articles/252295.php.

Pennington, Tess. "5 Naturally Occurring Salt Sources For When the SHTF," *Ready Nutrition*. Accessed March 22, 2017. http://readynutrition.com/resources/5-naturally-occuring-salt-sources-when-the-shtf_29012014/.

Perry, Lizzie. "Salt Injections 'Kill Cancer Cells' by Causing them to Self-Destruct ... And It Could Pave the Way for New Drugs to Prevent the Disease." *Mail Online* (August 12, 2014). Accessed March 22, 2017. http://www.dailymail.co.uk/health/article-2722869/Salt-injection-kills-cancer-cells.html.

Pimentel, Fernanda et al. "Chocolate and Red Wine – A Comparison between Flavonoids Content." *Science Direct* (2009). Accessed March 23, 2017. http://www.sciencedirect.com/science/article/pii/S0308814609011388.

Pollack, Andrew. "Genetically Engineered Salmon Approved for Consumption." *New York Times* (November 19, 2015). Accessed March 23, 2017. http://www.nytimes.com/2015/11/20/business/genetically-engineered-salmon-approved-for-consumption.html?_r=1.

Rack, Jessie. "Genetically Modified Salmon: Coming to a River Near You?" *NPR* (June 24, 2015). Accessed March 23, 2017. http://www.npr.org/sections/thesalt/2015/06/24/413755699/genetically-modified-salmon-coming-to-a-river-near-you.

Reinberg, Steven. "CDC Salt Guidelines Too Low for Good Health, Study Suggests." *Health Day* (April 2, 2014). Accessed March 27, 2017, https://consumer.healthday.com/public-health-information-30/centers-for-disease-control-news-120/cdc-salt-guidelines-too-low-for-good-health-study-suggests-686408.html.

Science Daily. "Oregon University – Potential Way to Repair Brain Damage in Multiple Sclerosis." *Science Daily*. Accessed March 22, 2017. https://www.sciencedaily.com/releases/2012/10/121031151611.htm.

Sugar Stacks. "How Much Sugar in Candy?" SugarStacks.com. Accessed March 22, 2017. http://www.sugarstacks.com/candy.htm.

Truth in Aging. "PEG-100 Stearate." TruthinAging.com. Accessed March 23, 2017. https://www.truthinaging.com/ingredients/peg-100-stearate.

US News. "Should Sugar Be Regulated?" *US News* (March 30, 2012). Accessed March 22, 2017. http://www.usnews.com/debate-club/should-sugar-be-regulated.

University of British Columbia. "Researchers Design Trees That Make It Easier to Produce Pulp." *UBC News*, Media Release April 3, 2014. http://news.ubc.ca/2014/04/03/researchers-design-trees-that-make-it-easier-to-make-paper/.

Wells, S. D. "70,000 Food Additives Approved by the FDA – What You Don't Know Will Hurt You." *Natural News* (June 26, 2014). Accessed March 22, 2017. http://www.naturalnews.com/045739_food_additives_FDA_toxic_chemicals.html.

Chapter 4: Conscious Choices

Acu-Cell Nutrition. "Boron." Acu-cell.com. Accessed March 23, 2017. http://www.acu-cell.com/b.html.

Acu-Cell Nutrition. "Germanium and Silicon/Silica." Acu-cell.com. Accessed March 23, 2017. http://www.acu-cell.com/gesi.html.

Acu-cell Nutrition. "Selenium & Sulfur (Sulphur)." Acu-cell.com. Accessed March 23, 2017. http://www.acu-cell.com/ses.html.

Acu-cell Nutrition. "Vanadium & Molybdenum." Acu-cell.com. Accessed March 23, 2017. http://www.acu-cell.com/vmo.html.

Adf.ly. "10 Fruits Rich in Omega-3 Fatty Acids." Adf.ly.com. Accessed March 23, 2017. http://adf.ly/332359/banner/http://mostnutritious. blogspot.ca/2010/09/10-fruits-rich-in-omega-3-fatty-acids.html.

Agency for Toxic Substances and Disease Registry. "Manganese 2. Relevance to Public Health, 2.1 Background and Environmental Exposures to Manganese in the United States." 11–38. Atdsr.com. Accessed March 23, 2017. https://www.atsdr.cdc.gov/toxprofiles/tp2-c2.pdf.

American Cancer Society medical and editorial content team. "Marijuana and Cancer." Cancer.org. Accessed March 24, 2017. https://www.cancer.org/treatment/treatments-and-side-effects/complementary-and-alternative-medicine/marijuana-and-cancer.html.

Anderson, Greg. "The Vitamin D Promise." *Healthy Directions*.

Annie's Remedy. "Top 65 Most Commonly Used Herbs." Anniesremedy.com. Accessed March 23, 2017. http://www.anniesremedy.com/chart.php.

Austin, Kirsta, and Bob Seebohar. *Performance Nutrition*. USA, 2011.

AVogel. "Herbs for the Immune System." Avogel.ca. Accessed March 23, 2017. http://www.avogel.ca/en/health/the-immune-system/herbs-for-the-immune-system/.

B & T Wild Seeds. "Poppy – Divine Herb of Joy or Evil Weed of Daemons?" Bandtworldseeds.com. Accessed March 24, 2017. www.b-and-t-world-seeds.com/Poppya.htm.

Balch, Phyllis A., CNC. *Prescription for Nutritional Healing*. Fifth edition, revised and updated by Stacey Bell. DCS, 2010.

Barrett, Mike. "Vitamin K Deficiency Symptoms – 5 Signs of Low Vitamin K Levels." *Natural Society* (April 15, 2013). Accessed March 23, 2017. http://naturalsociety.com/vitamin-k-deficiency-symptoms-5-signs-low-vitamin-k-levels/.

Beecher, Gary R. "18 - Flavonoids in Foods," *Science Direct*. Accessed March 23, 2017. doi:10.1016/B978-012543590-1/50019-6. http://www.sciencedirect.com/science/article/pii/B9780125435901500196.

Bembu. "26 Foods Rich in Vitamin A for Healthy Eyes." Bembu.com. Accessed March 23, 2017. http://bembu.com/vitamin-a-foods.

Bembu. "32 Foods High in Vitamin B12 to Keep You Energized." Bembu.com. Accessed March 23, 2017. http://bembu.com/vitamin-b12-foods.

Bitelog. "Magnesium in Lemons." Bitelog.com. Accessed March 23, 2017. http://www.bitelog.com/narrow-food-search.htm?q=Magnesium +in+lemons&action=Search&options=1&redir=redir&food_quantity _text=1&unit_no=piece.

Blessed Maine Herbs. "Herbs for the Immune System." Blessedmaineherbs.com. Accessed March 23, 2017. http://www.blessedmaineherbs.com/herforhealim.html.

Brown, Mary Jane. "What is Choline? An Essential Nutrient with Many Benefits." *Authority Nutrition*. Accessed March 23, 2017. https://authoritynutrition.com/what-is-choline/.

Caba, Justin. "Studies Claiming Vitamins And Supplements Useless, and Even Harmful, Are Bogus, Study Suggests." *Medical Daily* (December 20, 2013). Accessed April 9, 2017. http://www.medicaldaily.com/studies-claiming-vitamins-and-supplements-useless-and-even-harmful-are-bogus-study-suggests-266021.

Canadian Food Inspection Agency. "Food Irradiation." Canada. ca. Accessed March 24, 2017. http://www.inspection.gc.ca/food/ information-for-consumers/fact-sheets-and-infographics/irradiation/ eng/1332358607968/1332358680017.

Cerulli, J. et al. "Chromium Picolinate Toxicity." *PubMed* 32 (April 1998): 428–31. Accessed March 23, 2017. https://www.ncbi.nlm.nih.gov/ pubmed/9562138/.

Cheng, Maria. "Scientists Serve up World's First Lab-Made Burger." *Global News* (August 5, 2013). Accessed March 23, 2017. http://globalnews. ca/news/762108/scientists-serve-up-worlds-first-lab-made-burger/.

Clements, Rex, and Betty Darnell Betty. "Myo-Inositol Content of Common Foods: Development of a High Inositol Diet." *American Journal of Clinical Nutrition*, 33(9) (October 1980): 1,954–67. Accessed March 23, 2017. https://www.researchgate.net/publication/ 15783165_Myo-inositol_content_of_common_foods_development_ of_a_high-myo-inositol_diet.

Conis, Elena, "The Hidden Salt in Chicken." *Los Angeles Times* (June 22, 2009). Accessed March 23, 2017. http://articles.latimes.com/2009/ jun/22/health/he-nutrition22.

Conrad Stoppler, Melissa. "Iron and Iron Deficiency." *Medicine Net.* Accessed March 23, 2017. http://www.medicinenet.com/iron_and_ iron_deficiency/article.htm.

Consumer Lab. "Question: What Are Omega-7 Fatty Acids? Do I Need to Take These If I Already Take Fish Oil?" ConsumerLab.com. Accessed March 23, 2017. https://www.consumerlab.com/answers/ What+are+omega-7+fatty+acids+Do+I+need+to+take+these+if+I+ already+take+fish+oil/omega-7_fatty%20acids/.

Consumer Lab. "Recommended Daily Intakes and Upper Limits for Nutrients." Consumerlab.com. Accessed March 23, 2017. https:// www.consumerlab.com/RDAs/.

Consumer Reports. "Healthy Heart with Omega 3. Choosing a Tropicana Orange Juice Type." Consumerreports.com. Accessed April 6, 2017. http://www.consumerreports.org/cro/2012/04/juiced-up-juice/index. htm.

Corleone, Jill. "What Foods Contain Vitamin B7?" *Livestrong* (December 18, 2013). Accessed March 23, 2017. http://www.livestrong.com/ article/380934-what-food-contains-vitamin-b7/.

Curinga, Karen. "What are the Benefits of Eating Smoked Oysters?" *Livestrong* (February 17, 2014). Accessed March 23, 2017. http://www.livestrong. com/article/274635-what-are-the-benefits-of-eating-smoked-oysters/.

Diet. "Molybdenum." Diets.com. Accessed March 23, 2017. http://www.diet.com/g/ molybdenum.

Diet and Fitness Today. "Copper in Chicken Calculator." Dietandfitnesstoday.com. Accessed March 23, 2017. http://www. dietandfitnesstoday.com/copper-in-chicken.php.

Dietitians of Canada. "Food Sources of Magnesium." Dietitians.ca (October 28, 2016). Accessed March 23, 2017. http://www.dietitians.ca/ Your-Health/Nutrition-A-Z/Minerals/Food-Sources-of-Magnesium.aspx.

Dietitians of Canada. "Food Sources of Omega-3 Fats." Dietitians.ca (October 28, 2016). Accessed March 23, 2017. http://www.dietitians.ca/ Your-Health/Nutrition-A-Z/Fat/Food-Sources-of-Omega-3-Fats.aspx.

Dietitians of Canada. "Food Sources of Riboflavin (Vitamin B2)." Dietitians.ca (October 28, 2016). Accessed March 23, 2017. http:// www.dietitians.ca/Your-Health/Nutrition-A-Z/Vitamins/Food-Sources-of-Riboflavin-(Vitamin-B2).aspx.

Dietitians of Canada. "Food Sources of Vitamin A." Dietitians.ca (November 26, 2014). Accessed March 23, 2017. http://www.dietitians. ca/Your-Health/Nutrition-A-Z/Vitamins/Food-Sources-of-Vitamin-A.aspx.

Doctors' Research. "The Truth About Minerals in Nutritional Supplements." Doctorsresearch.com. Accessed March 23, 2017. http:// www.doctorsresearch.com/articles3.html.

Dr. Hoffman. "Iron: Deficiency and Toxicity." Drhoffman.com (October 4, 2013). Accessed March 23, 2017. http://drhoffman.com/article/iron-deficiency-and-toxicity-3/.

Dr. Mercola. "10 Important Facts about Vitamin K That You Need to Know." *Mercola* (March 23, 2014). Accessed March 23, 2017. http://articles.mercola.com/sites/articles/archive/2004/03/24/vitamin-k-part-two.aspx#!

Drake, Victoria J. "Cognitive Function." *Linus Pauling Institute* (February 2011.) Accessed March 24, 2017. http://lpi.oregonstate.edu/mic/health-disease/cognitive-function.

Drugs. "Potassium Content of Foods List." Drugs.com. Accessed March 23, 2017. https://www.drugs.com/cg/potassium-content-of-foods-list.html.

Earnest Pravel, Donna. "Horsetail and Oat Straw Are Two Powerhouse Herbs for Calcium." *Natural News* (August 25, 2012). Accessed March 24, 2017. http://www.naturalnews.com/036941_calcium_horsetail_oat_straw.html.

Engels, Jonathon. "Plant-Based Foods with the Highest Omega-3 Fatty Acids." *One Green Planet.* Accessed March 23, 2017. http://www.onegreenplanet.org/natural-health/plant-based-foods-with-the-highest-amount-of-omega-3-fatty-acids/.

Eversole, Gayle. "Magnesium & Calcium Aren't Always the Best of Friends." *Rense.* Accessed March 23, 2017. http://www.rense.com/general87/magnes.htm.

Fang, Fang et al. "Determination of Red Wine Flavonoids by HPLC and Effect of Aging." *Science Direct.* Accessed March 23, 2017. doi:10.1016/j.foodchem.2005.12.036. http://www.sciencedirect.com/science/article/pii/S0308814606000045.

Fawesome.tv. "Top 10 Boron Rich Foods for Children." Fawesome.ifood.tv. Accessed March 23, 2017. http://fawesome.ifood.tv/health/395760-top-10-boron-rich-foods-for-children.

Fitday. "Incomplete vs. Complete Proteins," Fitday.com. Accessed March 23, 2017. http://www.fitday.com/fitness-articles/nutrition/proteins/incomplete-vs-complete-proteins.html.

Food Facts. "- elements - 31: SULPHUR." Nhri.org. Accessed March 23, 2017. http://apjcn.nhri.org.tw/server/info/books-phds/books/foodfacts/html/data/data5g.html.

Food Facts. " - element - 37: CHROMIUM." Nhri.org. Accessed March 23, 2017. http://apjcn.nhri.org.tw/server/info/books-phds/books/foodfacts/html/data/data5m.html.

Food Facts. "- Fat-Soluble Vitamins - 14: VITAMIN E." Nhri.org. Accessed March 23, 2017. http://apjcn.nhri.org.tw/server/info/books-phds/books/foodfacts/html/data/data3d.html.

Foods matter. "Sulphates and Sulphites – The Good, the Moderately Bad and the Ugly." 2009. Foodsmatter.com. Accessed March 23, 2017. http://www.foodsmatter.com/allergy_intolerance/sulphites/articles/sulphates_sulphites.html.

Fosmire, G. J. "Zinc Toxicity." *The American Journal of Clinical Nutrition* (1990). Accessed March 23, 2017. http://ajcn.nutrition.org/content/51/2/225.abstract.

Geib, Aurora. "Top 10 Herbs and Spices for Strengthening Your Immune System." *Natural News.* (April 9, 2012). Accessed March 24, 2017. http://www.naturalnews.com/035530_immune_system_herbs_spices.html.

Gillaspy, Rebecca. "Sulfur Deficiency & Toxicity Symptoms." *Study.* Accessed March 23, 2017. http://study.com/academy/lesson/sulfur-deficiency-toxicity-symptoms.html.

Greek medicine. "Hippocrates." Greekmedicine.net. Accessed March 24, 2017. http://www.greekmedicine.net/whos_who/Hippocrates.html.

Green, Deane. "Purslane: Omega 3 Fatty Weed." *Eat the Weeds.* Accessed March 23, 2017. http://www.eattheweeds.com/purslane-omega-3-fatty-weed/.

Greenopedia. "Alkaline-Acid Food Charts," Greenopedia.com. Accessed March 23, 2017. http://greenopedia.com/alkaline-acid-food-chart/.

Grisanti, Ronald. "The CoQ10-Statin Secret." *Functional Medicine University.* Accessed March 23, 2017. http://www.functionalmedicineuniversity.com/public/883.cfm.

Group. Edward. "15 Foods High in Folic Acid." *Global Healing Center* (November 1, 2011), updated November 19, 2015. Accessed March 23, 2017. http://www.globalhealingcenter.com/natural-health/folic-acid-foods/.

Group, Edward. "What is Calcium Toxicity and Hypercalcemia?" *Global Healing Center* (February 18, 2013), updated November 11, 2014. Accessed March 23, 2017. http://www.globalhealingcenter.com/natural-health/what-is-calcium-toxicity-and-hypercalcemia/.

Guerrero, A. L. et al. "Serum Uric Acid Levels in Multiple Sclerosis Patients Inversely Correlate with Disability." *Medscape, Neuro Sci.* 32(2) (2011): 347-350. http://www.medscape.com/medline/abstract/21327401.

Guersche, Siegfried. "Silica – The Forgotten Nutrient." *Alive.* December 5, 2005, updated June 20, 2016. Accessed March 23, 2017. http://www.alive.com/health/silica-the-forgotten-nutrient/.

Haney, Rose. "Is Hemp a Complete Protein?" *Jillian Michaels.* Accessed March 24, 2017. http://livewell.jillianmichaels.com/hemp-complete-protein-5511.html.

Health Canada. "Archived–Boron as a Medicinal Ingredient in Oral Natural Health Products." *Health Canada.* Accessed March 23, 2017. http://www.hc-sc.gc.ca/dhp-mps/pubs/natur/boron-bore-eng.php.

Health Canada. "Dietary Reference Intakes Tables." *Health Canada* (2005). Accessed March 23, 2017. http://hc-sc.gc.ca/fn-an/nutrition/reference/table/index-eng.php#rvv.

Health Diaries. "10 Food Sources of Coenzyme Q10 (CoQ10)." Healthdiaries.com (April 4, 2011). Accessed March 23, 2017. http://www.healthdiaries.com/eatthis/10-food-sources-of-coenzyme-q10-coq10.html.

Healthaliciousness. "Top 10 Foods Highest in Copper." Healthaliciousness. com. Accessed March 23, 2017. https://www.healthaliciousness.com/ articles/high-copper-foods.php.

Healthaliciousness. "Top 10 Foods Highest in Vitamin K." Healthaliciousness.com. Accessed March 23, 2017, https://www. healthaliciousness.com/articles/food-sources-of-vitamin-k.php.

Healthknot. "Hypertension Risk: Time to Move beyond Salt?" Healknot. com (May 2010). Accessed March 23, 2017. http://www.healthknot. com/hypertension_risk.html.

Heinerman, John. *Heinerman's Encyclopedia of Healing Herbs and Spices.* New Jersey; Parker, 1996.

How Stuff Works. "What are Carotenoids?" Howstuffworks.com. Accessed March 23, 2017. http://health.howstuffworks.com/wellness/food-nutrition/vitamin-supplements/what-are-carotenoids.htm.

Iodine Research. "Iodine and Other Halogens." Iodineresearch.com. Accessed March 24, 2017. http://iodineresearch.com/goitrogen_ halogen.html.

Ipatenco, Sara. "Vanadium-Rich Foods." *Livestrong* (updated February 8, 2014). Accessed March 23, 2017. http://www.livestrong.com/ article/318066-vanadium-rich-foods/.

Jugdaohsingh, Ravin, et al. "Dietary Silicon Intake and Absorption1'2'3." *American Society for Clinical Nutrition* (2002). Accessed March 23, 2017. http://ajcn.nutrition.org/content/75/5/887.full.

Landsman, Jonathan. "Grocery Store Cinnamon Proves to Be Toxic." *Natural Health 365* (December 22, 2013). Accessed April 9, 2017. http://www.naturalhealth365.com/cinnamon_alert.html/.

Lind, Melissa. "List of Foods with Flavonoids." *Livestrong* (updated December 13, 2013). Accessed March 23, 2017, http://www.livestrong. com/article/73159-list-foods-flavonoids/.

Mayo Clinic. "Biotin (Oral) Route." Mayoclinic.org. Accessed April 6, 2017. http://www.mayoclinic.org/drugs-supplements/biotin-oral-route/description/DRG-20062359.

MD idea. "Constituents and Phytochemicals of Oat Straw." MDidea. com. Accessed March 23, 2017. https://www.mdidea.com/products/new/new03204.html.

Medical News Today. "Chemicals in Marijuana 'Protein Nervous System' against MS." *Medical News Today* (October 13, 2013). Accessed April 6, 2017. http://www.medicalnewstoday.com/articles/267161.php.

Medline Plus. "Calcium Carbonate Overdose." *Medline Plus.* Accessed March 23, 2017. https://medlineplus.gov/ency/article/002605.htm.

Merrill, Jamie. "The Clippings of a 300-Year-Old, 150 ft. Yew Hedge Can Save the Lives of Cancer Patients." *Independent* (August 7, 2014). Accessed March 24, 2017. http://www.independent.co.uk/;ife-style/gealth-and-families/natures/the-clippings-of-a-300yearold-150ft-yew-hedge-can-save-the-lives-of-cancer-patients-9655500.html.

Minera Vita. "Boron Sources." Mineravita.com. Accessed March 23, 2017. http://www.mineravita.com/en/boron-sources.html.

Murray, Michael T. "What is the Role of Sulphur in My Body?" *Sharecare.* Accessed March 23, 2017. https://www.sharecare.com/health/minerals-nutrition-diet/role-of-sulfur-in-body.

Mushrooms. "Mushrooms and Vitamin D." Mushrooms.ca. Accessed March 23, 2017. http://mushrooms.ca/nutrition/vitamins.aspx.

Muzaurieta, Annie Belle. "Top 10 Natural Sources of Vitamin C." *Good Housekeeping* (June 17, 2014). Accessed March 23, 2017," http://www.goodhousekeeping.com/health/diet-nutrition/g1926/top-sources-vitamin-c-44102808/#slide=1.

Myron, Duane R., et. al. "Vanadium Content of Selected Foods as Determined by Flameless Atomic Absorption Spectroscopy." *Journal of Agriculture and Food Chemistry* 25(2) (March 1977): 297–300. doi:10.1021/jf60210a036. https://www.researchgate.net/

publication/22315905_Vanadium_content_of_selected_foods_as_ determined_by_flameless_atomic_absorption_spectroscopy.

Natural endocrine solutions. "Zinc, Copper, and Hyperthyroidism." Naturalendocrinesolutions.com. Accessed March 24, 2017. http://www. naturalendocrinesolutions.com/articles/zinc-copper-hyperthyroidism/.

Natural Health 365. "Are Your Anti-Aging Foods Rich in Omega 5 and 7?" Naturalhealth365.com (April 28, 2013). Accessed March 23, 2017. http://www.naturalhealth365.com/anti_aging.html/.

Natural Remedies Review. "Co-enzyme Q10 Benefits (COQ10 or Ubiquinone)." Naturalremediesreview.com. Accessed March 23, 2017. http://www.natural-remedies-review.com/coenzyme-q10.html.

Nootriment editorial staff. "The Dangerous Effects of a Choline Deficiency." Nootriment.com. Accessed April 6, 2017. https://nootriment .com/choline-deficiency/.

Nootriment editorial staff. "Vitamin B8 Food Sources to Increase Inositol Levels." Nootriment.com. Accessed March 23, 2017. http://nootriment .com/vitamin-b8-foods/.

Nutrition. "TOPIC – Gout." Nutrition.com. Accessed March 23, 2017. http://nutrition.com.sg/atd/atdgout.asp.

Nutrition and You. "Dandelion herb nutrition facts." Nutrition-and-you. com. Accessed March 24, 2017. http://www.nutrition-and-you.com/ dandelion-herb.html.

Nutritional Supplements Center. "Inositol." Nutritionalsupplementscenter. com. Accessed March 23, 2017. http://www.nutritional supplementscenter.com/info/HealthSupplement/inositol.html.

Office of Dietary Supplements. "Chromium – Dietary Supplement Fact Sheet." *National Institutes of Health.* Accessed March 23, 2017. http:// ods.od.nih.gov/factsheets/Chromium-HealthProfessional/.

Office of Dietary Supplements. "Vitamin E." *National Institutes of Health.* Accessed March 23, 2017. https://ods.od.nih.gov/factsheets/ VitaminE-HealthProfessional/.

Pandal, Natraj. "Nutraceuticals: Global Markets." *BCC Research* (November 2014). Accessed March 23, 2017. http://www.bccresearch. com/market-research/food-and-beverage/nutraceuticals-markets-report-fod013e.html.

Pearson, Craig. "Angel Investor Boosts Windsor Dandelion Root Cancer Research (with Video)." *Windsor Star* (April 8, 2014). Accessed March 23, 2017. http://windsorstar.com/health/ angel-investor-boosts-windsor-dandelion-cancer-research.

Robberecht, Harry, et. al. "Silicon in Foods: Content and Bioavailability." *International Journal of Food Properties* 11(3) (July 2008): 639–645. Researchgate.net. doi:10.1080/10942910701584252. https://www. researchgate.net/publication/233428856_Silicon_in_Foods_ Content_and_Bioavailability.

Rogers, Joshua. "11 Chaparral Benefits and the Herb's Side Effects." *Natural alternative remedy.* Accessed March 23, 2017. http://www. naturalalternativeremedy.com/11-chaparral-benefits-and-the-herbs-side-effects/.

Rose, Amanda. "Iron Content of Oysters." *Daily Iron.* Accessed March 23, 2017. http://www.dailyiron.net/oyster/.

Rutto, Laban K. et al. "Mineral Properties and Dietary Values of Raw and Processed Stinging Nettle (*Urtica dioica L.*)." *International Journal of Food Science* (2013). Article ID 857120, 9 pages. doi:10.1155/2013/857120. https://www.hindawi.com/journals/ijfs/2013/857120/.

Science and Technology. "Manganese Poisoning, Subtle Effects, Exploring the Link between Manganese and Parkinson's Disease." *The Economist,* from the print edition *Science and Technology* (April 26, 2014). Accessed March 23, 2017. http://www.economist.com/news/science-and-technology/21601233-exploring-link-between-manganese-and-parkinsons-disease-subtle-effects.

Science Daily. "Coumarin in Cinnamon and Cinnamon-Based Products and Risk of Liver Damage." *Science Daily* (May 8, 2013). Accessed April 9,

2017. https://www.sciencedaily.com/releases/2013/05/130508123127. htm.

Science Direct. "Omega-3 Fatty Acid Intake Linked to Reduced Risk of Age-Related Macular Degeneration in Women." *Science Direct* (March 15, 2011). Accessed March 23, 2017. https://www.sciencedaily.com/ releases/2011/03/110314163439.htm.

Seafood Health Facts. "Omega-3 Content of Frequently Consumed Seafood Products." Seafoodhealthfacts.com. Accessed March 23, 2017. http://www.seafoodhealthfacts.org/seafood-nutrition/healthcare-professionals/omega-3-content-frequently-consumed-seafood-products.

Self Nutrition Data. "Chickpeas, (Garbanzo Beans, Bengal Gram), Mature Seeds, Cooked, Boiled, without Salt." Nutritiondata.self. com. Accessed March 24, 2017. http://nutritiondata.self.com/facts/ legumes-and-legume-products/4326/2.

Self Nutrition Data. "Tomatoes, Red, Ripe, Raw, Year Round Average [Includes USDA Commodity Food A238 and A233] Nutrition Facts and Calories." Nutritiondata.self.com. Accessed March 23, 2017. http://nutritiondata. self.com/facts/vegetables-and-vegetable-products/2682/2.

Seneff, Stephanie. "Sulphur Deficiency." Weston A. Price Foundation (July 2, 2011). Accessed March 23, 2017. https://www.westonaprice.org/ health-topics/abcs-of-nutrition/sulfur-deficiency/.

sheknows. "Are You Getting Enough Iron?" Sheknows.com (March 22, 2010). Accessed March 23, 2017. http://www.sheknows.com/health-and-wellness/articles/806550/are-you-getting-enough-iron.htm.

Smith, Robin L., Trafny, Tomasz, and Max Gomez. *The Healing Cell: How the Greatest Revolution in Medical History is Changing Your Life.* New York, Boston: Center Street, 2013.

Squadrito, G. L. et al. "Reaction of Uric Acid with Peroxynitrite and Implications for the Mechanism of Neuroprotection by Uric

Acid." *Medscape* (April 15, 2000). PMID (10775420). doi:10.1006/ abbi.2000.1721. https://www.ncbi.nlm.nih.gov/pubmed/10775420.

Taylor, Julianne I. "Omega 6 and 3 in Nuts, Oils, Meat and Fish. Tools to Get It Right." *Paleo Zone Nutrition*. Accessed March 23, 2017. http://paleozonenutrition.com/2011/05/10/omega-6-and-3-in-nuts-oils-meat-and-fish-tools-to-get-it-right/.

Underground health reporter. "Iodine Therapy for Fibrocystic Breast Disease Treatment." Undergroundhealthreporter.com. Accessed March 24, 2017. http://undergroundhealthreporter.com/ fibrocystic-breast-disease-treatment/#axzz3zQjZ7Kfo.

University of Windsor. "Human Clinical Trials on for Cancer Killing Dandelion Extract." *University of Windsor* (February 19, 2015). Accessed March 23, 2017. http://www.uwindsor.ca/dailynews/2015-02-18/ human-clinical-trials-cancer-killing-dandelion-extract.

Vegetarian Health Institute. "Which Foods Are More Nutritious Raw vs. Cooked?" Veganrecipes.com. Accessed March 23, 2017. http://www.veganrecipes.com/blog/vegan/which -foods-are-more-nutritious-raw-vs-cooked/.

Vesna, Rafajlovska et al. "Determination of Proteins and Mineral Contents in Stinging Nettle." *Quality of Life* 4(1-2) (2013): 26–30. Accessed April 6, 2017. doi:10.7251/QOL1301026R. https://www.researchgate. net/publication/271263619_Determination_of_protein_and_mineral _contents_in_stinging_nettle.

Vineetha in Rich Foods. "Top 13 Zinc Rich Foods You Should Include in Your Diet." *Health beckon*. Accessed March 23, 2017. http://www. healthbeckon.com/zinc-rich-foods/.

Vital Health Zone. "All About Nutrition — Silicon (Silica)." Vitalhealthzone. com. Accessed March 23, 2017. http://www.vitalhealthzone.com/ nutrition/nutrition-questions/Lesa-Rusher1/foods-with-highest-silica-content-amount-of-silica.html.

Vukovic, Diane. "14 Best Vegan Sources of Omega 3." *Plenteous Veg.* (March 13, 2017). Accessed March 23, 2017. http://plenteousveg.com/vegan-sources-omega-3/.

Web MD. "Q. What is the Recommended Dosage for Boron?" WebMd.com (April 14, 2010). Accessed March 23, 2017. http://answers.webmd.com/answers/1187782/what-is-the-recommended-dosage-for.

Wikipedia. "Bromine." *Wikipedia: The Free Encyclopedia.* Accessed March 24, 2017. https://en.wikipedia.org/wiki/Bromine.

Wikipedia "Coumarin," *Wikipedia: The Free Encyclopedia.* Accessed March 23, 2017. http://en.wikipedia.org/wiki/Coumarin.

Wikipedia. "Folic Acid." *Wikipedia: The Free Encyclopedia.* Accessed March 23, 2017. https://en.wikipedia.org/wiki/Folic_acid.

Wikipedia. "Omega-7 Fatty Acid." *Wikipedia: The Free Encyclopedia.* Accessed March 23, 2017. https://en.wikipedia.org/wiki/Omega-7_fatty_acid.

Wikipedia. "Oseltamivir," Wikipedia.com. Accessed March 23, 2013. http://en.wikipedia.org/wiki/Oseltamivir.

Wikipedia. "Quercetin." *Wikipedia: The Free Encyclopedia.* Accessed March 24, 2017. http://en.wikipedia.org/wiki/Quercetin.

Willett, Walter C. "Ask the doctor: 'Why is peanut butter 'healthy' if it has saturated fat?" *Harvard Health Publications* (July 2009). Accessed March 30, 2017. http://www.health.harvard.edu/healthy-eating/ask-the-doctor-why-is-peanut-butter-healthy-if-it-has-saturated-fat.

Wisegeek. "What are Flavonoids?" Wisegeek.com. Accessed March 23, 2017. http://www.wisegeek.org/what-are-flavonoids.htm.

Wisegeek. "What is Vitamin P?" Wisegeek.com. Accessed March 23, 2017. http://www.wisegeek.org/what-is-vitamin-p.htm.

Whole foods catalog. "Potassium Content of Nuts and Seeds (11-20)." Wholefoodcatalog.info. Accessed March 23, 2017. http://wholefoodcatalog.info/nutrient/potassium/nuts_and_seeds/2/.

World's Healthiest Foods. "Biotin." Whfoods.org. Accessed March 23, 2017. http://www.whfoods.com/genpage.php?tname=nutrient&dbid=42.

World's healthiest foods. "Broccoli." Whfoods.org. Accessed March 23, 2017. http://www.whfoods.com/genpage.php?tname=foodspice&dbid=9.

World's Healthiest Foods. "Choline." Whfoods.org. Accessed March 23, 2017. http://www.whfoods.com/genpage.php?tname=nutrient&dbid=50.

World's Healthiest Foods. "Flavonoids." Whfoods.com. Accessed March 23, 2017. http://www.whfoods.com/genpage.php?tname=nutrient&dbid=119.

World's healthiest foods. "Iron." Whfoods.org. Accessed March 23, 2017. http://www.whfoods.com/genpage.php?tname=nutrient&dbid=70.

World's healthiest foods. "Magnesium." Whfoods.org. Accessed March 23, 2017. http://www.whfoods.com/genpage.php?tname=nutrient&dbid=75.

World's Healthiest Foods. "Panthotenic Acid." Whfoods.org. Accessed March 23, 2017. http://www.whfoods.com/genpage.php?tname=nutrient&dbid=87.

World's Healthiest Foods. "Pineapple." Whfoods.org. Accessed March 23, 2017. http://www.whfoods.com/genpage.php?tname=foodspice&dbid=34.

World's healthiest foods. "Potassium." Whfoods.org. Accessed March 23, 2017. http://www.whfoods.com/genpage.php?dbid=90&tname=nutrient.

World's Healthiest Foods. "Vitamin B12 – Cobalamin." Whfoods. org. Accessed March 23, 2017. http://www.whfoods.com/genpage. php?tname=nutrient&dbid=107.

World's Healthiest Foods. "Vitamin B6 – Pyridoxine." Whfoods. org. Accessed March 23, 2017. http://www.whfoods.com/genpage. php?tname=nutrient&dbid=108.

World's Healthiest Foods. "What are Purines and How Are They Related to Food and Health?" Whfoods.org. Accessed March 23, 2017. http://www.whfoods.com/genpage.php?tname=george&dbid=51.

World's healthiest foods. "Zinc." Whfoods.org. Accessed March 23, 2017. http://www.whfoods.com/genpage.php?tname=nutrient&dbid=115.

Work safely with silica. "Work Safely with Silica, Know the Hazards." Silica-safe.org. Accessed March 23, 2017. http://www.silica-safe.org/know-the-hazard/what-are-the-health-effects/signs-symptoms.

Wright, Michelle. "Zinc Deficiency, Excess and Supplementation." *Patient*. Accessed March 23, 2017. http://patient.info/doctor/zinc-deficiency-excess-and-supplementation.

Printed in the United States
By Bookmasters